*R*emembering *R*ay

Remembering Ray

A Composite Biography of Raymond Carver

Edited by William L. Stull and Maureen P. Carroll

CAPRA PRESS
SANTA BARBARA

To Lane Ameen

LIBRARY OF CONGRESS CATALOGING-IN-PUBLICATION DATA
Remembering Ray : a composite biography of Raymond Carver / edited by
William L. Stull and Maureen P. Carroll.
p.   cm.
Includes index.
ISBN 0-88496-370-5 : $14.95
1. Carver, Raymond—Biography.   2. Authors, American—20th century—Biography.
I. Stull, William L.   II. Carroll, Maureen P.
PS3553.A7894Z85   1993
813'.54--dc20
[B]   93-11053
                                                       CIP

CAPRA PRESS
Post Office Box 2068
Santa Barbara, CA 93120

Permissions

"The Door" by Marvin Bell. Copyright © 1993 by Marvin Bell.

"My Crony" by Morris R. Bond. Copyright © 1993 by Morris R. Bond.

"New Hope for the Dead" by Lewis Buzbee. First published in *The San Francisco Review of Books*. Copyright © 1988 by Lewis Buzbee. Reprinted by permission of the author.

"Fish Stories" by Henry Carlile. Copyright © 1993 by Henry Carlile.

"What We Talk About When We Talk About Carver" by David Carpenter. First published in *Descant*. Copyright © 1987 by David Carpenter. Reprinted by permission of the author.

"Ray" by Hayden Carruth. Previously published in *Collected Shorter Poems, 1946–1991*. Copyright © 1992 by Hayden Carruth. Reprinted by permission of Copper Canyon Press, P.O. Box 271, Port Townsend, WA 98368.

continued on next page

CONTENTS

Editors' Preface   9

In the Year 2020 *Raymond Carver*   10

PART I: San Francisco, California, 1969

Carvering *William Heyen*   14

The Days with Ray *James D. Houston*   15

Just Listening to Stories *David Raphael Israel*   21

PART II: Arcata, California, 1961

Weedy Logic *Joyce Carol Oates*   24

The Most Unhappy Man *Jay Karr*   26

Bad News *Richard Cortez Day*   31

PHOTOGRAPHS   33–48

Secret Places *Dennis Schmitz*   49

All-American Nightmares *Morton Marcus*   53

Tell Me More About Salmon Fishing *Geoffrey Dunn*   68

A Nothing Generation *William Harmon*   71

PART III: Cupertino, California, 1974

The Message *Riccardo Duranti*   74

Dark Days *Jim Somers*   75

A Real-Life Carver Story *Michael Rogers*   78

No Blessed Calm *David Swanger*   80

Bulletproof *William Kittredge*   85

Happy Hour with Ray *Noel Young*   96

The Good Story *Jeffrey Skinner*   99

PART IV: El Paso, Texas, 1978

Odometer *Patricia Dobler*   102

The Ghosts of Dreams *Tess Gallagher*   103

Laughter's Creature *Stephen Dobyns*   108

New Hope for the Dead *Lewis Buzbee*   114

Raymond Carver, Mentor *Jay McInerney*   119
Read It Again *Kenneth Inadomi*   127
A Literary Comrade *Haruki Murakami*   130
Laundroma *Jay Woodruff*   136
Shameless *Tom Jenks*   141
The Door *Marvin Bell*   144

PART V: Port Angeles, Washington, 1984

My Crony *Morris R. Bond*   148
Fish Stories *Henry Carlile*   150
Lines of Force *Olivier Cohen*   161
What We Talk About When We Talk
   About Carver *David Carpenter*   166
Twice-Touched *Charles Wright*   187

PART VI: Port Angeles, Washington, 1988

The Letter *Jane Kenyon*   192
Do You Like It? *Dorothy Catlett*   194
Going Through the Pain *Ted Solotaroff*   199
Reunion in Yakima *Liggett Taylor*   207
American Light *Robert Coles*   215
Stories Change You *Stephen Hunt*   225
Salt Water and Fresh *Gary Fisketjon*   234
Something Else *Bibhu Padhi*   237

PART VII: Syracuse, New York, 1989

Carver's Medallion *Barry Spacks*   240
Appetite *Tobias Wolff*   241
Ray *Hayden Carruth*   251

Contributors   253

Index   258

Editors' Preface

If this sounds
like the story of a life, okay.

—R.C., "Locking Yourself Out,
Then Trying to Get Back In"

For years before his death in August 1988, Raymond Carver spoke of having lived two lives. The date dividing them was June 2, 1977. On that day Carver, his first life laid waste by alcohol, took his final drink. After that, as he said in one of his last-written poems, "it was *all* gravy": a ten-year second life of rising productivity, widening reputation, and sustaining love. "Don't weep for me," he wrote when told he had lung cancer at age forty-nine. "I'm a lucky man."

Remembering Ray bears witness to the fact that Raymond Carver was nowhere luckier than in his friends. The book's forty-three contributors include fellow writers who knew Ray personally during his first and second lives. Also included are students, teachers, and readers who knew him only through his work. In keeping with Carver's Chekhovian range of friendships, recollections by well-known writers stand next to letters, poems, and stories by previously unpublished authors. Among the contributors are Carver's Japanese and Italian translators, his French and American publishers, a poet from India, a novelist from Saskatoon. Present too is the most intimate companion of Ray's second life, the writer Tess Gallagher, to whom a dozen of his books are dedicated.

Ray Carver's claim to have lived two lives proves to be understatement. Viewed through so many eyes over a stretch of thirty years, his lives double and redouble like reflections on the swift northwestern waters that he loved. What results is not a static portrait but a moving picture—the life story of a memorable, many-sided man.

W.L.S.

M.P.C.

July 4, 1993

In the Year 2020

Which of us will be left then—
old, dazed, unclear—
but willing to talk about our dead friends?
Talk and talk, like an old faucet leaking.
So that the young ones,
respectful, touchingly curious,
will find themselves stirred
by the recollections.
By the very mention of this name
or that name, and what we did together.
(As we were respectful, but curious
and excited, to hear someone tell
about the illustrious dead ahead of us.)
Of which of us will they say
to their friends,
he knew so and so! He was friends with _____
and they spent time together.
He was at that big party.
Everyone was there. They celebrated
and danced until dawn. They put their arms
around each other and danced
until the sun came up.
Now they're all gone.
Of which of us will it be said—
he knew them? Shook hands with them
and embraced them, stayed overnight
in their warm houses. Loved them!

Friends, I do love you, it's true.
And I hope I'm lucky enough, privileged enough,
to live on and bear witness.
Believe me, I'll say only the most
glorious things about you and our time here!
For the survivor there has to be something
to look forward to. Growing old,
losing everything and everybody.

—RAYMOND CARVER
Where Water Comes Together with Other Water (1985)

PART I

San Francisco, California

1969

WILLIAM HEYEN

Carvering

All day I play these games, so when
I see a photo of Ray I've not seen before—
Frisco, '77, he's got long sideburns
& is petting the Siamese cat in his lap—
I say to myself, Bill, if you can ID
just one book on that shelf beside him,
Ray will rise from the dead, . . .
so I get out my magnifying glass—
it's even got a little light you can click on—
& try, but it's no use, the print's too small,
the one dustjacketed book doesn't compute,
the others are blurs. Again, I've played
a game I couldn't win, & why? Not
for the dead—they're welcome to spend
their own lives, to remain in their dark
& be dead. Just for the rush of it,
as Ray realized, and wrote. For this.

JAMES D. HOUSTON

The Days with Ray

I first met him at a collating party in San Francisco back in 1969. This was when George Hitchcock was editing and publishing *Kayak* magazine out of his house on Laguna Street. I had just come back from two months in Mexico and had to think twice about climbing into a car again to drive the eighty miles from Santa Cruz into the city. But it was considered something of an honor to be invited to one of these gatherings, a little nod of recognition from George, the small-press impresario. And I had been told that Ray Carver would be there. George was about to bring out *Winter Insomnia,* Ray's second book of poems. I had been seeing his stories and wanting to meet him for a couple of years.

Among other things, I was struck by his clothing, a plain white long-sleeve shirt and dark slacks. I liked him for that. The year 1969 was the height of the counterculture, which had its world head quarters right there in San Francisco. The streets were teeming with headbands and broadbrim hats, turquoise pendants, amulets, mocassins, roman sandals, shirts covered with handsewn embroidery and leather fringe hanging from every vest and jacket. But the Bay Area scene did not interest Ray much at all. He was not affecting the look of a hippie or a cowboy or a Buddhist or a trail guide or a lumberjack. Oblivious to the costumery of the times, he was a man of the West who dressed in a sort of midwestern way, conservative, though not entirely respectable, since the white shirt was wrinkled and the slacks were rumpled as if he might have spent the night in these clothes.

After an hour or so of snacks and drinks, George put everyone to work on his literary assembly line, someone to collate the pages, someone to add the cover, someone to trim the edges, to staple, to fold, to stack, and so on. I was assigned to the stapling gun. Ray ended up next to me, working the trimmer with its guillotine blade.

Neither of us was mechanically inclined. We had already talked about various forms of car trouble that had bewildered and defeated us. We wondered if our participation that afternoon would have any effect upon sales. That is, we wondered if readers would buy a poetry magazine spotted with the drops of blood that would inevitably fall upon its pages once we touched the machines we'd been asked operate. We wondered if Hitchcock might get sued, the way angry consumers will sue a food processer when a loose fingernail turns up inside the can of stewed tomatoes.

Then the joking subsided. We bent to our tasks. What I remember most about that day is standing next to him for the next hour or so, not talking much, standing shoulder to shoulder, stapling, trimming, stapling, trimming, as we worked along with George and the others to put this issue of the magazine together.

Ray was an easy and comfortable man to be with, to stand next to, or to sit with for long periods of time. He had a ready wit, and an infectious laugh, and no pretensions about him, no attitude. In every way he was unassuming. From the first meeting I felt a strong kinship, and I realize now that it was due, at least in part, to our similar origins. Years later we would finally talk about how both our fathers had come west during the early 1930s looking for any kind of work, his from Arkansas into the state of Washington, mine from east Texas to the California coast.

There was something else about Ray that I found enormously appealing. I think of it as a priestly quality. I never imagined I would be making such a statement about him, but as I look back I believe it's true. He could be very brotherly. He often seemed filled with wonder. And you knew he would never judge you for your sins, whatever they might be. That was my experience, at any rate. In later years he had the capacity for genuine forgiveness.

He also had a brotherly demon in him, and this was appealing in another kind of way. Ray could talk you into things, cajole you or seduce you into things you were not perhaps ready for: a pied piper on the prose and poetry circuit.

One afternoon stands out in my memory. This must have been

six years later. I was upstairs working on something, I can't remember what, when I heard footsteps down below. We have an old Victorian-style place with an attic that has been converted into a writing space. It's private yet still not entirely cut off because the building is old and poorly insulated. Rising toward me came the sound of large and deliberate footsteps, too heavy to be those of my wife or one of our kids. I listened until the footsteps stopped, in the room directly below me. A voice called my name.

I didn't answer. I didn't care who it was. I didn't want to see anybody just then or get into a conversation. It was about three in the afternoon. Whoever this was had now moved to the doorway at the bottom of the attic stairs.

"Houston, you sonofabitch, I know you're up there."

Again I didn't speak.

"Answer me!" he shouted.

I knew this voice, but I said, "Who is it?"

"It's Carver."

"What do you want?"

"Goddam it, come down here and say hello to some people."

"I'm busy. I'm working."

"Of course you're working. We're all working. We're busy as bees. Do you want to come down or shall we come up?"

"I'll be there in a minute."

He was traveling with Bill Kittredge and a big, red-bearded fellow named John, recently arrived from Alaska—all large men, large and thick. The four of us completely filled my living room. Ray was carrying two bottles, a gallon of vodka and a half gallon of grapefruit juice, which he carefully set upon the rug. From a plastic bag he withdrew a plastic cup and began to fill it.

With his rascal grin he said, "You tell me when," though he paid no attention to my reply. They had been at it since lunch, or earlier. Ray was living in Palo Alto at the time. On and off he'd been teaching here at UC Santa Cruz. He had them on a kind of sightseeing tour with no clear agenda, making it up as they went along. I surrendered to the inevitable and began to quench my thirst with the drink he had prepared, which ran forty-sixty in favor of the vodka.

I don't remember all that we talked about. Kittredge was down from Montana as a Stegner fellow at Stanford, so we must have talked about that. Ray's second book of stories, *Will You Please Be Quiet, Please?*, had been put together, so we must have talked about that. It was a rambling conversation about books and writers and schemes and plans, that grew noisier as I caught up with them, as we sat and sipped and argued and laughed, and while Ray, self-appointed host, refilled and refilled the plastic glasses.

I guess an hour had passed when someone mentioned starting back.

"What do you mean?" said Ray.

"Who can drive?" said Kittredge.

"My God, you're right," said Ray. It was his car. "Who's going to do it?"

This led to a long debate over who was most qualified to navigate Highway 17, the curving mountain speedway that connects Santa Cruz to Santa Clara Valley and the peninsula.

"Maybe Houston should," said Ray, at one point, "while he can still see."

"Gladly," I said, "though there is a problem with that. Once we got to your place, I would need a ride over the hill."

He leaned toward me with a raspy and infectious giggle. "Well, it goes without saying. One good turn deserves another. We'd just have to give you a lift back home."

The next thing I knew they were lunging through the house, down the hallway, out the back door and into the yard. While they piled into the car we shouted our good-byes. It was a big unkempt American car, a car from a Ray Carver story, with low tires and a rumbling exhaust. It lurched a couple of times, kicking up dust. Ray took the corner without braking. The rear end swung wide, he gunned it, and they were gone.

There was no wind. The sky was clear, ordinarily a great time to be outdoors. But my head was throbbing. I was alone in a sudden stillness. In those days my driveway wasn't paved. It had not rained in a month or so. Dust hung in the slanting light of late afternoon and slowly settled around me, and I stood there wondering what I was now supposed to do, stunned with drink at quarter to five and abandoned in my own driveway.

Later on we would talk about that trip and others like it, and Ray would always laugh the hardest, hearing his escapades repeated. But it doesn't seem so funny now. It fills me with sadness, thinking back on the turmoil of those mid-1970s days, when he was always on the run. I prefer to remember him as he was in the years after the running ended, after the drinking stopped.

The last time I saw him was in February 1987, maybe six months before he learned about the cancer in his lungs. By that time he had gone back home to Washington. He and Tess were living in Port Angeles. He had come down to the Bay Area to spend a few days as the Lane lecturer at Stanford, which included a public reading at Kresge Auditorium. It was a triumphant return to the campus and to the region where he had honed his writing style. To a packed house he read "Elephant," which had recently appeared in the *New Yorker*, and got a standing ovation. Ray had a hulking, self-effacing way of receiving praise. At the podium he looked a bit surprised. He also looked genuinely prosperous. He was wearing an elegant suit, light beige, almost cream colored. It had an Italian look, single-breasted, with narrow lapels.

As I stood there applauding with all the others I was thinking about a time I had flown to Tucson, fall of 1979, on my way home from a trip to Albuquerque. Tess had a one-year appointment at the University of Arizona, and Ray was on a Guggenheim. He'd been moving around so much I hadn't seen him for a while. I'd heard about the big changes in his life, from him, and from others, but I wasn't sure quite what this meant, until we went out that night for Mexican food. "You have whatever you want," Ray said, when it came time to order the beverages. "I'm sticking with the iced tea."

As we began to talk I saw that the crazy restlessness had gone out of his body. He had lost some weight. He was calmer, clearer, his laugh was softer. He had spiraled all the way down, he told me, drunk himself into the final coma, which he described as being at the dark bottom of a very deep well.

"I was almost a goner, I see that now. I was ready to go out. I could have. I was ready to. But I saw this pinpoint of light, so far up there it seemed an impossible distance. It seemed completely beyond my reach, and yet something told me I had to try and reach it. Somehow I had to climb up toward that last tiny glimmer. And by God, I managed to do that. What do you call it? The survival instinct? I climbed out of that hole and I realized how close I had come, and that was it. I haven't had a drop from that day to this, and I've never felt better in my life."

He had always had the will to write, no matter what. Now he had joined that with the will to live. It made a powerful combination. You can see the effects in his later stories, and you could see it in his face the night he read at Stanford.

After the reception that followed the reading we found some time to chat, catch up on things, old times, new times—a chat that turned out to be our last, face to face. I had never seen him so happy. There was a lot of light around him, the kind of light given off by a man who feels good about himself and his work, a light enhanced by the ivory-tinted cloth of his tailored suit. Ray had quite a bit of money tied up in that suit, and he liked it. That is, he liked the *idea* of it, though my guess is he was not entirely comfortable wearing it.

He had a way of leaning in and lowering his voice, even when no one else was around, as if what he was about to say should not be overheard or repeated. "I have to tell you something," he said. "Every day I feel blessed. Every day I give thanks. Every day I am simply amazed at the way things have turned out. All you have to do is look at what I'm wearing. Look at this suit. . . ."

He laughed his high, light, conspiratorial laugh. "Can you imagine me wearing anything like this? It's just astounding!"

DAVID RAPHAEL ISRAEL

Just Listening to Stories

She was a woman whom
    I admired we shared
        an interest in Sufism

    her husband was decent
        and tolerant we shared
            a liking for literature -

So I went with the fellow
    (the wife was home studying)
        on a drive down to Stanford

    to hear Raymond Carver
        give a reading from his prose
            that last year of his life -

Too bad on the outskirts
    of campus the guy's car
        broke down we finally

    found a tow truck for the long
        ride home 40 miles
            back to Walnut Creek -

never glimpsing Ray Carver
    just listening to stories
        from the driver of the tow truck

PART II

Arcata, California

1961

JOYCE CAROL OATES

Weedy Logic

for Tess and Ray

Shaken and jubilant at the edge of the woods knowing
we'd seen Death but Death had not seen us.
And that night midnight jazz from San Francisco, saxo-
phone, trumpet, notes so pure the future
became suddenly possible.

Friends living their lives year following year,
disasters at their feet, small ignoble failures like
wood shavings they kick aside, seeming not to notice
and why not? The logic of survival.
Why not.

Oh, Jesus, he was speaking of the beauty of white.
The mad white rim of the eyeball above the iris.
Ice. Ivory. Paper. Snow. White-walled rooms
with white-framed windows fixing the Absolute.
How present tense resolves itself whitely to past.

Don't look. *Don't* look—circling the dead deer
at the edge of the woods: a doe, and how mute. And
how heavy lying on its side, the girth of its belly
that seemed swollen, stiffened legs, the gaping muzzle
and a bright buzz of flies. And wonder seized us.

That morning of grasses now Death. The fresh-painted
room smelling of Death. Steam rising from gratings
in the street that is Death but mysterious, the way
the poem is always a love poem, always in love with
its subject—helpless, chagrined. The way fireflies

drifting against the window demonstrate that the Absolute
doesn't matter. Do you know, he said, that sensation
driving into a city you've never seen before, mile upon
mile of houses, streets, *So many human beings who don't
know us* and it's a child's amazement denied at once,

like the discovery of jewelweed, named because of the glittering drops of moisture at the corners of the leaves
in the early morning, or daisy, named for the day's eye,
the creek you'd seen as a child miles from home and someone would say, There, that's our creek! and you'd have

to take it on faith, so much existence wider than you
know. And plaques for the dead, like poems no one reads,
crusted in birdlime and the birds close by with their
sun-sparked song, persisting, *It's always the same morning!*
And why not? Already the asphalt is cracking, giant
weeds pushing up from beneath. Weedy logic.

JAY KARR

The Most Unhappy Man

August 5, 1988

Dear Tess,

You do not know me. I feel I know you a little, through your poems and a story I have read, and from a piece *Vanity Fair* did on the two of you some time in '86, a copy of which Ray gave me when he read here, and in another respect through him, which is the point of what follows.

When I saw that Ray had died of cancer in an item in the *Post-Dispatch* two days ago, I was stunned. Having known nothing of his illness, I was stricken with a sensation close to outrage. It seemed of life not so much unaccountable as perverse. What can I offer of any consolation? You will be flooded with sincere and powerful tokens of sympathy from everywhere, from everyone great and small. I can only give you a small contrast montage to explain why, knowing you so remotely, I am sure you are not among those to whom condolences supply a kind of aching need or fill a lacuna caused by something lacking, unfulfilled.

I knew Ray only at the very beginning and again for a brief reencounter near the end of his writing career. There was a void of more than half a decade when I heard nothing of him after I left Humboldt State College. The first story of his I read in a national publication was in the Martha Foley collection, I think, back about '67. After that, he rose steadily in literary recognition and, more important, in realization of all his promise, and then he went out in the time it takes a meteor to arc down. Thus, my sense of outrage. But yesterday it came clearly. I put the two Ray Carvers side by side in my mind.

My wife and I moved from Idaho to Arcata, California, in the summer of '61 when I took a job teaching English and journalism at Humboldt State. I met Ray and came to know early on the nearly unvarying keynote of his nature during the whole time he was there. At a summer production of a play he had written, a one-act called *Carnations,* I watched him build the climactic tantrum of the main character (the other character in the play was a woman, and she had left the stage by then) from breaking the dishes on the table, until he destroyed the room, and finally flung down the very walls of the set, sparing not even the essential illusion that it was a play!

During the next years, because Ray was a talent, older, married, and an English major, he was with the language arts faculty crowd when we partied. He was an assistant in the English comp program; he was often in the cafeteria with Dick Day or others for coffee. And so we knew each other. I mean, always, under that thin membrane of the taciturn that carried him through the ordinary obligations of the day was that volcanic core. One realized after a while that it was always there, roiling, waiting to be turned on like a flamethrower. Ray only had to point it and pull the trigger. There was a variety of targets: the forestry majors; a professor who did light musical comedies, or perhaps the musical comedy itself, the genre; and most ferociously there was the Vietnam War. In that Humboldt State setting, it drove Ray nearly crazy to be almost the only anti-Vietnam militant in Humboldt County. And, of course, he turned the flame on himself. Our parties often lasted till four a.m. or later. As they say of people trapped in a Yukon winter with cabin sickness, they weren't happy parties. I've often wondered how much that milieu affected him. But with or without the parties, it was crystal-clear to me that Ray was one of the most unhappy men—I've hardly ever met anyone who struck me as matching the description "desperately unhappy," but Ray did. My wife and I had to get out of that soup, but Ray left first.

The first winter I was at Humboldt, I placed half a big novel with an option to Houghton Mifflin. So, though I wasn't teaching creative writing there (Dick Day was), I was known by Ray as a writer type. I'd gone to the Iowa Writers' Workshop and was supposed to know what good it was. And on the other hand, Dick Day was always passing on something of Ray's to me, "Ray's latest story." It would be a page, two pages.

I'm sure Ray would have put the question to Day also, but one afternoon at the office I shared with a stuffy, totally old-line mandarin-style senior professor named Giles Sinclair, Ray sought me out. In Sinclair's presence but ignoring him, Ray asked which I would recommend: the Writers' Workshop or a conventional English Ph.D. program. Which would be better for him?

I had no time for more than an excruciating moment of regret that as a student Ray was oblivious to the way the department had divided itself about the issue of creative writing, a division familiar to anyone who carried an M.F.A. rather than a doctorate into an English department in those days. At Humboldt State Giles led the old guard, and I knew his campaign against my job would be hardened by what I had to say to Ray. But it was my conference, and, to give him credit, Giles didn't butt in.

I encouraged Ray no more than I have some others; this is not that sort of story. My partiality was to his poetry promise then, and I did not see he had the "wind" for long distances. But I told him I had seen enough of his stuff to say he might make a writer. I said I didn't even have to think of what he still lacked to tell him the odds were heavily against his making it. Since he had published nothing, his decision had to be made almost purely subjectively. I had been the route myself, so all I could do was to crystalize the decision into two alternatives. I said, Go to the Workshop and you won't get any help. All you will get will be intangible. But if you do have the potential, having gone will be valuable. On the other hand, if you go for the Ph.D., you will be able to count on some help: freshman classes to teach, etc. And after you've deep-sixed creative writing for five to seven years, as you *will,* you still might pick it up and make a writer anyway. I told Ray that only if he knew in his gut that life wouldn't be worth living if he didn't go to Iowa, and he was prepared for a protracted period when it might be pretty near not worth living anyway—in every sense except that he would have the freedom to write—then he should go. But if he felt in any way shaky about that, he should take the academic way.

I never talked to Ray of such things again after that session. When he left Arcata in '63 there was a party, and then he was gone.

If there was any favorable sign for Ray's hopes to be drawn from his interlude at Humboldt, it was fixed in Hemingway's remark "Great writing comes from a sense of injustice."

Giles notwithstanding, I stayed on at Humboldt till I was offered the chance to start a creative writing program at Westminster College in Missouri. I never saw Ray again until the Iowa Workshop's fiftieth anniversary in May '86, though by then through phone calls and correspondence we had arranged that he would come here for a reading in the fall.

So, a twenty-three-year hiatus before we meet again. Of course I have his stories, and the letters and phone calls. The latter simply do business: he remembers me and is willing to come for thus and so. And the former, the stories—which I have grown to like, grown almost addicted to—the stories in no way prepared me for the Ray Carver I was to meet. The stories were so much a true extrapolation of the younger Ray and the life at Arcata in the sixties that, to tell the truth, I stayed away from them for several years after I read the first one. The first one brought me down so much, was so purely distilled Arcata, the *daemon* of the place, that at first I just didn't want to be taken back there the way Ray could do it.

I won't go on about the reception he made here, except to note that the people in the department who went out to dinner with him were well acquainted with some of his stories. They didn't ask any stupid questions, and they made him feel at ease. Later, at the auditorium, students listened to "A Small, Good Thing" and one or two other stories with a kind of avid responsiveness I've seldom seen in them at readings. My creative writing students knew his work as well as they knew Hemingway's. Most of them seemed to have acquired this taste on their own, before I put Ray on the assignment sheet two weeks earlier. But many of the folks he read to were freshmen. With them, he had to make his case orally, on the spot. And you know he didn't major in histrionics and declamation. He simply won them into the stories.

All right. I was proud and pleased as punch with the whole thing. We're such a small school (seven hundred), and sometimes we're overprogrammed. That is, the obligation of providing an audience falls to too small a pool, and the students' response can be flat. But Ray had won them, and they had taken him to heart. On the other hand, he was a very successful writer, and we sometimes get the perfunctory on-the-way-to-somewhere-big treatment. And it had been twenty years. Who was Ray now?

After the reception following the reading, Ray and I and Phyllis, my wife, sat around and visited awhile. I began to get in touch with him a bit then. It wasn't easy to make the connection. Except for his height, his appearance offered few reference points to the Ray of Arcata days. He'd gone from youth, when I'd last seen him, to middle age. Thin as a rail then, now stooping, heavier, his face lined, an air of detachment, a preoccupied-ness that wasn't easy to pierce at first contact. But as we talked and he obviously relaxed, he spoke about his life now and you and his projects. I remember his mentioning that *Where Water Comes Together with Other Water* was just out, or just coming out. More things were being published, more projects were on than he'd ever had before. One got the distinct impression that Ray responded to his rather stunning success with simple satisfaction muted with a touch of amazement. Then he crossed the street to the bed-and-breakfast where I'd gotten him a room.

The conversation continued the next day as I drove him the twenty miles to the airport and waited with him for the plane. I remember that even before we parted, sitting there drinking coffee, I had a sense of the total revision I'd made in my interior image of Ray. Gone was the edged, impersonal, bladelike personality. A warmth, I thought, has come into him and filled him out, made him whole. Then the plane came, and everything was finished except saying so, and I extended my hand. Ray grabbed it with his big hand and tugged. I was getting *hugged!* I was muffled for an instant in the folds of that Burberry trenchcoat. Then we looked at each other, something passing about "next time," and he was gone.

I was numb with a reflected glow all the way home. "Ray's happy now. He's complete," I told my wife. It had to be that. You see, we had been no more than close and sympathetic acquaintances in the Arcata days.

With my very best,
Jay Karr

RICHARD CORTEZ DAY

Bad News

Strip away some twenty-six years and there sits Ray, dejected, in a booth at Tracy's. It is early in March 1963. He has called me at 2:00 a.m. to say, "Bad news. Meet me."

Tracy's Cafe in North Town, Arcata, where drunks and philosophers fetch up, beached, after the bars close. All-night breakfast, the air blue with grease smoke. Cracked laughter, an occasional shriek, a general muttering against unkind fate. I sit down and order coffee.

Ray is the editor of the 1963 *Toyon,* the literary magazine of Humboldt State. I'm the adviser. He says there's not enough good stuff to fill the issue, so if I don't mind he'll fill it out with his own work, using various names. I say, "It's skulduggery, but probably not felonious."

"That's not the bad news," he says. The bad news is that William Carlos Williams died this week. Hemingway dead, and now Williams. The great ones are gone or going fast, and Ray is far from ready to take their place. He's still writing under names true and false for *Toyon.*

"Cheer up," I tell him. "You're young—you've got time."

His gaze drifts to the short-order cook behind the counter, a dead-pale fellow with a bent nose, nearly no chin, and black hair oiled and slicked. A real fry cook, that one—intent, detached, sliding a pan back and forth over the gas flame. A flick of the wrist then, and two eggs fly high, turning once, twice, another half, and land over-easy in the pan again.

"Jesus," Ray says, "did you see that?"

Pure magic. Art is possible. Anything can be done. "Keep working," I tell him.

Over the years I've never known anyone who worked harder. I still see him in that long-gone cafe, in time's backwash: young Ray Carver, just starting out.

Above: 1941. Three-year-old Ray with his parents, Ella and
Raymond Clevie Carver.

Below: 1949. Mother, brother James, father, with Ray
standing behind.

Right: 1950. Ray and father back from fishing. Yakima, WA.

Below: June 1956. High school graduation, Yakima.

Ruth Ziony

Far Left: Nov. 1977. Ray at the time he and Tess Gallagher first met.

Above: Summer 1978. Ray with Page Stegner (conter) and Jim Houston.

Left: 1978. Ray and Tess at Chuck Kinder's for Thanksgiving.

Right: Spring 1979.
Rowing in Mexico City.

Below: Spring 1983.
Behind Ray are
Sally Daniels,
Hayden Carruth
and Tess Gallagher.
Syracuse, N.Y.

Far Right: 1983.
On Sky House deck,
Port Angeles.

Above: 1967. Ray with his children, Vance and Christine.

Below: Summer 1974. From left: Judy and Noel Young, Jim Houston and Ray at the Second Annual Writers Stampede, Casa Coyote, Santa Barbara.

Above: 1984. Ray holding granddaughter Jennifer, and Tess.
Below: 1985. With Marvin Bell and Tess.

Above: 1986. Ray and Tobias Wolff.
Below: 1986. With Gary Fisketjon at Sky House.

Tess Gallagher

Above: September 1986. Goose hunting in Saskatchewan with, from left: Bob Calder, Peter Nash, Ray, Dave Carpenter and Bill Robertson.

Below: With Henry Carlile.

Left: 1987. Fishing in Alaska.

Below: Summer 1987. Visiting V.S. Pritchett in London.

Far Left: 1987. At State Capitol in Olympia, Washington where he received the governor's award.

Left: January 1988. With William Kittredge on Four Seasons Ranch.

Below: May 15, 1988. With William L. Stull at the University of Hartford where Ray received an honorary doctor of letters degree

Right: June 1988. Ray planting a Japanese maple at Ridge House.

Below: July 1988. With son Vance.

Above: June 17, 1988. Tess and Ray after their wedding in Reno.
Below: July 1988. Last photo of Ray and Tess together. Ridge House.

Betty Udesen, Seattle Times

July 30, 1989. Tess has a quiet moment at the graveside of her late husband.

DENNIS SCHMITZ

Secret Places

Ray was a master storyteller—in the poems too. If you want to know what sort of person Ray was, read the poems. The short stories suggest his program as a writer, but in the poems he was able to say "I" more easily, was able to say how he felt. Ray's short stories and his poems were concurrent; the stories tell about his troubles in an objective way, but the poems, first-person, redeemed him. He could speak in a level voice, directly, in a conversational way that often rose to a tone of reverence, praise, wonderment.

Ray was a shy man with a low voice, a short, barking laugh that you heard as often as you heard mere words, his cigarette smoke curling around his eyes. He was a delight in the spun-out joke or story two people could build in conversation, a reminiscence, always interrupting the story with laughter. He was not a talker but a conversationalist. The stories and poems are that intimate, disarming. The horror tales of the bad jobs he had always turned in retrospect to foibles: though humans were never big enough for their dreams, the life that was given them was enough. That's why he loved Chekhov's short stories his whole writing life, and why it's appropriate that the story of Chekhov's death (a parallel?) is the final story in his collected stories.

The bad jobs sometimes turned into good jobs. He was a graveyard-shift sweep-up man at Sacramento's Mercy Hospital during the late sixties, the years when I first knew Ray. We laughed then about how the job was a writer's sort of job. We laughed almost the same way about it years later. He wondered if he'd ever had such a wonderful job, writing by day, working so little by night. Bad jobs were good jobs if the writing you did meanwhile was good. The poem "The Autopsy Room" in *Ultramarine* shows the other side of that job and of his personal life.

Maryann, his first wife, selling encyclopedias door-to-door, working as a waitress, had bad jobs too, both she and Ray trying anything, even a short term as live-in managers of a Sacramento apartment complex. Then there was the abortive student exchange situation for her in Tel Aviv (they came back midway through the term)—all the years of dead-ended dreaming from the time of their late-teen marriage. The small towns, seedy rentals, the piecemeal college study, the intermittent bursts of relative prosperity, through it all she was avid for Ray's work. They grew up together. They worked so hard for one another. Ray understood the characters in his stories who were knocked about by circumstance because he was one of them.

Eventually, Ray had teaching jobs which came as a result of the success of his early stories (many of them with Sacramento settings) collected in *Will You Please Be Quiet, Please?* Meanwhile, he fought alcoholism and quit drinking. His subsequent life with Tess Gallagher changed him and his work. The stories and poems came richer, fuller, and there were more of them. He was happy. The ten years he speaks about in the poem "Gravy," years that he had earned, were the gift that Tess gave him. They shared their writing, probably pushed each other farther than each could have reached alone. But he was never satisfied with grief. Look at the later stories which transcend accommodation, and the poems, all of them, which tell you right out the richness and diversity of the lives one person has.

The last poem in *Ultramarine,* "The Gift," is one of the many thank-you poems to Tess; *tenderness,* the gift that the narrator speaks about, is the ability to give as much as to receive compassionate love. We should address and perhaps are able to address one another with tenderness because one really can't know what the other feels. Secret places.

Humans wrestle one another—it's one-to-one in the stories—and the wrestling sometimes turns into embracing. In the poems, Ray could turn to monologue, to the lyric, to a person embracing himself; he could show that he understood the ironies he turned on himself and not be hurt. The poems have renewal after renewal.

"The Gift" contrasts the changes in spiritual states of the narrator's life by naming the places in which the changes occurred. Ray uses this device in other poems; the process gives the poems grounding, locale. You verify something happened by saying where it happened, verifying memory by association but also allaying the power of bad events by putting them in context. Not that Ray was ever afraid to face what he had to, deny himself good or bad luck. "Glad to be here, and nowhere else," he says in "The Gift."

Ray never hid in his work; integrity was the stake even in the bad stretches of his life when he thought he had no integrity. You would have thought that because of the frankness of the early- and middle-period stories that he'd have no more secrets. But he kept discovering new things in himself; Tess made those places accessible. There are several versions of some of the stories when he felt he had not gone far enough.

Ray wanted to write for everyone, to be clear, and if you see the statistics about his popularity in the countries in which his work was translated (some twenty different languages), you understand that what he wrote was universal because familiar. He'd found the point of contact, the place where a person rubs up against another, living brand-name domesticity, often not having the words to talk to one another or name their condition but having the products to identify how they lived. The stories have a kind of sad Kmart specificity in the listing of the signs of the culture.

When Loretta and I saw him the last time in July 1988, I gave Ray back a Carver anecdote. There's a stretch of the Pacific coast between Jenner and Fort Ross where northbound Highway 1 climbs through switchbacks to maybe nine hundred feet. Below, I had discovered a pocket-sized rocky beach you could see only when you're coming south on the road through the last straightaway into the descent, a secret place.

Back in the late sixties, Gary Thompson, Ray, and I spent a weekend there, talking, climbing, splashing around. I remember the event because I have the place: the driving is slow, maybe a little scary there; I pass it every trip thinking the same thing. We were young, we had literary causes, and we had fears which could be burned off in the sun or washed with small talk. We had a fire for cooking and telling late-night stories; we slept.

Ray's sleeping bag was empty the next morning. The way out was up. Finally, we saw where Ray had scrambled, slid back, climbed; in the half-dark, he'd hiked to the car and driven the miles to a place where he could get coffee, he later told us. Coffee, coffee. Which was more amazing—Ray's push for the coffee, or the care he took not to disturb us for it? It wasn't much of a secret place, nor much of a quirk to reveal. The climb was hard, and he went up and away from us without our knowing.

Generally, most of us like the same things in poems that we like in human beings. If the contact is to be casual, we will forgive pushiness and some self-indulgence, but for the long run, we love the humans and poems that will show us our secrets; we welcome trust and what the Sunday supplements call vulnerability.

Ray was a noble and generous man; he never held back as a writer or as a person. Who had more life? But he died too soon for all of us who loved him and anticipated other secrets his writing would give us.

MORTON MARCUS

All-American Nightmares

One of the most often-used later publicity photos of Ray Carver shows him seated, leaning forward, hands crossed in front of him, wearing a soft leather flying jacket, eyes peering intently, almost challengingly at the viewer. His hair is mussed but recently razored to fashionably fit his face. He looks like he's just come from a polo match or his fortieth bombing mission over Schweinfurt. He's cool, in control, almost aggressively, intimidatingly self-confident. There are several variations of this photograph, most taken by Marion Ettlinger, but they all insist on the intensity of those eyes, on that self-confidence, and on the hair razored fashionably short and mussed.

The Ray Carver I knew looked nothing like that. He wore ties and rumpled sport jackets and never appeared quite right in them. Not that the jackets didn't fit, but that he seemed awkward, even uncomfortable wearing them: he held his shoulders too high, away from his body, like adolescent weights, giving the impression that there was an iron bar lashed across his upper back and that his body hung slackly from it. Sometimes it seemed as if that bar was the only thing holding him up. As for his hair, it grew over his ears and sat in uncombed chunks around his head. A nervous, raspy laugh punctuated his sentences and he had trouble looking people in the eye. The word *youthful* comes to mind, and *shy, bashful, ingenuous.* Or *boyish. Eternally boyish.* A boy who woke in a nightmare to find himself in an adult's body hemmed in on all sides by sport jackets and snatches of menacing conversation.

As for props, he usually had a glass in one hand and a cigarette in the other. Like the imagined bar across his back, they held him up in their own way, although now I can't help seeing that cigarette as a piece of chalk he used to chart his lifeline on the cosmic blackboard, or as a baton with which he was learning to conduct his own requiem.

At the outset, I want to say that my relationship with Ray never reached the boozy intimacy he had with others. I knew him from 1967 to 1977, his most notoriously alcoholic period, and even though I can still sit and talk in bars for hours on end, I don't drink now and I didn't drink then. We were an unlikely pair in more ways than one: Ray internalized everything—his pains, his uncertainties, his humiliations, his fears—whereas I gushed them in a torrent of emotions and operatic gestures. Add to this that Ray was a small-town boy, and a small-town boy from the Northwest at that, while I was a city boy from the East Coast, and the differences are clear.

On the other hand, Ray and I didn't put on airs. Although I was from New York City, I never pretended to be cool or hip. Ray—and Maryann, too—were open and generous-spirited from the start. I knew they had no rocks in their hands and they knew I had none in mine. We never analyzed our friendship or even once questioned why we liked one another because whenever we saw each other we talked, laughed, shared our work, and generally enjoyed one another's company. No matter how many months would go by between meetings we resumed our friendship where we had left off.

In 1981 Ray sent me a copy of *What We Talk About When We Talk About Love*. In it he had inscribed this dedication: "For Mort, with nothing but love, and admiration." That about says it, although the word "admiration" needs to be explained. I'd like to think it refers to the writing, which truly cemented the friendship, the recognition on both our parts that under the sport coats we were two kids trying to figure out what this life meant, no matter how horrendous the revelations, and that we were both pursuing that goal through a mutually ferocious dedication to words. That commitment was our inseparable bond.

Besides this, I was a poet whose work Ray liked, and poets were something special to him. He said toward the end of his life that he would like to be remembered as a poet, and I wish now I had told him more often how good I thought his poetry was. There is a lack of pretentiousness in his poems—in tone and diction—which is unique in contemporary American poetry, and we can all learn from it. It is disarming and therefore makes the implications, ironies, and juxtapositions of images that much more powerful. Ray wrote poetry as if it were written with a small, not a capital, *p,* conveying an impression of naturalness that no other American poet of his generation—and maybe any other generation—has been able to evoke. In his last volume, *A New Path to the Waterfall* (1989), this naturalness reaches its apex, spilling with an appearance of artlessness that resembles nothing so much as water, which assumes the shape of every channel it enters yet remains itself, and which appears as swirls, slurs, elongations and a variety of textures and colors under the shifts of light and the sediments it travels over, yet remains as transparent and ephemeral as breath when you attempt to lift it in your hands.

Ray always insisted that we knew each other in Iowa, and so did Maryann, but I can't recall it. And our dates of tenure there don't correspond. Sometimes I think he meant that he knew of me from Iowa. Maybe that was it. As far as I'm concerned we met at George Hitchcock's house on Laguna Street in San Francisco at one of those parties Hitchcock gave four times a year to put *Kayak* magazine together. There were always about twenty of us, an interchangeable group of contributors, friends, actors, and writers or painters passing through, all turned into happy workers by Hitchcock, a commanding presence with a voice like a wave booming in a sea cave, who directed us to collate and staple pages, stuff and address envelopes, and encouraged us to meet each other, while he kept bread, cold cuts, beer, and pies stacked on the kitchen table.

At that time *Kayak* was one of the important literary magazines in the country and fostered a sort of deep image or "near surrealist" approach to poetry. But as a kayak is a one-man vessel, so the magazine was a product of one man's taste, a man who abhorred categories, George Hitchcock. The magazine displayed his many talents as poet, editor, printer, visual artist, and organizer. He was the sun from which all things grew and ideas radiated, the center we looked toward for direction. Well over six feet, a recognized playwright, and an actor in the grand manner—on those Sundays he directed the closest thing to an American-style Parisian salon I have ever attended.

It was at the collating party in the spring of 1967, I think, that Hitchcock introduced me to Ray and Maryann, an indulgence to which George's laissez-faire attitude towards social etiquette usually didn't succumb. Ray said he remembered me from Iowa and was an admirer of my poetry, but even then I wondered if he had asked George to introduce us. As I have said, I still don't remember Ray from Iowa and it wouldn't be until many years later that I learned he had been the student of two special and talented friends of mine, the fiction writer Richard Day at Humboldt State University and the poet Dennis Schmitz at Sacramento State University, both of whom could have exposed Ray to my work. When I learned that, I suspected even more that Ray had asked Hitchcock to introduce us and that he hadn't said he *knew* me from Iowa but rather had *heard* about me there.

Whatever the reason, Ray and I were soon chatting like old friends. There was an openness about Ray and Maryann that could win over anyone. There was nothing morbid or precious about them. They weren't ego-centered or self-absorbed as are so many of the literati I have met. We talked about everything—from literature to sports to politics—and kept talking from one collating party to the next. Within a year or two Hitchcock and his wife broke up and Maryann's sister, Amy, a vivacious, talented actress, began coming to the collating parties. She and George were entranced with each other immediately, and I remember staying late a number of times to watch them perform some hilarious, ingenious, spontaneous bit of nonsense after which the five of us would go off to dinner somewhere, joined by any odd member of the collating squad who wanted to come with us.

At about this time (1969) Hitchcock put out my first book of poems, *Origins,* and a year later he brought out Ray's first major collection, *Winter Insomnia.* During this period, I knew Ray as a poet. That is what we talked about mostly, and I'd seen some of his poems in *Kayak* and other magazines. He never lost this focus on poetry and I think the extreme concentration he exercised in his prose at times can be traced to his poetic practices. Gradually he showed me one or two stories, then added others, many in manuscript or in pages stripped from magazines. I was astonished by them, to say the least. As I remember, the first one I saw was "The Student's Wife," and soon after that "Will You Please Be Quiet, Please?" and within the next year or two, in the early seventies, "Fat" and "Neighbors."

What was astonishing, even unique about Ray's stories at that time was not that they engaged everyday American life and went behind the doors of suburban middle-class and blue-collar homes, but that they were scenarios of our worst dreams about the reality of our neighbors' existences, scenarios about the spiritual barreness at the heart of American life which the majority of us were living, whether we admitted it or not. Ray had the courage to face this barrenness and the genius to make it come alive.

I sensed that a lot of Ray's writing was autobiographical, things that had happened to him and Maryann or, more, things he feared might. That's why I call them scenarios. He was writing his worst dreams, readying himself for whatever might happen to him and his family, innocent small-town American kids moving through the world like victims in search of an oppressor.

That's the reason Ray's acclaimed realism is so strange, or rather "unrealistic" in the end, and seems to be steeped not in bleakness but in nightmare and approaches the surreal. His poetry, especially. It is a poetry of the threatened. *Winter Insomnia* is propelled by a kind of paranoia, a fear that everyone the speaker encounters means him and his family harm or poses the possibility of it. Menace is everywhere, especially in the poems that deal with the Middle East. It is the paranoia one finds in an Alfred Hitchcock film or an Eric Ambler thriller. Everyone out there is a threat. This is not "realism" or "superrealism." It is, if anything, expressionism, a reality shaped and shadowed by the mind of the artist. That is why I think Ray's poems and stories were so admired by the *Kayak* crowd and why *Winter Insomnia* came out under the *Kayak* imprint.

One more word about the work. Not so much those of us around *Kayak*, but later, in Santa Cruz from 1970 to 1976, just before *Will You Please Be Quiet, Please?* hurled Ray to the heights of the literary world, a number of writers I knew thought Ray's stories too depressing. I wonder if they would think that now, not because Ray has become a legend, but because in the last few years what he imagined about America has become the truth of our lives—the unemployment, the fear of homelessness, and the lack of medical security; I mean the terror of being poor or disenfranchised in this land of milk and acid. Intuitively Ray knew what that part of America was all about and the terror of that knowledge drove him to the bottle and cigarettes, or so I thought then and think to this day.

Now it might seem too simple to assign the fear of the small-town boy with the weak father, the father who didn't even provide him with a location of good places to fish, as the reason for Ray's drinking and smoking, but I did, as many of us do with our friends. The bottle lip and cigarette tip were nipples on a milk bottle that gave Ray security, pacifiers that let him relax—pacifiers he didn't need any more when he met Tess and that he had needed with Maryann because he and Maryann were both young and he had to grow *through* his fears and *out* of them when he was with her. Maybe these notions are too easy. And, again, maybe they're not.

By late summer of 1968 I'd moved seventy miles south of San Francisco to the small coastal town of Santa Cruz, where I had gotten a job teaching English at a community college. I still journeyed to San Francisco for the *Kayak* collating parties, but within a year Hitchcock followed me to Santa Cruz and was teaching poetry and acting at the local University of California campus. He continued printing *Kayak* magazine and books from his Santa Cruz address.

Ray and Maryann were living in Cupertino, a suburban town thirty miles south of San Francisco and ten miles north of San Jose, the center of a middle-class residential area which in the late sixties and early seventies served the families of the burgeoning computer microchip industry called Silicon Valley. Ray and Maryann were living the TV version of the American good life. As I remember, one of the houses they rented was a one-story, upper-middle-class showpiece complete with swimming pool, fieldstone walls, and huge bay windows set in angles like transparent guillotines—although I suspect my hyperbolic imagination has galloped off here with the frail damsel of memory. I do recall that at night you could see all the way to the bay, several miles away, street lights and house windows along the way glittering like an overturned jewel box. I remember at least several memorable parties there, each with dozens of people—a lot of writers and businessmen and engineers, the last two groups obviously neighbors and fellow workers.

I'm not sure but I think Ray was still employed as a textbook editor at Science Research Associates and Maryann was teaching high school in Los Altos. What is certain is that they were living beyond their means and soon it was difficult to reach them by phone. The creditors were descending and any friendly "Hi!" chirping from the receiver could be followed by demands for payment of overdue bills. Was it that year, 1970, or five years later, that Ray's mother or Maryann would answer the phone explaining that the Carvers no longer resided at that address? When I came to visit once, Ray's mother, who didn't know me, insisted I had the wrong house, until Ray, who was standing behind an inner door, rescued me.

At about this time Ray showed me the manuscript of a new story called "What Is It?" (later renamed "Are These Actual Miles?"), one of the most terrifying pieces he ever wrote. It was about the day in the life of a man burdened with bills whose wife goes off to sell the family car. At different points during the afternoon and evening the man receives calls from his wife who says she is on the verge of making a "great deal" on the car. Finally, in the early hours of the next morning, drunk, she is covertly dropped at home by the car salesman, and the husband stoically puts her to bed. But the salesman returns to place the wife's handbag, which she had left in his car, on the porch. Observing the salesman through the window, the husband wrenches the door open to confront him, but he is unable to say anything to the man, who retreats and drives off behind a nervous spattering of excuses.

The story is filled with a sense of humiliation for both husband and wife, a sense of hopelessness for anyone caught in our socio-economic treadmill. Few writers anywhere have portrayed economic degradation this nakedly. At the time I was overwhelmed by the story and wondered if it was yet another scenario of Ray's terrors, but I never asked him. Now I assign the story to the category of those chilling pieces of literature that depict the end of an age, a time such as Ray's beloved Chekhov wrote about so relentlessly in plays and stories. The cultures and times are different, but the vision and subject are the same, although Chekhov's vision is not as raw as Ray's.

During this period I was teaching a course I had designed for the University of California Extension called "Writers off the Page." The class met all day Saturday. In the morning we discussed a novel or book of poems by a contemporary author, and in the afternoon the author met with the class to read aloud, answer questions, and discuss the work.

I asked Ray to be one of the participants and select several stories. He chose "What Is It?" ("Are These Actual Miles?"), "Neighbors," "Fat," and an initiation story he had just finished called "The Summer Steelhead" (which appeared renamed and revised, not for the better, as "Nobody Said Anything" in *Will You Please Be Quiet, Please?* and later as the first piece in Ray's selected stories, *Where I'm Calling From*). The story is about a boy who does combat with a giant fish in the river on the other side of his hometown. What makes the story unique is its frame, which comments ironically on the boy's coming-of-age ritual: at the beginning and again at the end of the story, the boy is witness to his parents' arguing. This intrusion of the dreary adult world of 1950s America destroys the boy's heroic undertaking, which had charged his imagination by making the everyday world marvelous. All of this was suggested in the original story by medieval quest imagery paralleling the contemporary images, but was cut by the time the story was collected as "Nobody Said Anything."

The class was composed mostly of teachers taking the course for graduate units. Ray's stories excited and horrified them because of the fresh way he had of directly facing the dark side of American life. The group was filled with admiration. His stories generated the kind of energy people feel when they discover someone in their midst who is going to be a celebrity.

This was the third time I had given the class, and the powers that be had decided to move its location to Palo Alto, fifty miles northeast of Santa Cruz, as an experiment to draw new students. Weather permitting, we would meet for the afternoon session under a shady clump of trees in a rolling, open park.

When I met Ray to guide him to our glade, I was surprised by how nervous he was. He was more jumpy than I had ever seen him. I pretended not to notice at first, but as he tremblingly lit one cigarette after another I finally asked what was wrong.

"This is the first time," he said.

"For what?" I replied.

"This is the first time I ever taught a class."

"On your own work?"

"On anything."

It had never occurred to me that Ray hadn't taught before. I tried to calm him down, give him confidence and a few basic pointers— a coach's pep talk. I tried to make him see that he had already introduced himself through his stories, that everyone in the class thought they knew him to the quick because of who they imagined the writer of those stories to be. I don't think that set him at ease at all.

He was dry-mouthed and twitching as he began the class. But many of the women, seeing his nervousness, gave him maternal encouragement; and the outright admiration of the entire group was so apparent that within fifteen minutes my rhetorical questions and other verbal aids were no longer necessary. Ray's shy, humble manner won everyone over, and he warmed to the serious conversation about his work. I like to think he developed his unassuming, open classroom style because of what happened that day, but the truth is he was just being Ray and sooner or later he would have realized that simple secret of teaching. As I remember, I invited him to talk to the class for several successive semesters; those who took the course repeatedly insisted on it.

One more thing. Neither the class nor I could convince Ray that "The Summer Steelhead" ("Nobody Said Anything") was a first-rate story. I nagged him about it endlessly over the next several years and he did finally send it out and get it published in the *Seneca Review*. But he always felt unsure about it. Maybe he thought it was too much like Hemingway's *The Old Man and the Sea*. Maybe he was piqued at himself for writing an initiation story, the kind of tale he had been raised on and knew had become clichéd by the late fifties. I don't know. But I was happy to see it as the lead-off story in *Where I'm Calling From,* even in its severely revised form.

By 1972 Hitchcock had gotten Ray a teaching assignment at the University of California Santa Cruz. That had to have been accomplished through the man who had hired Hitchcock, the well-known short story writer James B. Hall, who had been made the provost of the new creative arts college on campus, which was called, for lack of a financial donor, College V. George worked there and now so did Ray.

While he was at the university, Ray influenced a lot of students, including a number of my former pupils who would tell me how much they loved him as both a teacher and a human being. I, of course, would tell those of my students heading up to the university to be sure and take a class with him. Although he was only working at the university part-time and would soon begin a dizzying travel week teaching at both Santa Cruz and the University of Iowa (a schedule reminiscent of the feverish peregrinations across Siberia of Vassily Sergeyitch in Chekhov's "In Exile"), Ray had the energy to convert UC Santa Cruz's literary magazine, *Quarry,* into a publication of national stature, under the name *Quarry West,* by lobbying many of the poets and fiction writers he knew to submit work to it.

It was during Ray's tenure at Santa Cruz that one of the more revealing episodes in my relationship with him took place. As I recall, it was in 1973. Ray had been chosen to host Charles Bukowski, who was to give a reading at the university. When he met Bukowski at the airport he discovered that the irascible poet had been on a binge for more than a week. I wonder if Ray saw a future image of himself in the creased, pockmarked face of his older contemporary. I know something early on made him decide not to drink glass for glass with Bukowski, and when we met before the reading Ray was completely sober—and worried. He didn't have any idea of how Bukowski was going to behave, and had quickly realized that the Los Angeles poet operated on both insult and shock.

"Stick close," Ray said to me, "and be sure to come to the party after—please."

Bukowski, for his part, must have taken one look at Ray in his corduroy trousers and rumpled sports jacket and decided to dismiss him as an insipid academic. The reading drew a full audience and was a wild affair. Bukowski punctuated each poem by sucking from a large bottle of gin and tossing raspy insults at the audience— all spoiled middle-class students and prissy professors, as far as he was concerned. The professors grinned condescendingly or left. Or grinned and then left. But by and large the students were titillated, and warmed to this old drunk telling them what little shits they were. I got the impression that Bukowski delighted in parading his image and that the students were experiencing the taboo excitement of slumming, or being in touch with "real life"—at least for the evening.

Ray wasn't amused by any of it. His worried expression was a mask stuck to his face throughout the reading. As host, he said later, he felt responsible for whatever happened and I translated this into meaning that he saw his credibility slipping with his superiors at the university with every insult Bukowski growled.

At the party, held in the house of two former students of mine who were currently students of Ray's, things got wilder. Only students were present after the first ten minutes. Rock music and pot smoke engulfed the shabby room. Bukowski, drinking everything in sight, muttered, bragged, cursed, and getting drunker by the minute, grabbed the girls and mashed his whiskery face against theirs, or shot his hand to the crotch of their jeans or down their shirts. Several of the girls screamed and ran from the house. A number of the more cerebral students sat back and stared straight ahead, probably stoned. A group of rough town poets watched Bukowski's every move adoringly, as if they were learning how to be real poets with every belch or snort. Ray started drinking.

Bukowski blinked when he saw me coming up the stairs. "Allen," he said, "I didn't know you were here. Why doncha recite some lines from *Howl?*" (Even in his drunken haze, Bukowski recognized my tribal resemblance to Allen Ginsberg—albeit an Allen Ginsberg who had swallowed an orange crate.)

I shot back some stupid remark to the effect that "My name isn't Allen. It's Kenneth, Kenneth Patchen."

A malevolent smile lit Bukowski's face, making him look like a sinister pumpkin, as he turned toward Ray. "Hey, professor, why didncha tell me that Allen was gonna be here?" Then he turned back to me and said, "Come on, Allen, give us some *Howl*."

My former students were so poor they didn't own a couch and Bukowski was seated like a malicious Buddha on a mattress set on the living room floor, stubbing out his cigarettes on the floorboards until one of the students who lived in the apartment stopped him.

Bukowski kept turning to Ray between drinks and grabs, derisively calling him "professor" and treating him like the most menial servant, every once in a while turning to me with that sinister pumpkin face and saying, "Come on, Allen, let's hear it."

I smiled back as malevolently as I could. Bukowski continued drinking. More students ran squealing from the house. Soon Ray, fed up, and by now drunk himself, stalked out. There was no one left but my two former students, Bukowski, and two or three others. Bukowski had not risen from the mattress in several hours. Now, obviously exhausted, he subsided into a stupor, his chin on his chest. "So, Allen," he muttered one more time, "what do you think of this shit?"

At this point Ray clumped up the stairs. Bukowski spied him and raised his head for a moment. "Professor," he said with the last bit of derision he could muster. "Professor . . ."

Ray looked down at him, swaying, but said nothing, his expression caught midway between disgust and pity. But maybe it was neither. Ray was drunker than I'd ever seen him. Something about Bukowski's behavior struck deep inside him, like a pickax sinking into the wall of a mine, something he never spoke to me about. My sense of the extremity of Ray's reaction, however, suggests that there was something more to it than just disgust or pity. I'm convinced he saw in Bukowski's drinking and behavior intimations of his own future, a sort of Mr. Hyde who would be released by his incessant boozing. On the other hand, this is said with a good deal of hindsight and may be just literary balderdash.

It was a revelatory evening, an historic non-meeting of two major American writers. For the first time I saw Ray act uncomfortably, feeling responsible for someone else and not knowing how to handle the situation. Bukowski was too much for him: Ray couldn't deal with his continual insults and venomous behavior. But

Bukowski was more revealing to me. He showed that the self-image he chose to establish in his poems, an image that limited the poems in both reach and meaning, had taken him over. He had become the mask he chose to face the world wearing. More than this, he was so overwhelmed by this image, and the easy assumptions that went with it, that he stereotyped Ray. Bukowski never realized that he was in the presence of the one artist whose work on the same subjects and themes had achieved what he himself rarely if ever could, for the very reasons he failed to recognize who Ray was—lack of real interest in others and compassion.

The upshot of the incident was a nasty poem by Bukowski about the uptight academic host who took care of him in Santa Cruz and a reply from Ray, the collage-barrage of lines he heard or thought he heard Bukowski speak throughout the evening incorporated into the poem "You Don't Know What Love Is," a poem that can be found in *Fires*.

I've often wondered if Bukowski ever read any of Ray's work and realized that *that* Ray Carver, that "uptight academic" host, was no prissy professor but the author of stories of more depth, passion, and authenticity than Bukowski allowed himself to write.

During the winter of 1972, Noel Young of Capra Press asked to bring out two of my books. That request grew into a friendship. Over the next several years I sent along a dozen or so writers to Capra for Noel's burgeoning chapbook series, a dozen or so West Coast writers, I should add, for there was a feeling among us of neglect and downright hostility from the publishers and editors of the good green East.

The first author I introduced to Noel was James D. Houston, a novelist whose subject matter and themes are the mores and life-styles of the California central coast, a thinker who in book after book has insightfully defined what California means to the psyches of those who live here. Jim, also a friend of Ray's, was completing a group of stories at that time about a character named Charlie Bates whose very existence, often depicted in Kafkaesque comic situations, was bound up with cars and freeways, certainly a most California subject. Noel immediately took one of the stories for the chapbook series and a year later brought out all the Charlie Bates stories in one volume. Now both Jim and I were feeding Noel authors, and I'm sure that both of us urged him to get in touch with Ray, while urging Ray to get in touch with Noel.

Nothing happened until the spring of '72 or '73, and Jim and I were both involved in it. It was at the annual Swanton Corn Roast, a spring ritual in those years when all the local craftspersons— potters, weavers, jewelry makers, and leather workers—showed their wares in makeshift stalls set up in the wilds off a rural road north of the coastal hamlet of Davenport. The scenery was the epitome of old California, open farmlands surrounded by woods. The corn roast was held in a meadow hemmed in by redwoods, madrone trees with their sweet-potato-colored bark, lime-colored lichen-splotched coast live oaks, and spicy-smelling California bay trees, all tangled together by vines and jumbles of weeds and poison oak still green and succulent from the winter rains.

The corn roast drew people from as far away as San Jose and San Francisco. Hundreds of cars lined the narrow road. The roast was an event, a reason to get into the country for city dwellers and come away with a pitcher or belt or beaded necklace made by local artisans, not mass-produced by anonymous factory workers. The roast was part of the return-to-the-earth movement that gripped the nation in the early seventies.

As Noel remembers it, I was strolling with him, both of us looking at the displays. Jim Houston was playing bass with a bluegrass band called the Red Mountain Boys, a traditional part of the day's entertainment, and as the banjos caplunketed and the fiddles whined and the guitars thwanged and Jim plucked baritone sounds of gastric disorder from his phlegmatic bass, Noel and I came upon a tall galoot lying on his side in the grass with his head propped in one hand, listening to the music. Noel remembers that the man had "a purple wine mustache." I remember that there were several paper cups on the ground nearby.

I turned to Noel and said something like "Remember I told you about a terrific short story writer you should get ahold of? Well, here he is." Then I spoke to the reclining figure. "How you doing, Ray? Remember that publisher from down south I've been urging you to send stuff to, Noel Young? Well, here he is. Noel, Ray; Ray, Noel."

Now that may sound like one of the great shaggy dog stories of all time, an anti-anecdote, the report of one of the great non-events in any memoir. But truth to tell, it was an historic meeting. Out of it Noel would eventually publish Ray's short story collection *Furious Seasons* in 1977 and the potpourri of short stories, poems, and essays, *Fires,* in 1983. Capra would become the publishing house where the original and restored versions of some of Ray's best stories would be permanently maintained. That Ray returned to Capra to publish *Fires* after he had become one of the nation's most publicized writers was a symbolic return to the West from the frenetic East, a move he would make physically within two years after the book came out. *Fires* contains the definitive versions of those stories that first appeared in *Furious Seasons* and that, in two instances, appeared in *What We Talk About When We Talk About Love,* the book that made him famous but that also contained drastically revised versions—to my taste, far too drastically—of many previously published stories. In *Fires* Ray re-revised (actually restored) two of the stories that I consider among his best, "Distance" and "So Much Water So Close to Home." For that reason, and its plenteous helping of poems, *Fires* is an important source for understanding Ray's work. We can thank Noel Young for that as well as for the original versions of the stories in *Furious Seasons.*

In a letter to an editor inquiring about Ray, I wrote that "I knew him before the fame, before he became a legend. I knew him as he groped his way through the thicket of his problems, and I can tell you that even then he was a lovable man who, despite the debt and drinking, I would trust with my life, and for me that is the test of a human being's mettle." A friend who is a therapist told me that such values are typical of people abandoned in childhood, which I was. Who knows? But loyalty and a good heart go a long way to winning my affections, and Ray had both. Do those words smack of sentimentality? So be it. There was a man here I loved who is a hole in the air now, a doorway the wind shuttles through. This man left us gifts at great personal expense, a suitcase full of small trick mirrors in which we can see our distorted inner selves. I remember this person as someone who shaped and polished those mirrors day after day through cigarette smoke, alcohol fumes, unpaid bills, and domestic dogfights. He came and is gone, but the gifts he made for us remain, each one a kiss on our lives.

GEOFFREY DUNN

Tell Me More About Salmon Fishing

for Tess Gallagher

It was just starting to get dark when he pulled over to pick me up in his old Ford sedan. Some books and dirty shirts and what looked like a shaving kit were scattered on the back seat.

"Where are you going?" he asked as I opened the door.

"Downtown," I said. "Anywhere into town is fine."

"I'm just going to the bottom of the hill," he said. "End of Mission Street."

I thought about it for a moment. There weren't many cars leaving campus at that time in the evening. "Sure," I nodded. "Okay."

He wasn't all that friendly. I'd seen him at the university coffee-house a couple of times and figured him to be a professor. He was a big guy with fair skin and thick dark hair brushed forward and not much of a smile. He seemed lost in thought.

We turned down the hill at the west end of campus. It was a gorgeous view. In the distance you could make out the lights of the Santa Cruz waterfront and the last trace of a sunset over the Pacific. I don't think he noticed.

"I'm going to stop for a drink at Paul's Lounge," he said. "Then I'm going 'cross town. You can wait around if you like."

I had just turned twenty-one but didn't look it, so he may have thought I was too young to go inside. "I'll have a beer with you if it's okay," I said. He nodded.

There were lots of regulars at Paul's that evening, guys just off work from the Wrigley's plant playing pool and shuffleboard. The room was full of smoke, and Buck Owens was blaring from the juke.

I think he was surprised to find out that the bartender at Paul's was my Aunt Sally. I leaned over the bar to give her a kiss and she grabbed me by the hair. "When you gonna cut that stuff?" she growled in mock anger. I just laughed. Paul's was pretty much redneck in those days. It wasn't a place for university types.

He ordered a mixed drink, a bourbon and soda or something like that. Aunt Sally gave me an Oly on the house.

"How the hell's your mother?" she asked.

"Working her ass off. Still living with that drunk."

"But he's a nice drunk," Aunt Sally said. "Treats her good. Remember that."

The guy who gave me the ride lit a cigarette. "My name's Ray," he said. "I'm teaching at the university this semester." He let go the slimmest of smiles. We shook hands. Ray's grip wasn't all that firm.

I'd like to say we talked about writing, but we didn't. We talked mostly about fishing. I was working part-time on a salmon boat back then, and the conversation focused on baits, currents, trawling gear, and wages.

"So what were you doing at the university?" he asked.

"I'm a student," I said a little brashly. "I only fish weekends." I took a sip from my beer. "I'm a politics major. Right now I'm reading a lot of Marx and Tocqueville."

"Never have read 'em," Ray said. He lit another cigarette. "Politics don't interest me."

He wasn't being mean about it, nor even emphatic. I suppose he was just being honest. "Tell me more about salmon fishing," he said.

About a year later, I was in a bookshop when I saw Ray's picture on the back of a hardcover. I recognized him right away. I sat down and read a couple of his stories. They were pretty bleak and dark and, well, apolitical. I didn't like them all that much at the time, but you know, they stayed with me.

I told my Aunt Sally about the book. She said she hadn't seen Ray in quite a while. "Used to come in here two, maybe three nights a week. Always just after work, 'cept once he came in around noon and really got loaded. He put it away that day, I tell ya. Never said much. Never tipped much neither."

From time to time I'd see his stories in magazines, and then there'd be a new book and reviews. Somewhere I read that he'd cleaned up his act and had given up drinking. He was getting to be pretty famous.

I was in a train station in southern Italy years later when I saw his name on the cover of a magazine. Inside was a story of his about a writer and his ex-wife. I read it once at the station and again on the train. I liked it. By then I'd been married and divorced myself. That Ray's really got marriage down, I thought. And then I remembered the deep lines running across his forehead.

A few more years go by and I'm in Seattle with my girlfriend and my nine-year-old daughter on our way home from Canada. We've just stopped off for breakfast, and there's Ray's photo again, only this time it's on the obituary page of the *Seattle Times*. "Fifty years old," it says. "He grew up in Yakima."

A guy in the booth next to us is smoking a cigarette and it's bugging the hell out of me. "Put that damn thing out," I yell at him. "Put it out now!" My girlfriend gives me one of her looks.

I settle back down and continue reading. "When it became obvious that the hospital had done all it could, he asked to go back to his home to die. Tuesday morning it happened in the arms of his wife, the writer Tess Gallagher, who once told him, 'God has given you to me to take care of.' "

My daughter reaches for some syrup and spills her orange juice. She wipes it up very carefully with her napkin, then squeezes the juice back into her glass. I finish the article about Ray. "He will be buried in Port Angeles," it says. "Graveside services will be private."

There's no mention of his interest in salmon fishing.

WILLIAM HARMON

A Nothing Generation

Henri Coulette died earlier
this year, only sixty, and now another. . . .
For one reason or another
I never
thought so very much about Raymond Carver
(1938–1988) while
he was alive, I
guess I
figured he worked his side of the world, I mine, the
same goes for Billy Carter, a year older
than us but dead now too, and that
what
mattered would matter whether
I reckoned so or not, and so on;
but now that Carver is dead
I think a little at least
about what it may mean to have been born
as he and I both were
in 1938—not much
of a year for being born in,
so few '38s amounting to anything much,
unless
you want to count Henry Adams, and I
don't, especially, but, spottily or inchoately,
I recognize that all of us "b. 1938" people

have things in common that put us apart, too old
to be hippies, too
young to be beatniks, can
say, even so, we
were born before WWII,
patronizing those students who're now too young
to remember J.F.K., Vietnam, Beatles,
and, although I'm not retired, I'm
eligible for AARP. . . . I sent
in my application three months or so ago but
haven't heard:
a young friend, a friend's son,
actually, says Well, that's understandable,
their office
being staffed by all these non compos old
people whose . . . attention . . . span . . .
you
know. To
die at fifty in this day and age is to die young,
even though somebody like Fielding
who died at forty-seven in the eighteenth century
could be said to have lived a full life—
no: never full enough,
not even if you lived forever, Carver.

PART III

Cupertino, California

1974

RICCARDO DURANTI

The Message

for Ray Carver

Pain takes a terrible revenge
against whoever
                    unmasked it
giving it the shape it deserves,
revealing, from inside,
its four dimensions:
length, width, depth and silence—

It waits
            crouching
                        in the background
filing its claws
for maximum hurt power
and waste effect
on a finally found ease.

You knew this all the time
and have been trying to tell us.

Roger.

JIM SOMERS

Dark Days

February 2, 1991

Dear Tess,

I have long pondered writing to you but often fought the sense that perhaps what was deep within my spirit would come off on paper as one more "I knew Ray" letter. I suspect when they are well intended these letters are at some level an offering of love, and in any case helpful in understanding more fully Ray's pilgrimage. My decision to write has come finally from a realization of a deep regret I carry in putting off contacting Ray some years ago when I began to see his books appear. . . . I no longer have that option, and when I saw *Carver Country* in a bookstore in Kent, Washington, I was taken, if not swept away. It was a bittersweet journey, at the end of which I felt in some painfully mystical sense "hugged." That evening I attempted to contact you by phone and was informed that you have an unlisted number. I contacted what appeared to be, in the Yellow Pages, a quality bookstore in hopes they would know you, and perhaps relay this letter to you. It was yes to both questions. I was grateful and just perhaps, if it is any concern, I have no intention of contacting you in the future, unless I hear from you. I will most likely contact "Rick" at the Elliott Bay Book Company to see if you received this letter and leave it at that.

At the outset I would like to say that my relationship with Ray was short-lived yet intimate. On the grand scale of things it carried no lasting weight, I suspect. But what poured from Ray's heart, what he wrote, who I knew Ray to be, tells me it does matter. Ray had eyes that saw clearly what so many missed. A wonderful gift . . . He picked up the pennies most walk past and ended up with a treasure.

In 1974 Ray lived with his then wife and two children in a home on Cupertino Road, Cupertino, California. This home had an attached rental unit where I lived with my girlfriend, Frances Yoshinaga. Attached to the back of our bedroom was a small office where Ray did his work. I was a bartender in San Mateo. Frances worked in an office position in Sunnyvale. I have a poor memory for names but from what I remember his wife was Maryann, daughter . . . Christine, and son Vance (?). In any event, I remember quite well, beyond the names, who we were.

I know now that for Ray these were dark days that by 1976 all but killed him. As I look back on my own life, those were for me years of ignorant waste and rebellious arrogance. I returned from twenty months in Vietnam in 1971 at the age of nineteen. The years between 1971 and 1975 were filled with fear, confusion, and violence. There was little time redeemed. Yes, there were many light moments and laughter. And as a crazy kid from Queens, New York, I grew up in a drinking family and around the bars. I was open to the general insanity of existence and enjoyed observing life.

My memories of Ray are fond, and I remember the extremes of emotion. We would drink to excess and laugh and laugh. We would banter back and forth and then Ray would commonly run with a theme or concept until we ached. He was a lovable, hypersensitive, alive drunk. There were tough times as well. He and Maryann came over one night when one or both of the kids ran away. It was when I first met him. He asked for a drink, "Scotch." So I fixed him a nice tall Scotch and water. Ray had a gentle way about him and each time I freshened his drink he would sort of hint, "A little less water." About the fourth drink I woke up and understood what he wanted was Scotch and nothing. Oh, he hurt that night. His face was drawn and sober. The Scotch did little to alter that. He asked a lot of questions. I think all he heard was the echo of his own voice.

I saw Ray angry, and on a few occasions in a rage. I think when he was sober he would become susceptible to those moods. I never felt he was trying to hurt anyone. I think maybc hc felt trapped. He didn't enjoy hurting anyone. He was a lover.

I knew Ray was in trouble with his drinking. He would sneak into our place when we were not home and steal our liquor, and it became so obvious that he started watering it down. I never said anything because I knew he meant no harm. He would sometimes drink Nyquil or mix it with vodka. Tough stuff ... Frances and I would go over to Ray's house and spend time with the family, eating, drinking, talking, watching TV, whatever. They were a lively bunch and we all seemed to get along quite naturally.

On occasion Ray and I would have talks when he was calm and sober. He talked a lot about Yakima, the lumbermills, life in the Northwest. I always enjoyed and looked forward to time spent with him. Self-destructive or not, Ray was authentic and that meant a lot to me.

Ray appeared to have a lot of friends, although at that time he seemed isolated, low on funds, and stayed at home much of the time. I think he stayed in touch by phone mostly. I remember James Dickey calling drunk from Georgia playing "Deliverance" over the phone. Also the author of *ZAP Comics* seemed to be around by phone. Maryann's sister would visit. I think she was "friends" with James Earl Jones at the time.

I am most happy to say that I also remember Ray working. As I mentioned, his office was behind our bedroom, and every so often I would hear the clicking of his typewriter. . . . And that was good.

My relationship with Frances ended that year, and I left the house. I was married in 1976, have two children, and lived in the Santa Cruz mountains until last March when we moved to Grants Pass, Oregon. The years have been tough, filled with much stark reality and transition. Although a course of pure destruction ended in 1975, it wasn't until ten years later that the light of pure spirit blossomed in my heart. But that is another story.

I want to tell you how grateful I am for your years with Ray. And for his sobriety. I read *A New Path to the Waterfall* and it helped me catch up with Ray's heart, and to get to know you. Well, . . . at least a glimpse, anyway. I miss Ray and hope to hear from you, perhaps just a few words if you care to. Thanks, in any event, thanks.

Keep smiling,
Jim Somers

MICHAEL ROGERS

A Real-Life Carver Story

I met Raymond Carver at a poker game in downtown Palo Alto, California. I was seventeen, studying fiction and physics at Stanford. He was charming, mildly drunk, and that night badly off his poker game. I cleaned him out. We also struck up an acquaintance that lasted. At the time we shared a taste for risky behavior. But it turned into more than that. One hesitates to say "mentor," but that's what Ray—understanding, supportive—meant to me, even when he was confusing my own life.

Confusion? One Saturday, for example, we drove down to Monterey to hear a mutual friend, novelist James D. Houston, play bluegrass music. It was a pleasant outdoor afternoon involving a certain amount of drinking. I was with my girlfriend, quite young, with whom I was entirely infatuated. On the way back from Monterey, Ray suggested we stop in San Jose, where he had a relative who lived in an apartment complex with a hot tub. This turned out to be a bad idea.

Details are vague in recollection, but around midnight six people were in the hot tub, with vodka bottles bobbing about in the water. Perhaps we were noisy; at any rate, soon the manager, a fiftyish woman, emerged from the darkness in her bathrobe, walked up to the hot tub and confronted Ray's relative, the apartment resident: "What do you think you're doing here?"

"I live here," she replied.

"Not anymore you don't."

Having managed to trigger an on-the-spot eviction, we put on our clothes and drove home to Palo Alto in silence. I never heard from my heartthrob again. The event, in retrospect, was probably a little distressing for a teenager. It was also my first but hardly last experience living out a real-life Carver story.

Over the next few years, trying to learn to write fiction, I spent much time with Ray and a handful of other writers, hours occasionally accompanied by violence or accidents or financial crises. There was a stabbing once, at a big party; other times, walking out of restaurants neglecting to pay the bill. Once one of Ray's relatives jacked up his car and stole his tires. Everybody always just seemed to have bad luck. Then Ray chose to stop drinking. His life changed dramatically: suddenly everything started to go his way.

When I graduated from school, I sold my first novel, but had my own bad luck and went to jail for smuggling marijuana. When I decided to stay straight, Ray volunteered to become my sponsor in a twelve-step program. In life he was precisely as he'd been as an adviser on writing: sweet, understanding, tentative in his criticism but ultimately very firm. His own life had turned around dramatically by then—he was well on his way to international fame. But he still took hours to talk about my greatest fear: whether one could be an artist without having a crazy existence. He was a clear instance that it was not only possible but powerful. In demonstrating that case, I'm certain he saved my life.

DAVID SWANGER

No Blessed Calm

Several years ago, Ray Carver sent me a postcard that delighted my wife, Lynn. In Switzerland, Ray, drinking no more, claimed to have become a chocoholic. The card is generic, alps and chalets; but in a corner of the sky Ray drew a face with an arrow pointing to it. At the other end of the arrow he wrote, "Me, in chocolate heaven."

It was his boyish charm again, the same that inspired our friendship in Santa Cruz from the time I met Ray in 1971. We were both new here, both embarking upon our first "real" jobs in academia; and it was splendid. The sun shone continuously, the students believed that art mattered, deer lightfooted among the shadows of the redwoods, and our prospects seemed as panoramic as the view commanded by the university.

Not that Ray had reason to be boyish. He and his high school sweetheart, Maryann, had married so young they already had two half-grown children. They had moved from one nondescript apartment to another, from one insignificant job to the next, and even this job was tenuous. Also, in those days, Ray and Maryann drank like crazy. And they teetered always on the edge of bankruptcy.

It was Maryann, I think, who kept things more or less together for the Carvers; she had a teaching credential and worked full time in a succession of high schools as she and Ray migrated from town to town. Now they were living in Ben Lomond, a hamlet in the valley below the university. There was a poignant surge toward normalcy, impelled by Maryann despite the boozy film she and Ray spread over everything. Ray both complained and bragged that among their expenses was the boarding fee for a horse Maryann had bought their teenage daughter. How was he, a man of perilous finances, going to support a horse?

Despite himself, Ray edged toward the middle class even then—a nice enough home, albeit rented; two cars, both reasonably reliable; a schoolteacher in the family; a horse and riding lessons for his daughter. Lynn and I barbecued steaks on the backyard grill Saturday afternoons with the Carvers. We did this at our house, or at theirs in Ben Lomond, or later in Sunnyvale, where Maryann and Ray moved to another rented house in a middle-class neighborhood, and Maryann again taught school. We and they might be participating in the ordinary weekend ritual of respectable middle America, except for the drinking. There was nothing ordinary about the amounts of gin and Scotch Ray, Maryann, and I, though not Lynn, consumed.

How did Ray do it, manage to stay boyish, write, and hold down a job at the university while drinking so heavily? The booze was as constant as the domestic discord; the Carvers sent each other to the emergency ward for stitches after hurled objects, such as cast-iron frying pans, hit their mark. I think both Maryann and Ray were sustained, for a while, by the separate but overlapping visions they had of their lives. Maryann was devoted to the idea of a normal family, as well as to Ray's talent, and labored mightily to sustain the illusion of the first, the reality of the second. For Ray's part, his writing, often drawing on the violence he and Maryann experienced—a violence both psychic and physical, manifest and latent—wove a whole of his life. Although the domestic chaos took a terrible toll, Ray was able to use it in his stories. It was Maryann who had a nervous breakdown. Ray was (relatively) free to be boyish.

So here we were, Ray and I, and other *nouveaux arrivistes,* in an academic Arcadia, the University of California at Santa Cruz. All we had to do was live up to the new university's promise and our own. During his first year as lecturer in College V (now Porter College), Ray not only taught fairly conscientiously, but organized a reading series and began a literary journal. The journal, *Quarry West,* survives to this day. Its first issue included poems and stories by Leonard Michaels, Richard Hugo, Bill Kittredge, Morton Marcus, and John Haines, as well as by UCSC students and faculty. (There was also an essay that seemed to me incongruous: Gordon Lish's

"How I Got to Be a Bigshot Editor.") The visual layout was elegant, as were the folios of drawings. And Ray was excited. He galloped up to my table in the cafeteria carrying the university newspaper, *City on a Hill,* which contained Victor Perera's favorable review of the magazine, and raised the paper overhead like a trophy.

This same enthusiasm infused the readings Ray organized. When Dennis Schmitz came to campus, his performance was followed not by perfuctory wine punch and chips, but rather by a full spread at the Carvers' house in Ben Lomond: hard liquor, cold cuts, and cake. This was emblematic of the generosity Ray brought to literary endeavors. He would criticize a colleague's manuscript (for example, mine) with a combination of care and candor; he read attentively and, within the purpose and context of the work as he perceived it, offered major advice—how better to order the poems, why this one is inaccessible, or that one sags in the middle. And when he saw a piece of work that was a knockout, he said so.

Whatever violence Ray and Maryann inflicted upon each other in private, Ray was, publicly, a gentle man. This public gentleness was especially prominent because Ray had no intimations of high culture about him, and was a big guy. He was almost chivalrous toward both men and women, and considerate of students and colleagues. In professional matters, he could not be relied on to be punctual, nor always to be prepared; still, he would take the matter at hand and consider who was talking and why these things were being said. Then he would respond gently, his voice low enough that he seemed to be sharing a confidence. What's more, he would be optimistic. There was a way the thing—the literary or other public thing—could be fixed; he really believed that.

Ray once told me that it wasn't until he hit forty that life seemed manageable. This makes sense: in his forties, Ray was on the wagon, divested of his marriage to Maryann (and of the kids, from whom he was then estranged), in love with Tess Gallagher, and firmly established as a major writer in America. But while there was newfound financial ease and considerable happiness, no blessed calm had descended, at least so far as I could see. The last time Ray stayed at our house was for a couple of days after he had just worked at a writers conference in Texas and had come for one here in Santa Cruz. This may have been in 1983. The new Ray resolutely drank mineral water while I consumed beer; and his clothes bespoke not only money but also a recently acquired concern for appearances. He gleefully told me how it felt to walk into a Mercedes showroom and drive away in a hugely expensive sedan, bought on the spot and with cash. He could hardly believe this new prosperity—the way the event was described, Ray might as well have stolen the Mercedes.

Even so, I don't think Ray had banished all his demons. He was restless, deeply on edge. Perhaps he was uncomfortable returning alone to this part of his past, the place where he and Maryann, and Lynn and I, had spent so many intense, boozy evenings together. Also, I imagine he was missing Tess. But that wasn't all of it. He was smoking more now than before, those years when cigarettes were punctuated by the rituals of assembling and drinking all those Bloody Marys and Scotch and sodas. At the time, I had on hand a coffee can full of homegrown marijuana. When we said goodnight, Ray asked if he could take the can with him out to the garage I had converted into a guesthouse and study. He smoked not only a couple of packs of cigarettes each day, but an awesome amount of pot each night, solitary in the garage. We know it killed him, the smoking. But why then, in his forties and by his own account a most fortunate man, did Ray continue to commit slow suicide?

I don't claim to have the answer to that question. But one thing I know is that earlier, in his thirties and during what Ray came to describe as his dark days, he was, despite everything, having a hell of a good time. While he wasn't yet renowned, the struggle to write and receive recognition seemed joyous, even celebratory. At first we'd exult over stories and poems taken by any magazine, for example, the *Western Humanities Review,* to which he introduced me. Then came *Esquire.* As Maryann put it, Gordon Lish had taken an interest in Ray's career. Not just a story or two, but Ray's *career.* The next we heard, Ray's stories were to be collected in a book. Then the publication parties took place more often in San Francisco, in rooms full of people I didn't know. I'd arrive still breathing Santa Cruz mountain air, and stare into the smoky crowd. Ray would find and embrace me while simultaneously nudging me toward the door—we'd go to the tavern across the street, boys sneaking away from the grown-ups. One elbow on the bar, his body inclined toward mine, his voice soft enough to be conspiratorial, he'd ask how I was, and Lynn, and things in Santa Cruz. As always with Ray, it wasn't what he said but how he said it.

WILLIAM KITTREDGE

Bulletproof

It is often said that something may survive of a person after his death, if that person was an artist and put a little of himself into his work. It is perhaps in the same way that a sort of cutting taken from one person and grafted onto the heart of another continues to carry on its existence even when the person from whom it has been detached has perished.

—Marcel Proust, *Remembrance of Things Past*

Which is no doubt a strange way to begin a story about traveling to visit Ray Carver, who had just missed dying. Or, as it turned out, not escaped. In fact he was dying. But of course we all are. That was what I told myself.

In December of 1987, just after Christmas, Annick and I drove the freeways from Montana to visit my children and grandchildren and some friends in Seattle. We ate fresh oysters; we played frivolity and cultivated the idea that it is possible to live without guilt amid the pleasures of paradise; we tried to ignore the idea that Ray was dying not so far away, at least I did; then Annick and I drove over to Port Angeles on the Olympic Peninsula, where Tess Gallagher and Ray were seeing to what was the end of his life.

The rhododendron were flowering, and the azalea (or so it seems in memory), and Ray was fragile (a large, awkward man gone breakable) but not at all what you would think of as killed. Annick and I bought cut flowers in a shop on the main street in Port Angeles, and took them up through the incessant rain to Ray's big old-fashioned two-story house on the hill above the harbor; Ray made us some of his good coffee (he'd gone to coffee when he quit booze; coffee was one of his specialties). We sat in the bright kitchen with the cut flowers on the drainboard, and drank the coffee and pretty soon we were talking. It was raining outside and quiet and Ray told us his story about healing from the almost literally unimaginable operation, the removal of about two-thirds of one cancerous lung. He'd coughed up some blood one September morning in a kind of innocent, almost painless way, and the nightmare began. That was how he put it.

"It was a nightmare," Ray said. Sunlight broke through, casting long streaks of gunmetal brilliance across the seawater toward Vancouver Island. He smiled. "But now we're all right," he said. Something like that.

What I was doing was watching Ray like he was in possession of some secret message I could read if only I could pay close enough attention. I realize this acutely now and knew it at the time. The thought did not last but a second, a sort of easily forgettable twinge I put away as if such self-interest while face-on with the oncoming death of a friend were shameful. And maybe it is. The message I was looking for had something to do with taking care of yourself by cherishing what there was to cherish, moment into moment, and not holding to it, something like that, some secret Ray knew, and I didn't, some story he had learned.

For a while that evening Annick and I were alone in Ray's house, and I sat in the chair where Ray sat when he read; I held his books and opened them to the place where he had closed them. There was a good tape deck and dozens of classical tapes. I played some Vivaldi, trying to fathom this man who had been my friend in another life, before he was dying, trying to hear what he heard, as he heard it. He was reading mostly European poets. Milosz, some others I can't remember. I'm moved to think of something I know closer to heart, Philip Levine:

> Earth is eating trees, fence posts,
> Gutted cars, earth is calling her little ones,
>
> . . . .
> They Lion grow.

Ray was a man who had stared himself down in the mirror of his imagination, and now he was dying without allowing himself to descend into any rattled bitterness so far as I could discern. I was trying to see how he got to where he was; I was trying to understand how it could be that he could absorb the terrifying joke of this perfect metaphysical injustice into his calmness and turn it reasonable, at least into something no more unnatural than the running water which drowns some mother's sacred child.

Ray and I had been friends since the spring of 1970, and we liked to tell ourselves, as he said in one of his stories, that we had *seen some things.* We met one spring evening in the old Olympic Hotel in Seattle, perfectly by accident, and we fell for one another as inebriates will, like playmates in love with the same possibilities.

There was some college comp-class English teachers gathering in the Olympic. The lobby was given over to a vast display of books, a hundred or so yards of publishers' booths. But it was empty when I wandered through in the early evening.

Empty, that is, except for one scruffy fellow who was way down the line. As I was looking through a book called *Short Stories from the Literary Magazines,* this fellow came right up to my elbow and tried to look over my shoulder. "I've got a story in there," he said.

"Yeah," I said. "I'll bet you do."

"Please be quiet, please," he said.

I knew what he meant, but I didn't believe it.

"It is," he said. "It's mine. Curt Johnson put it in there. He printed it in a magazine called *December.*"

It was not a lie anyone would have bothered telling, at least in those days. It was clear this man was Raymond Carver, and I was one of the few people in the world who would have found significance in that fact. This stranger had written the story called "Please Be Quiet, Please." It was already a kind of famous story in my mythologies.

A couple of years before, I had read that story in a hotel room in Portland, sitting with my feet up in the bed and disengaged from the world and waiting for my second wife to come back from somewhere, and that story got me started again in my wondering if I had already ruined my life. "Please Be Quiet, Please" caused me to hang my head with heartbreak over my own situation in the world and yet to admire myself for even trying to confront those troubles as a writer.

However stupid it sounds, that is pretty close to what I thought right after I read "Please be Quiet, Please" one rainy afternoon in the old Benson Hotel in Portland while I yearned to be actual at something. For a little moment that story led me to think I was doing the right thing with my life.

And here I was, better yet, in another hotel, with the guy who wrote the story. This was indeed the life; we were shy for some moments, then we touched, we shook hands, we talked about a cup of coffee. Wait a minute, he said, why not a beer? I said, why not a drink? A drink would be fine, maybe a couple of drinks, what the hell; all things lay before us. It was that moment between drunks which is known as Exchanging Credentials. Would you have a drink? Well, maybe, sure.

Even on the morning of this writing, a brilliant blue day which began with the temperatures well below zero, after an evening of Christmas celebration and decency with family, I think of the old days and going down to the taverns in Missoula to join the people I know. They are still there, some of them, and I still love the thought of their company. There was a time when we would be drunk by noon.

The days after Christmas, in the taverns, were always splendid in their timelessness. At heart loomed that perfect irresponsibility, long hours when it was possible to believe we were invisible and shatterproof, walking on water for at least a little while, and beautiful in our souls.

But those afternoons are gone. Ray took a hard fall on the booze. Drink became his secret companion in a more profound way than anything, even love, ever really works for most of us.

We pulled our tricks. It was our only sport; it would never end; we were free, invulnerable. In June of 1973, running on getaway bravado and whiskey, I took a long run from Missoula and found myself at Carver's house in Cupertino.

My first day in town we made our way over to a literary party in Berkeley, in some public room on the campus. I found myself talking to a famous critic with a glass of white wine in my hand, thinking in my drunken self-pretense that I knew some never-before-revealed thing about *texts*. Ray lifted a sack of ice over his head, crashed it down on the corner of a trestle table, and three half gallons of gin danced off to shatter on the stone floor. We hired a graduate student to drive us back to Cupertino.

And we lived there a week in dreams, drinking two bottles of vodka every day, one for each of us. In the morning I would come out of my bedroom to find Ray in the living room with vodka, orange juice, ice, my drink mixed.

Toward the end of the week we wandered up to the little liquor store at the high end of Cupertino Road and ordered a half gallon. "Christ," the clerk said. "You guys together?"

One evening, crossing the twilight of a moving-picture six-plex parking lot on the west side of San Jose, I looked back to see Maryann looking back another fifty yards to the place where Ray stood beside their little yellow Japanese automobile. He had waited until we moved off toward the theater, and then come up with a pint from under the seat and now he was downing the last of it, chin to the china pink of the evening sky and oblivious to us in what he thought of as his selfishness.

That fall Ray was teaching full time in Iowa City, in the Writers' Workshop with the likes of John Cheever, feeling like maybe he was some semblance of the real thing since there he was with Cheever, who was damned sure the real thing and as much a drunk as anybody.

Every Friday afternoon Ray was supposed to meet a beginning poetry writing class at College V, UC Santa Cruz. It was possible; he could fly every Thursday afternoon, meet his class, and fly back in time to meet his workshop on Tuesday. And he had worked a deal with one of the airlines. Free tickets in swap for an essay (which of course never got written) for some airline magazine.

No problem. Two jobs, two paychecks, home every weekend.

And he showed up on the airplane each Thursday evening for a number of weeks. Always drunk. I had left my second wife behind in Missoula and was thrashing around in the single life again, temporarily, according to my plans anyhow, at Stanford with a Stegner fellowship. So I was available and I drove him down the fifty or so miles to Santa Cruz, and he ceremoniously pinned a notice to the door of his classroom: *Can't teach. Sick.* And it was true.

The next week Ray lay down in the backseat of my car so no one could possibly see him, and it was my job to pin up the notice. The next week Chuck Kinder and I went down without Ray. The class was mostly hippies with no shoes. We faced a circle of their bare grass-stained feet propped up around our conference table. Kinder refused to look. I carried on like some prideful piss-ant. That was the last of those classes; Ray stopped coming altogether.

That Christmas there was a great swaying in the warm winds; Ray flew to Missoula, then drove south with my second wife and Ed McClanahan, who was taking my place in Missoula. It sort of seemed like we all might couple up again and make peace and be lovey. And we kind of did, for a week or so.

Ray and Maryann looked to be bemused by happiness as they drifted off from a small party at McClanahan's house in Palo Alto. It wasn't until the next day that I got a full report. It was one of our sports in those days, getting the full report.

Ray had lost Maryann. I mean lost her. He got in the car and drove the twenty-some freeway miles from McClanahan's to his place in Cupertino, innocently, without Maryann. Ray left her standing at the curb, door locked on her side. Rather than come back into McClanahan's, Maryann hitched a ride with an old couple. There was lots of hitching rides in those days; people fell out, temporarily. The old couple drove Maryann right to her door. Ray was rummaging in the refrigerator, building a great sandwich. "Oh," he said, when Maryann came in the door. "I wondered where you were."

At least that was how it was reported. Ray said he was slicing a great sweet onion, a Walla Walla sweet, for a huge thick sandwich. Later on he never ate. That was one way you told the beginning of the end; some people stopped eating.

Maybe Ray was the more easily wounded, maybe he was physically fragile, or maybe he was simply capable of taking all of what was happening more seriously than most of us, maybe he saw through our joke in a clearer way, maybe he was more open to certain kinds of wounding, to witnessing what became our war zone with a heart not so securely boarded up and barricaded as, at the least, was mine.

Maybe Ray recognized that in the long run we weren't reaping freedom after all; maybe we had been tricked.

I hope there is not anything about this recital of antics which sounds prideful. I hope these are not seen as the kind of stories you dine out on. Once they were, once I used them that way, I suppose. At least I recall telling them in bars while we all had a swell time; they had a certain currency.

Ray suffered some sight of chaos deep in his soul and turned away and sobered up in the late 1970s, and moved up to McKinleyville on the coast of California just north of the little university town of Arcata, where he had gone to school in the old days and friends like Dick Day could help see him through the drying out. I visited there a couple of times on my way to San Francisco. I asked Ray if he was writing. By this time he had been sober for most of a year. "No," he said. "I could. But I'm not."

I asked him why.

"Because I can't convince myself it's worth doing." That was the first time he surprised me. I thought about that for days afterwards. It implied a kind of consequence I had never anticipated. We had seen a lot of our things by then, but it had never seemed to me possible that even the fractured marriages and falling down, bite-your-tongue convulsions in the streets could lead to this kind of seriousness. Ray must have witnessed some things I had not imagined.

The thing I had believed in was work, the stories, and if that was not worth doing, well then, there was no way to make good on anything, there was no justifying anything in your life. I had let myself believe that good writing was like a license to steal; anything was forgivable so long as you were writing well.

Which is a line of bullshit a lot of people like me have used to excuse endless rudeness, selfishness, cruelty, and general cheap-shit misconduct. It's a line so stupid and so demeaning I have to wonder if I believed it at the time.

This is what I think: No one thing justifies any other thing. Each thing you do stands alone; they don't add up, not in any direction; nothing accumulates; there is no magic, the work you do is the work you got done, good or bad, and it doesn't earn you any moral privileges. No points. If you have the good luck to do some good work, that's a fine thing. But it has nothing to do with making you anything but lucky.

A lot of the long-term Sunday afternoon sadness in taverns

where I go, among people I know, has to do with wasted possibilities, fine and capable people who didn't do any work and
collapsed into serving their own selves and pleasures, as I was so
inclined, for so long. Drunk in the morning. Those were fine times,
I have to say, with fine friends. I loved them dearly.

But it has been a good idea, for me, to attempt putting away the
indulgence and make-believe, and to try to identify some decencies
to serve. I do not mean God or country, but community, which is a
larger, extended version of our own selves. We are responsible;
nothing is bulletproof.

All these were not thoughts I wanted to let myself dwell on in
those days. Most of what I did was support a set of all-day excuses
for seldom doing any work. I thought maybe Ray saw some visions,
maybe that was his trouble. Maybe he had the heebie-jeebies and
scared himself. But I was not scared.

And there we were, not so many years later, he was famous, and
dying, and I was studying him for hints.

In the months before his affliction revealed itself Ray had taken
to inspecting condominiums on the downtown hills of Seattle
overlooking Elliott Bay and shipping lanes to the Orient, right near
the Public Market with its perfect produce and living geoducks you
could kill and fry for dinner, and flowers picked just that morning.
He liked to talk about living close to such amenities.

Just out the windows you could witness sunset over the Olympic
Mountains. This was the saw filer's son from Yakima, and he was
finally getting his chance at the world. He wanted properties.

A few years before, in the fall of 1982, while I was visiting in
southern Vermont, Ray showed up driving an immaculate new
Mercedes. He had been going home to Syracuse from John Gardner's funeral, he said, and he had decided you might as well enjoy
some things, if you could afford them. "So what the hell," he said.
"So I bought this car. Who knows?"

And that was what we were all studying, on that visit to Port
Angeles, "Who knows?"

What I was most concerned about, that last time there in Port
Angeles, was watching myself as I watched Ray and wondered who
to be, studying him like a stranger, envying his equilibrium. He had
survived some series of transformations, and I wanted to share the

wisdom, if it was wisdom. Ray was dying and I wanted to know how he could conduct himself as he did. I wanted to see what he saw when he looked out from his seashore to the flow of his ocean. I wanted to hear his music as he heard it.

The summer before, I had gone to Port Angeles for some salmon fishing. It all seemed so very easy, that dream, and natural enough. We caught salmon, the day was brilliant, Ray was the generous center of it all, our prince of good fortune, proof that some rewards were justly rationed out by the way of things. And now his life was over, soon now, forever. Someone had canceled his ticket to the rest of the party.

On a bright chill morning, Ray and Tess and Annick and I took a short hike on a downhill path to the edges of the beach, where we were stopped by driftwood logs. Ray was still healing from his operation and moving like an old man. He refused to go climb over the logs and we turned inland along the soggy fairways of a little golf course bordering a tiny creek, and looped back to a bridge over the river. It was a small expedition into the native world, but longer than we ever took before. Back at Tess's house, Ray opened a tin of canned salmon, we ate a little, and that is what there is to tell. There is no insight here, no moment, no recognition.

There is just my friend in his gentle patience with his terrible fate, and with us.

He could have been impatient; he could have thought we were exhausting what little remained of his life. And maybe he did. Or maybe he was glad of the company.

On August 3, 1988, in warm morning sunlight on a patio outside a mental health clinic in Aspen, Colorado, I was meeting with a fiction writing class. "I see in the paper," one of them said, "where your friend is dead." He was talking about the *New York Times*. Ray was dead at fifty, leaving the example of his conduct while dying.

In December of 1988, coming home from the beaches near La Push, Annick and I passed by a chaos of clear-cut logging near the little Washington town of Forks, heedless wreckage, mile-long swatches of torn earth and the jagged rotting stumpage of the great cedar trees, limbs crushed into the black mud. Imagine paradise perfectly violated.

We stopped in Port Angeles and visited the highland over the seacoast where Ray is buried. Tess had worn a little path around the grave. She went down there and talked to him, she said. I tell him the news, she said. Like all of us, Ray was given to a love of gossip and scandal. His eyes would gleam, and he would lean into the talk. But as I stood there by his grave I had nothing much in the way of things to say to the dead, except to make a game of my question. How is it, old sport? Maybe I was too scared for much fun.

I said to myself: how many happy, contented people there really are! What an overwhelming force they are! Look at life: the insolence and idleness of the strong, the ignorance and brutishness of the weak, horrible poverty everywhere, overcrowding, degeneration, drunkenness, hypocrisy, lying—Yet in all the houses and on all the streets there is peace and quiet; of the fifty thousand people who live in our town there is not one who would cry out, who would vent his indignation aloud. We see the people who go to market, eat by day, sleep by night, who babble nonsense, marry, grow old, good-naturedly drag their dead to the cemetery, but we do not see or hear those who suffer, and what is terrible in life goes on everywhere behind the scenes. Everything is peaceful and quiet and only mute statistics protest: so many gallons of vodka drunk, so many children dead from malnutrition—And such a state of things is evidently necessary; obviously the happy man is at ease only because the unhappy ones bear their burdens in silence, and if there were not this silence, happiness would be impossible. It is a general hypnosis. Behind the door of every contented, happy man there ought to be someone standing with a little hammer and continually reminding him with a knock that there are unhappy people, that however happy he may be, life will sooner or later show him its claws, and trouble will come to him—illness, poverty, losses, and then no one will see or hear him, just as now he neither sees nor hears others. But there is no man with a hammer. The happy man lives at his ease, faintly fluttered by small daily cares, like an aspen in the wind—and all is well.

—Anton Chekhov, "Gooseberries"

Chekhov understood that stories, when they are most valuable, are utterly open in their willingness to make metaphor from our personal difficulties. Our most useful stories focus simultaneously on our most generous and betraying ways. These troubles could be yours, the story says, this unfairness *is* yours, and so are these glories.

Ray must have spent lots of time listening to Chekhov's person with the little hammer. It is easy to see that his most profound sympathies lay, as did Chekhov's, with the disenfranchised, the saw filers like his father.

Ray's last story, "Errand," is about the death of Chekhov, drinking champagne as you die, celebrating what there is to celebrate, which is this, what we have. It is one of his put-yourself-in-my-shoes, try-my-blindness stories, like the story in which a man stands before a mirror in his neighbor's bedroom in his neighbor's wife's lingerie, making a try at being *someone else.*

Ray gave the world all the strength and decency he could muster and died out of an unnaturally foreshortened life (and we do; each of us). By his time of dying Ray had come to what seemed a learned and objectified sense of his own beliefs; he found it to say, Sure enough, sadness all over town—but, like my man Chekhov, I'm going to forgive myself, and try happiness anyway.

However terrifyingly misguided our lives may have been, we have to pray they are ultimately forgivable. My culture has poured burning napalm on babies; they did it on purpose; I didn't think I had any politics; much of what we do is madness.

We know the story of civilization; it can be understood as a history of conquest, law-bringing, and violence. We need a new story, in which we learn to value intimacy. Somebody should give us a history of compassion which would become a history of forgiveness and caretaking.

Ray's best work continually suggests the need for attempting to keep decent toward one another while deep in our own consternations. His best stories are masterworks of usefulness; they lead us to imagine what it is like to be another person, which is the way we learn compassion. It is the great thing: In intimacy we learn to cherish each other, through continual acts of the imagination. Nothing could be more political.

NOEL YOUNG

Happy Hour with Ray

Ray seemed at peace with the world, sprawled in a meadow with a drowsy grin and a moustache of beer suds, idly listening to Dago Red bluegrass while folks carefully stepped over his outstretched legs. Jim Houston made the introductions and before long I was down on his level with a cup of foamy beer, soaking up the glories of a Santa Cruz festival. This was how the seventies began, with no one feeling any pain. Several good writers were caught up in the crowd; besides Houston, they straggled by, one by one—Peter Beagle, Mort Marcus, Joe Stroud, Vic Perera, William Everson, if memory serves me. Of them all, Carver seemed the least likely, the least driven, at one with the sun.

So much for that first impression of Ray; recumbent and gentle as though awaiting the Lilliputs and their ropes. Our paths kept crossing during the following years, mostly at stuporous hallway parties, with a lot of goodwill and male bonding. During that time we had our chapbook series going and Ray's story "Put Yourself in My Shoes" became its twenty-first volume, a tale that detonated inside my skull a half hour after putting it down, an uncanny quality lurking in most of his stories.

Suddenly, one day came word that he was moving to Santa Barbara with a lectureship at UCSB and would arrive next week with his family and no place to land. (I think the English department solved that.) The Carvers settled in a month before the fall semester opened and Ray lost all his equanimity, confessing he wasn't at all looking forward to this stint. "Let's find a Happy Hour somewhere, for god's sake," he muttered. It wasn't students or the campus itself, but some invisible torment that had come upon him to grapple with. We were putting together his poetry collection, *At Night the Salmon Move,* which gave us the excuse we needed to have Happy Hour conferences. We found the perfect place, inappropriately named Jacques's Family Restaurant. The decor was totally decadent as one might expect in a Victorian brothel, with curtained booths and nude paintings framed in baroque gold hanging against walls of flocked *fleurs-de-lis.* A wise and comely waitress saved a certain booth for us night after night, and brought us our rums and Scotches and seemed to enjoy loitering. (We later learned she was a graduate student at the English department where Ray would be lecturing and a poet in her own right.)

It wasn't easy to get out of there before dark and a drink too many. Sometimes Ray brought his wife Maryann, which belied the Happy Hour's name, to handle the drive home. This was not the Ray Carver I met, blissfully sprawled in the Santa Cruz meadow. A day of reckoning was almost upon him. Thus came a fateful Friday, with his teaching to begin on Monday. He drank faster than usual and the waitress brought plates of hors d'oeuvres to slow him down.

Maryann didn't appear that night so we stayed on for dinner. Ray's blink rate accelerated and he began praising a book I didn't know—Jack London's *John Barleycorn,* a morality story dealing with demon rum—urging me to bring it back into print. "It's a great book," he exclaimed. "It deals with *invisible forces.*"

It could have been a tragic night. Ray had two for my one simply because he was twice as big, but even so he was begging for trouble. I was thinking of calling us a cab, but he must've read my thoughts. He rose to his feet, lumbered toward the men's room and simply never came back. He pressed a wad of money into the waitress's hand and eased out the back door. I didn't see him again until dawn and it wasn't what anyone would call a Happy Hour.

The phone woke me in the middle of the night. Ray had been busted and needed to be bailed out and a ride home. By the time I got to him he looked like anyone who had dozed on a stinking concrete floor in the county jail.

As we trudged toward the parking lot he suddenly turned and gave me a bear hug. "I'm sorry, but it's just not going to work," he said pointedly. It didn't. After two or three appearances in the classroom he pulled stakes and left town.

He hit bottom not long after, before the transformations began that led him to Port Angeles and into the arms of Tess Gallagher. There he became the resurrected Ray, bought a boat and went after salmon, captain of his own ship. The rest is history and I read *John Barleycorn.*

JEFFREY SKINNER

The Good Story
for Raymond Carver

The story was so right he wouldn't leave it
for fear the words might go on unreeling
in his absence and when he returned the story
would be over, the pages blank *I should hit*
the john, he thought, and went on with his reading.
It concerned the death of a child
and what happened to the parents for three
days following the death. The man reading
the story felt each needle of its language and event
flowing out inseparable, even though a TV
issued spiky voices from another room, and the draft
of a ceiling fan made his hands
uncomfortably cold. The urge to urinate grew
as the story lifted bandages of random pain
from his own life, and he squirmed in his chair, angry
he could not hold the parents' grief
outside himself, or even stop reading.
Someone turned the TV up and he cursed and kept on
reading. The cold in his hands passed through unbearable
to numbness and he kept on reading. The need
to piss was so intense he had to clamp
himself through his jeans and hold the book
with one hand to go on reading. . . .
Gradually the man realized he had wasted

much, though not all of his life,
that his own sorrow was real and bound up in time;
that the child would not return miraculous
but leave the parents to go on after the story
ended. And the man kept reading, himself
invisible as music, until the last unsweetened word.

PART IV

El Paso, Texas

1978

PATRICIA DOBLER

Odometer

Kids and all, we shored up on El Paso,
rode that prehistoric ocean floor, that backside
of the moon, held on to one another for dear life,
unpacked in the cheap apartment near the Rio Grande's
dusty crooked line. And called you up, Raymond,
because our yellow two-door Chevy's odometer was due
to turn 100,000 miles, and we knew you wouldn't
want to miss that. So around the apartment's
parking lot we drove and drove—it took
longer than we thought, to drive two miles
in a circle—then the odometer turned over
and we cheered and got on with our lives,
mostly frantic in those days, trying to stay on top
of all the payments that had all come due.
We dug out, patched up, pieced it together;
then we had ten good years. And now I've heard
that at the end you couldn't sit still.
That on the last night you circled the room,
pacing from chair to bed; you wouldn't sleep,
tried to stay awake, no one knows how. We think
you were afraid, and that you stayed inside, circling,
trying hard not to move on to where you had to go.

TESS GALLAGHER

The Ghosts of Dreams

The tall, hunched man who stepped to the lectern in Dallas, Texas, in November of 1977 to read from his stories seemed so shy and visibly shaken at finding himself before the small audience of other writers, that at first, I wanted to rescue him, to rush up to him and say, "You don't have to do this, you know."

But soon I was lost in a world of chance and ordinary loss brought into consequence. The characters and scenes came haltingly from the man's soft, humbled voice and seemed taken from my own life and the lives of my working-class parents. The speaker's recognitions were heartbreakingly real, yet they were also beyond the simply "realistic." This writer, Raymond Carver, had somehow managed to write in a multidimensional way that combined fable with what passes for that evasive surface called "the real" to produce an entirely new entity. There was not the slightest trace of irony in the voice, and the sentences sparkled cleanly in the air as if they had been flown in from some mountaintop, accompanied by the genial, self-effacing spirit before us.

I didn't know it then, but this was the man whose work and life would inextricably accompany my own in a companionship and marriage that for the next eleven years would change both our lives and end only with his too early death at age fifty on August 2, 1988, from lung cancer.

The first Carver stories I heard that day in Dallas were from *Furious Seasons* and from *Will You Please Be Quiet, Please?*, this last book having won him a modest amount of attention, though he was still relatively unknown. He was recovering from a ten-year bout with alcoholism and had only been sober about five months.

By the next time we met he would have left a twenty-year marriage and embarked on what he would later call his second life. I listened that day in Dallas while he read "Fat" and "Why Don't You Dance?" I wondered, Why are we all laughing? The poignancy of the loss being expressed had somehow carried us into the tragic in such a bold, unapologetic fashion that we were delivered (with hardly a breath in between) into a sense of the ridiculousness and palpability of human misery of these particular people and, by extension, all human lives. The loneliness and despair Carver delineated brought us into a communal recognition of hardships that seemed ordinary on the surface but were profound and mysterious as he passed his vision over them. Arthur Miller's *Death of a Salesman* had put before us the unacknowledged struggle of the American working class, but the fates of the Willy Lomans of the country had not been absorbed into the fabric of the literary and national consciousness as they ultimately would be in the work of Raymond Carver.

Carver's stories had the kind of impact on American fiction that Einstein's theory of relativity had on science. We couldn't quite fathom how it worked, but it changed the way we regarded the lives of middle-class working people. They were at last given full dignity. Their suffering was made emotionally palpable, for Carver was first of all a poet. While these stories appear to be written in the kind of accessible prose one finds in the newspaper, they are, at the same time, instruments of extreme precision. The stories culminate with what one critic has called "negative epiphanies." That is, especially in the early stories, our wish to be delivered is very much frustrated. Life is allowed to be as hard and baffling as it is. The dilemmas of the characters might best be expressed by the fat man in "Fat": "No, he says. If we had our choice, no. But there is no choice." This line seems to carry the starkness of Kafka's *Metamorphosis,* and it is emblematic of a larger truth expressed throughout Carver's work, that very often there is no choice. Many lives are simply trapped and have to proceed on the ghosts of dreams. Indeed, the early vision of his writing was forged during the late 1950s and throughout the 1960s. He came of age in an America that still believed in the American dream in which the traditional values of self-improvement and individual striving were assumed to prevail. People were led to expect that hard work and perseverance would win out, would allow average Americans to own a home and send their children to college, to improve their circumstances.

This dream gave way in the seventies and eighties to the discovery that hard work would often only certify people as members of the working poor, disenfranchised heirs in a country that more and more had surrendered to a spiritually bankrupt materialism. Carver manages to bring the inarticulateness of these lives into fresh credibility without violating the condition or idiom of their suffering. He does not impose intellectual theories or the superiority of irony. In fact, his French translator, François Lasquin, told me in Paris that he had translated all of one book by my husband when he happened to see a photograph of Raymond Carver. "I looked at the face and I knew I had made a terrible mistake," he said. "I had translated the book in a rather ironic, skeptical tone, and the man before me, I realized at once, would never set himself above his characters." Lasquin had to retranslate the entire book with this in mind.

Carver's taut, honed prose is refined with the precision of a diamond cutter. With chilling accuracy he describes the lives of men between jobs waiting for the break that may never come, of women who feel the loneliness of being with men who treat them like extensions of their own disconsolate needs. In the later books Carver would extend characterization and allow some glimmers of hope in the resolutions of stories, but he felt no obligation to provide answers that just weren't there for the lives of his characters. Throughout the work he maintained an obsession with the tormented nature of ruined love between men and women. He even told many of his stories, notably "So Much Water So Close to Home," "Chef's House," "Fat," and "Intimacy," from the viewpoint or in the voice of a woman.

Perhaps no other American writer yet has been able to remain compassionate while recording so unflinchingly the distortions of heart and soul that afflict contemporary lives. No wonder when he died the *London Times* called him "America's Chekhov." In their storytelling these two writers shared an intensity of spirit and directness of means that was uncanny.

I have watched the critics and journalists while he was alive and since Raymond Carver's death try to subdue his work with smart-sounding phrases—"minimalist," "dirty realist," "hick chic," "white trash fiction," "freeze-dried fiction"—as if these terms could confine and characterize his style and content. Yet the work itself continues to reject all such labels. Its mystery remains intact. Perhaps this is one of the qualities that defines a great writer. Yes, I think so. No matter what is said, the mystery remains intact.

I'm reminded of a story told by some hunters here in the Northwest along the Strait of Juan de Fuca where we lived together and where my husband wrote many of his stories. These hunters told me of how in the days before such hunting was banned, the houndsmen would be tracking a cougar and suddenly would find that the scent had strangely disappeared. They would discover what the cougar had killed, but the dogs would go wild for loss of the trail. The cougar would have escaped, become invisible to them. It was believed, the hunters told me, that the cougar was able to hold in its scent, to conceal the essence of its movement in times of danger. Raymond Carver seems not unlike the cougar in the elusiveness of his effect and wide appeal. As the critic Harold Schweizer has said in homage to Carver, quoting a line from "The Purloined Letter" by Edgar Allan Poe: "The mystery is a little too plain." Schweizer was appropriately pointing out, I believe, that the writing seems to conceal nothing while concealing all. Carver does this, in part, by making accessibility the least of our worries. This is why we are affected by Carver's spell without being able to locate the precise source of the energy in his writing. The voice has so fully assumed the tragic as its means, according to Schweizer, that it has shed any apparent affectation of art.

One of the things the critics have just begun to discover is that Raymond Carver did not simply cling to the early short, clipped style and treatment of his characters. As his art deepened he began to extend his characterizations and to add a complexity of resolution and voice in stories such as "Cathedral," "Intimacy," and "Blackbird Pie." This deepening culminates in the elegiac "Errand," a story that combines the moving facts of Chekhov's death with fictional overlays, amplifications of characters who would have been mere bystanders in someone else's account.

Another element that continued to be present in the middle and later stories was Carver's humor. When, in his last public reading in the Northwest, he read "Elephant" aloud in a small Seattle bookstore that was jammed with listeners, there was so much laughter he had to stop again and again, gazing up once in a while with a shy smile on his face, trying to contain his own enjoyment enough to get the story out. But also his breathing was difficult and he was drawing energy from the crowd's enthusiasm.

Raymond Carver is a writer who can be read again and again, aloud or silently, for the simple pleasure of the story or for the rich undertexture of what he has purposefully left out. His work with the short story has revived the form and given it a currency whose reverberations are now being felt around the world. Meanwhile, the tensed and supple muscles of the cougar flex their way from page to page—and we are snow and branch to his leaps and silences.

STEPHEN DOBYNS

Laughter's Creature

I first met Ray Carver in January 1978, at Goddard College, where we were both teaching in a two-week creative writing residency. He was just coming out of a bad time. Although he wasn't drinking, he was broke and feeling very fragile and uncertain about himself. He wanted to get away from his life out west and start a new one. He spent a lot of time in his room smoking and pacing around.

He wasn't equipped for the Vermont winter and wore a brown jacket that appeared to be made of vinyl and small shiny shoes that looked like a dancer's shoes, shoes oddly at variance with his great bearlike body. I remember him tiptoeing through the snow, setting his feet carefully in other people's tracks, and shaking his head as if the weather were just one more thing in an astonishing world.

He believed faithfully in catastrophe. Something awful would happen and all the stores would close. Consequently he was always leaving the dining hall with little packages of food wrapped in white napkins. Mostly they were sweet things because he had a terrible sweet tooth: packages of cookies, doughnuts, maybe a sandwich. One time someone took his package of brownies, replacing it with a package of stale bread. Ray carried it back to his room and eagerly opened it late at night. I would have been angry and hurt. He laughed, and for days he told everyone of the funny trick that had been played on him. And he was always forgetting these packages and leaving them around: in a classroom or after a reading. For years there were occasions when he would ride in my car and a week or so later I would discover a little white package of stale cookies under the seat.

At night at Goddard we would sit around and tell stories. His were always full of wonder: strange fish he had caught, narrow escapes he had had, outrageous behavior he had witnessed or participated in, dastardly deeds where one human being had let down or betrayed another. He had a story about how he had amused himself after he quit drinking by going to bingo games in California and how he had learned to cheat at these games and how the cheating was more interesting than the playing. He and his first wife would go up and down the coast seeking out bingo games while a posse of elderly women tried to catch them. And there was a story about how he and John Cheever, when they were both teaching at the University of Iowa, had walked a check at a fancy restaurant and got caught but never had to pay.

He would never tell a story to show himself off or brag. They would all deal with the strange predicaments we can find ourselves in. There wasn't much judgment. What Ray hated was cruelty and betrayal, but he had done those things too and sometimes a person couldn't help himself.

He read "Why Don't You Dance?" during the residency at Goddard. There were about a hundred of us in the audience. It was as if someone had slapped us. Most of us knew Ray's stories but this was something beyond *Will You Please Be Quiet, Please?* What was wonderful about the story was how it dug its way inside your chest and squeezed your heart, also how it was about the impossibility of communication and how it communicated so perfectly. Ray loved stories that worked on as many of the reader's emotions as possible. He hated stories that were simply idea and surface.

When he left the residency at the end of two weeks, he borrowed a hundred bucks from one of his students and a hundred bucks from me and headed out to western Illinois. Somebody had given him the use of an empty house, and he thought he could hole up there and write. The house turned out to be fifteen miles from the nearest town. He bought an old Oldsmobile. I think it was a '63 or '64. He called it his Okie car. It was February and about fifteen below and after the first night the car wouldn't start. The house was a cheap little place furnished entirely with lawn furniture. He lasted about a week, then called me in Iowa City where I was teaching. The next night he was sleeping on my couch.

He stayed in Iowa City until the summer and we saw each other often. He got a room, then another, then his wife joined him, and they moved to a succession of rental cottages. Okie places he called them. He was writing a lot, both poems and stories, but he was beginning to feel trapped again. When he answered the phone it was always with a quick "Yes?" or "Lo?" as if he thought his creditors had finally found him.

He loved what he called swapping stories, a group of friends sitting around, each telling a story in turn. There were many evenings like that in Iowa City that spring. Ray would scratch his head and lean forward with his elbows on his knees and say, "You know, I remember a funny thing," then he would be off with some story about how a lawyer had sued him, trying to get his dog because Ray hadn't paid his bill, and how the judge had grown indignant, saying, "You actually want to take this man's dog away from him?" And there was another story about finding a corpse on the beach in California.

He was a great listener and when someone else was telling a story he would burst forth with oddly archaic interjections like "you don't say" and "think of that." Then he would shake his head and look around in amazement. And he had a great laugh. His whole body would collapse backwards as if he had been struck in the chest with something happy and his face would wrinkle and a high raspy noise would burst out again and again. There was nothing restrained about it. For a moment he was laughter's creature, then he would wipe his eyes and the story would resume or a new story would start.

He was also a tremendous enthusiast, and when I read a book I liked or a poem, or heard a piece of music or saw a movie that I liked, he was the person I thought to share it with, and we would have great talks about it. And he also always had a list of books or poems or stories that he would urge on people and they would be about how a person had lived, how he or she had survived and loved, how this person had dealt with being alive in a difficult time.

His writing was always original and critics loved to natter about his language, but the writing was the medium for something more important: the apprehension of human emotion—how does a person live, how does he connect with other human beings? This is what he loved about Chekhov and why he saw Chekhov as his main teacher. Emotion was the most important part of the story and he liked to quote that remark of Kafka's that literature should be an ax to smash the frozen sea of the heart. It is this emotion that makes many of his poems so wonderful. They are not a critic's poems. They are not decorative. They need no one to interpret them. They are reader's poems. They exist to define moments of emotion and wonder. Often the moments are very simple, like getting a haircut from his wife. Here is one called "Near Klamath."

> We stand around the burning oil drum
> and we warm ourselves, our hands
> and faces, in its pure lapping heat.
>
> We raise steaming cups of coffee
> to our lips and we drink it
> with both hands. But we are salmon
>
> fishermen. And now we stamp our feet
> on the snow and rocks and move upstream,
> slowly, full of love, toward the still pools.

I can think of no contemporary American poet who could locate this sort of small yet intensely emotional moment as well as Ray could. They are the moments we mostly don't have time for. Unfortunately, they are also the moments that give life its significance. Ray's work constantly tried to remind us of that. He was the celebrator of those small occasions of fragile contentment, of time lived instead of time passing. Without him, we return to the constant rush, the crowded streets and honking horns.

Now he has been dead for three years and his work is increasingly popular and the critical work accumulates. He would have been both amused and proud of the attention. A few weeks ago I gave a copy of Ray's last book of poems to a truck driver who is a recovered alcoholic and after reading and rereading it he said, "I been there. That man lived my life!"

I can't remember Ray's reading much criticism. Although a passionate reader, he had no interest in the various isms and all the theories. His language worked to establish a particular tone and that tone became the vehicle for the emotion. In any case, although he took care of his stories and made sure they got published, the story or poem he liked best was always the next one. He was constantly pushing away from the confines of the present and into the future. In a letter I received from him two weeks before he died of cancer, he wrote that in a week or ten days his new collection of poems would be done. "Then we'll take a holiday—a week's salmon fishing in Alaska." And he also wrote that he wanted to go to London and Amsterdam in August where selections of his stories were being published. "I've been feeling very housebound," he added.

Writing itself was a form of exploration for him. I once asked him how he had happened to write the story "Put Yourself in My Shoes" and he said that the first sentence popped into his head and he had to follow it. The first sentence reads, "The telephone rang while he was running the vacuum cleaner." That's all. But Ray knew that something had to come after those words, so he set off looking, which meant opening his mind to possibility and discovery.

I was also struck by how many of the odd details of his stories came from stories he had heard or from his own experience. In the story just mentioned one of the characters tells about a son beaning his father with a can of tomato soup and sending him to the hospital. This was a story Ray used to tell long before he wrote "Put Yourself in My Shoes." He'd tell it and shake his head and say, "Think of that," in his hollow, breathy voice that sometimes reminded me of a great owl.

But strange things happened to him as well. That first January at Goddard he returned to the dorm one day and it looked as if some vicious animal had attacked his head. His hair seemed half chewed off. He had gone for a haircut to the one barber in Plainfield. The old man was just recovering from a stroke and had been forced to learn how to cut hair with his left hand. And his left hand shook terribly. Ray was the barber's first customer since returning to his shop. Looking at the man's shaking hand, Ray had considered not getting a haircut after all, but he had been afraid of hurting the man's feelings.

Then in Iowa City Ray rented a room from a man whose first name was the same as his last name. The man had a fierce wife who slept in a king-sized bed and made her husband sleep nearby on the floor. The man spent long hours telling Ray his troubles, until Ray could stand it no more and fled.

One of the things that made Ray a wonderful writer was the honesty with which he approached the endeavor of writing. He would begin without knowing where he was going and he would turn away from nothing that might show up. The story was in charge and it didn't matter how odd something was or who it might offend or that the *New Yorker* might find it in bad taste. After those initial drafts, of course, he would revise sometimes for years, until he could think of nothing else, until he found himself putting back commas he had taken out earlier. For him starting a story was like getting into a fast car with a questionable driver. There was no telling where they would wind up. Yet he trusted it and gave himself over to it. Even though dangerous, the story required that he surrender himself to the mystery. The poet Rainer Maria Rilke once wrote in a letter, "Works of art are indeed always products of having-been-in-danger, or having-gone-to-the-very-end in an experience, to where one can go no further." Ray always tried to do this in his writing. He was a brave man and the stories and poems we are still gladly reading are the results of that bravery, the results of his passionate investigation of the world.

In his last letter to me in July 1988, he described his marriage to Tess Gallagher in Reno about three weeks earlier. "[We] got hitched by the world's oiliest minister, a pomaded man who was wearing a string tie, cowboy boots and a $15.00 sport coat. But it was official, and then we walked a block into the heart of the gambling center, and played roulette (Tess won nearly $400.00; I lost). But we had a good time."

Had Ray lived, the world's oiliest minister would have turned up in a short story.

LEWIS BUZBEE

New Hope for the Dead

There are many good stories about Raymond Carver; here is one of my favorites. A college friend of mine spent one year delivering potato chips to make some quick money. Ken was the youngest of the drivers and took a lot of flack because of his education. The other drivers were strictly middle-class, long-term union guys with families, houses, divorces, and debts. At one of their weekly lunches Ken arrived early and read *What We Talk About When We Talk About Love* while he waited, but when he left, he forgot the book, and one of the older drivers picked it up. The next week the driver pulled Ken aside and told him that, while he normally didn't read, he had been intrigued by the book's title and read the book from beginning to end, unable to stop. He told Ken that he had never read anything like it, that his life just wasn't the same, and that he'd had trouble at home. "Listen," he said, returning the book, "where did this guy come from? Can you get me some more?"

On August 3, 1988, the day after Ray died, I was reading the paper and had just found his obituary, when the phone rang. It was Ken. What was he going to do? There was a big hole in his life. He insisted that because I had introduced him to Carver's writing I had to find him someone new to read. Carver had changed his life.

As for me, I first encountered Carver when *Will You Please Be Quiet, Please?* was published. I borrowed the collection of stories from the university library and selfishly kept it for the whole year. Those stories spoke to me so directly I felt that I indeed owned that volume. I was feeling what Ken felt; what would we now do?

Now is not the time to judge or place Carver's work; the years and decades, perhaps even the centuries, will do that for us.

However, there are some things we can say with certainty. In a career that spanned over twenty-five years, he proved to be a masterful craftsman. He added to our literature an original body of work that gave voice to a world that had, until him, no voice of its own, a world of working-class tract homes and the quiet and powerless families who live in them, a voice that strove to win a struggle with silence. And this can be said with utmost confidence: Carver's stories have the power to move people deeply, immediately. He once told me, sternly, "It's not about personal expression; it's about communication."

I first met Ray in 1979 when he was reading at the Intersection gallery in San Francisco. He was tall and lanky with a dark, concentrated, brooding face, in many ways an imposing figure. Seeing him at the podium, and knowing his work and its darker sides, I was ready to be scared. But he read his stories in a voice that was high and airy and thin. He clipped his words, as if sealing each one, and he punctuated his sentences with decided, often smiling pauses. He occasionally laughed at his own jokes. Contrary to what I'd expected, I was comforted by his reading, and his wry humor drew me even farther into the stories.

Three other writers read that night, all of them good, but they suffered from reading after Ray. When Ray finished, and it was this way at any reading he gave, an impenetrable silence followed, as if the audience were waking to a world much different from the one they'd left when they were drawn into the story. Then there was electric applause.

After the reading I nervously approached Ray, a copy of my first published story in my back pocket. I had never met a real writer and wasn't sure I'd actually give the story to him, but youth quickly forgets decorum. As Chekhov was to the aspiring writers who came to him for advice, Ray was kind and encouraging. We exchanged addresses as I tried to hide my elation behind what must have seemed an awfully thin veneer of cool. Ray wrote to me soon with a careful and considered critique of my story. I've heard the same many times from other writers.

The following year I saw him again at the Intersection, where he read with the poet Tess Gallagher. Ray went first again, as he always seemed to, and this time he read nothing but his poetry. He called poetry his love. I talked with him after the reading, and he introduced me to Tess. He looked happier and healthier than the year before. I presumed to be even bolder this time and proposed doing an interview. He liked the idea, told me to outline it and send it to him. He gave me a new address, saying he was always moving.

We decided to do the interview by mail and worked on it for the next three years. In reading those letters recently I found this appropriate colophon. Each letter, no matter how long, begins with "Just a note, in haste." Like his work and his life, just a note, in haste.

I ran into Ray many times over the next few years while he was busy on the literary circuit, and indeed things were changing for him, as he said. It seemed that overnight he had become a central figure in our literary world.

In 1983 Ray came to Palo Alto to give a reading at Printer's Inc. bookstore. *Fires* had just been published, and *Cathedral* was in the final stages of preparation. He had recently been awarded the Mildred and Harold Strauss Living Award for five years of tax-free writing, he was very much in love with Tess, and he had a new Mercedes and a houseful of matching furniture. The drinking and hard times seemed very far away; he called his life a miracle.

After the reading, Ray came to our house for the night. I was married at the time (in fact, I had met my wife because I chose a graduate school where Ray was teaching), and we were living on the same street where Ray had once lived during the bad times. The *Paris Review* had just accepted the interview and to celebrate we got stoned and made cocoa and popcorn, and then Ray began talking, while my wife and I sat back and absorbed his words.

He told us stories about the bad times. He told us how through his first marriage, when he was working in obscurity, he often went out to the car at night after work and wrote on a pad on his knee, the only place to find a little privacy. He told us how he used to steal food from the dormitory cafeterias of the colleges where he taught, hoarding the food for the weekends because he was so broke. He told of carousing with John Cheever in Iowa City and how one night, the two of them drunk and broke, they had skipped a check in a restaurant together.

One time, completely at odds, he drove for hours through a

blizzard to get to a friend's summer house that had been loaned to him. He turned on the heater and within an hour was besieged by thousands of hibernating flies. "Imagine that," he told us, laughing, tears rolling down his face. "Imagine that."

There were lots of drinking stories, and the best of them was how he quit. He'd been to a dry-out clinic, he told us, but had no place to go after that, so he went to a friend's cabin and drank himself into a coma. When he woke up some days later, he made his decision. "I haven't had a drink since, God willing," he told us, rapping the arm of his chair. He said he'd once been told he was going to die within six months and figured if he lived, he'd be cheating someone. He liked that.

"New Hope for the Dead," he said. "That's a bumper sticker Bill Dickey told me about. Isn't that great, isn't that a scream? A border of lilies. That's me. New hope for the dead."

He laughed out of control at his own stories, as much amused by the sordid tales of his past as exhilarated by the changes in his life, incredulous at his fortune.

As the night wore on, he began to talk very quietly, focusing on the struggle to keep writing against adversity, and my wife and I both realized, I think, that he was no longer speaking of himself particularly, but speaking to us, two young writers living very much the way he had lived. He talked for a long time about this, telling us in his thin voice that we had to keep working, keep fighting to find our own voice. He told us that what we were trying to do was crucial. Although Ray had to catch a very early flight, he talked to us until four that morning.

The last time I saw Ray was in Anaheim in May 1988, but I did not recognize him; he seemed small, stooped, very old, his body beaten by the cancer that would kill him. But when I heard his controlled, airy voice, I felt relieved. He told me that things were changing for him and that I should come for a visit. At a reading that weekend he had trouble breathing and seemed very tired, but the voice was still there, and so was the magic. "Why don't you dance?" he said, and the crowd swayed to his music.

The last story in *Where I'm Calling From* is the most unusual of Carver's stories. "Errand" is an account of the advance of Chekhov's tuberculosis and the night of his death. But the heart of the story is pure Carver. In the final scene, the hotel waiter who delivered Chekhov's last bottle of champagne has come to clean up. Realizing he is in the presence of a great man, the waiter stoops to pick up the last champagne cork and pockets it. Carver's stories are much like this gesture. In the midst of a terrible world, he allows us to steal away from our common moments, simple but meaningful, and seeing those moments through his "bright, wild eye," our world is altered. Ray Carver has left behind, to those who knew him through his work and those who knew him as a man, a legacy of "small, good things."

JAY McINERNEY

Raymond Carver, Mentor

A year after his death, the recurring image I associate with Raymond Carver is one of people leaning toward him, working very hard at the act of listening. He mumbled. T.S. Eliot once described Ezra Pound, qua mentor, as "a man trying to convey to a very deaf person the fact that the house is on fire." Raymond Carver had precisely the opposite manner. The smoke could be filling the room, flames streaking across the carpet, before Carver would ask, "Is it, uh, getting a little hot in here, maybe?" And you would be sitting in your chair, bent achingly forward at the waist, saying, "Beg pardon, Ray?" Never insisting, rarely asserting, he was an unlikely teacher.

I once sat in and listened while Carver was interviewed for two and a half hours. The writer conducting the interview moved the tape recorder closer and closer and finally asked if Carver would put it in his lap. A few days later the interviewer called up, near despair: Ray's voice on the tapes was nearly inaudible. The word "soft-spoken" hardly begins to do justice to his speech; this condition was aggravated whenever he was pressed into the regions of generality or prescription.

As I say, he mumbled, and if it once seemed merely a physical tic, akin to cracking knuckles or the drumming of a foot, I now think it was a function of a deep humility and a respect for the language bordering on awe, a reflection of his sense that words should be handled very, very gingerly. As if it might be almost impossible to say what you wanted to say. As if it might be dangerous, even. Listening to him talking about writing in the classroom or in the living room of the big Victorian house he shared with Tess Gallagher in Syracuse, you sensed a writer who loved the words of the masters who had handed the language down to him, and who was concerned that he might not be worthy to pick up the instrument. You feel this respect for the language—humility bordering on dread—in every sentence of his work.

Encountering Carver's fiction early in the 1970s was a transforming experience for many writers of my generation, an experience perhaps comparable to discovering Hemingway's sentences in the twenties. In fact, Carver's language was unmistakably like Hemingway's—the simplicity and clarity, the repetitions, the nearly conversational rhythms, the precision of physical description. But Carver completely dispensed with the romantic egoism that made the Hemingway idiom such an awkward model for other writers in the late twentieth century. The cafés and *pensions* and battlefields of Europe were replaced by trailer parks and apartment complexes, the glamorous occupations by dead-end jobs. The trout in Carver's streams were apt to be pollution-deformed mutants. The good *vin du pays* was replaced by cheap gin, the romance of drinking by the dull grind of full-time alcoholism. Some commentators found his work depressing for these reasons. For many young writers it was terribly liberating.

One aspect of what Carver seemed to say to us—even to someone who had never been inside a lumber mill or a trailer park—was that literature could be fashioned out of strict observation of real life, wherever and however it was lived, even if it was lived with a bottle of Heinz ketchup on the table and the television set droning. This was news at a time when academic metafiction was the regnant mode. His example reinvigorated realism as well as the short story form.

Though he was a teacher for much of his life, Carver never consciously gathered a band of disciples around himself. But when I was knocking around between graduate schools and the New York publishing world in the late seventies and early eighties, no other writer was as much discussed and mimicked by the writers one met at readings and writers' conferences. Probably not since Donald Barthelme began publishing in the 1960s had a story writer generated such a buzz in the literary world.

Having fallen under Carver's spell on reading his early collection, *Will You Please Be Quiet, Please?*, a book I would have bought on the basis of the title alone, I was lucky enough to meet him a few years later and eventually to become his student at Syracuse University in the early eighties. Despite the existence of several thousand creative writing programs around the country, there is probably no good answer to the question of whether writing can be taught. Saying that Faulkner and Fitzgerald never got M.F.A.s is beside the point. Novelists and short story writers like to eat as much as anyone else, and tend to sniff out subsidies while they pursue their creative work. For writers in the twenties, the exchange rate was favorable in Paris, and in the thirties there was the WPA, and a gold rush of sorts in Hollywood. The universities have become the creative writers' WPA in recent years.

Carver was himself a product of the new system, having studied writing at the University of Iowa Writers' Workshop and at Stanford, and later earned a living teaching. It was something he did out of necessity, a role he was uncomfortable with. He did it to make a living, because it was easier than the other jobs he'd had—working at a sawmill and a hospital, working as a service station attendant, a janitor, a delivery boy, a textbook editor. Though grateful for genteel employment, he didn't really see why people who had a gift for writing should necessarily be able to teach. And he was very shy. The idea of facing a class made him nervous every time. On the days he had to teach he would get agitated, as if he himself were a student on the day of the final exam.

Like many writers in residence at universities, Ray was required to teach English courses in addition to creative writing courses. One was called Form and Theory of the Short Story, a title Ray inherited from the graduate English catalogue. His method in these classes was to assign a book of stories he liked each week, including contemporary and nineteenth-century authors as well as works in translation. We would read the books and discuss them for two hours. Flannery O'Connor, Chekhov, Ann Beattie, Maupassant, Frank O'Connor, John Cheever, Mary Robison, Turgenev, and more Chekhov. (He loved all the nineteenth-century Russians.) Class would begin with Ray saying something like, "Well, guys, how'd you like Eudora Welty?" He preferred listening to lecturing, but he would read his favorite passages, talk about what he loved in the book he had chosen. He dealt in specifics, stayed close to the text, and eventually there would come a moment when the nervousness would lift off of him as he spoke about writing that moved him.

One semester, a very earnest Ph.D. candidate found his way into this class, composed mainly of writers. At that time, the English department, like many around the country, had become a battle-ground between theorists and humanists, and poststructuralism lay heavy upon the campus. After a few weeks of Carver's free-ranging and impressionistic approach to literature, the young theorist regis-tered a strong protest: "This class is called Form and Theory of the Short Story but all we do is sit around and talk about the books. Where's the form and the theory?"

Ray looked distressed. He nodded and pulled extra hard on his cigarette. "Well, that's a good question," he said. After a long pause, he said, "I guess I'd say that the point here is that we read good books and discuss them. . . . And then you *form* your own *theory*." Then he smiled.

As a teacher of creative writing, too, Carver had a light touch. He did not consider it his job to discourage anyone. He said that there was enough discouragement out there for anyone trying against all odds to be a writer, and he clearly spoke from experience. Criti-cism, like fiction, was an act of empathy for Ray, putting yourself in the other guy's shoes. He couldn't understand writers who wrote negative reviews and once chided me for doing so. He believed fiction and poetry were fraternal enterprises. Among the very few people that Ray vocally disliked were a poet who had refused to lend him fifty dollars when his car broke down in Salt Lake City, two critics who had attacked his own work, and writers who had attacked any of his friends. For a shy man, his gregarious generosity of spirit was remarkable. He kept up a correspondence with dozens of other writers, students, and fans. He wrote letters of recommendation and encouragement; helped people get jobs and grants, editors and agents; accompanied friends in need to their first AA meetings.

One day when I berated him for going easy on a student I thought was turning out poor work, he told me a story: he had recently been a judge in a prestigious fiction contest. The unanimous winner, whose work has since drawn much praise, turned out to be a former student of his, probably the worst, least promising student he'd had in twenty years. "What if I had discouraged her?" he said.

His harshest critical formula was: "I think it's good you got that story behind you." Meaning, I guess, that one has to drive through some ugly country on the way to Parnassus. If Carver had had his way, classes and workshops would have been conducted entirely by students, but his approval was too highly valued for him to remain mute.

Once he sat through the reading of a long, strange story in his graduate writing workshop: as I recall, the story fleshed out two disparate characters, brought them together, followed their courtship and eventual marriage. After a series of false starts they decided to open a restaurant together, the preparations for which were described in great detail. On the day it opened a band of submachine-gun-toting terrorists burst in and killed everyone in the restaurant. End of story. After nearly everyone in the smoky seminar room had expressed dissatisfaction with this plot, we all turned to Ray. He was clearly at a loss. Finally he said softly, "Well, sometimes a story needs a submachine gun." This answer seemed to satisfy the author no less than those who felt the story in question had been efficiently put out of its misery.

My first semester, Ray somehow forgot to enter my grade for workshop. I pointed this out to him, and we went together to the English office to rectify the situation. "You did some real good work," he said, informing me that I would get an A. I was very pleased with myself, but perhaps a little less so when Ray opened the grade book and wrote an A next to my name underneath a solid column of identical grades. Everybody did good work, apparently. In workshop he approached every story with respect—treating each as if it were a living entity, a little sick, possibly, or lame, but something that could be nursed and trained to health.

Though Ray was always encouraging, he could be rigorous if he knew criticism was welcome. Fortunate students had their stories subjected to the same process he employed on his own numerous drafts. Manuscripts came back thoroughly ventilated with Carver deletions, substitutions, question marks, and chicken-scratch queries. I took one story back to him seven times; he must have spent fifteen or twenty hours on it. He was a meticulous, obsessive line editor. One on one, in his office, he almost became a tough guy, his voice gradually swelling with conviction.

Once we spent some ten or fifteen minutes debating my use of the word "earth." Carver felt it had to be "ground," and he felt it was worth the trouble of talking it through. That one exchange was invaluable; I think of it constantly when I'm working. Carver himself used the same example later in an essay he wrote that year, in discussing the influence of his mentor, John Gardner. "Ground is ground, he'd say, it means *ground,* dirt, that kind of stuff. But if you say 'earth,' that's something else, that word has other ramifications."

John Gardner, the novelist, was Ray's first writing teacher. They met at Chico State College in California in the 1950s. Ray said that all of his writing life he had felt Gardner looking over his shoulder when he wrote, approving or disapproving of certain words, phrases, and strategies. Calling fouls. He said a good writing teacher is something like a literary conscience, a friendly critical voice in your ear. I know what he meant. (I have one; it mumbles.)

After almost twenty years Carver had a reunion with his old teacher, who was living and teaching less than a hundred miles from Syracuse, in Binghamton, New York, and Gardner's approval of his work had meant a great deal to him. In the fall of 1982, I happened to stop by Ray's house a few minutes after he heard that Gardner had died in a motorcycle crash. Distraught, he couldn't sit still. We walked around the house and the backyard as he talked about Gardner.

"Back then I didn't even know what a writer looked like," Ray said. "John looked like a writer. He had that hair, and he used to wear this thing that was like a cape. I tried to copy the way he walked. He used to let me work in his office because I didn't have a quiet place to work. I'd go through his files and steal the titles of his stories, use them on my stories."

So Ray must have understood when we all shamelessly cribbed from him, we students at Syracuse, and Iowa, and Stanford and all the other writing workshops in the country where almost everyone seemed to be writing and publishing stories with Raymond Carver titles like "Do You Mind If I Smoke?" or "How about This, Honey?" He certainly didn't want clones. But he knew that imitation was part of finding your own voice.

I encountered Carver near the beginning of what he liked to call his "second life," after he had quit drinking. I heard stories about the bad old Ray, stories he liked to tell on himself. When I met him I thought of writers as luminous madmen who drank too much and drove too fast and scattered brilliant pages along their doomed trajectories. Maybe at one time he did, too. In his essay "Fires," he says, "I understood writers to be people who didn't spend their Saturdays at the laundromat." Would Hemingway be caught dead doing laundry? No, but William Carlos Williams would. Ditto Carver's beloved Chekhov. In the classroom and on the page, Carver somehow delivered the tonic news that there was laundry in the kingdom of letters.

Not that, by this time, Ray was spending much time at the laundromat, life having been good to him toward the end in a way for which he seemed constantly to be grateful. But hearing the typewriter of one of the masters of American prose clacking just up the street, while a neighbor raked leaves and some kids threw a Frisbee as the dogs went on with their doggy life—this was a lesson in itself for me. Whatever dark mysteries lurk at the heart of the writing process, he insisted on a single trade secret: that you had to survive, find some quiet, and work hard every day. And seeing him for coffee, or watching a ball game or a dumb movie with him, put into perspective certain dangerous myths about the writing life that he preferred not to lecture on—although he sometimes would, if he thought it might help. When we first became acquainted, in New York, he felt obliged to advise me, in a series of wonderful letters, and a year later I moved upstate to become his student.

Reading the dialogues of Plato, one eventually realizes that Socrates' self-deprecation is something of a ploy. Ray's humility, however, was profound and unselfconscious and one of the most astonishing things about him. When he asked a student, "What do you think?" he clearly wanted to know. This seemed a rare and inspiring didactic stance. His own opinions were expressed with such caution that you knew how carefully they had been measured.

For someone who claimed he didn't love to teach, he made a great deal of difference to a great many students. He certainly changed my life irrevocably and I have heard others say the same thing.

I'm still leaning forward with my head cocked to one side, straining to hear his voice.

KENNETH INADOMI

Read It Again

April 29, 1991

Dear Ms. Gallagher,

I once knew Raymond Carver; I wish I'd known him better. Having recently read your moving tribute to him in *A New Path to the Waterfall,* I wanted to share a few, albeit too few, firsthand experiences I had with the man nearly two decades ago.

In the fall of 1972 Raymond Carver was my professor at the University of California at Santa Cruz in a class that I believe was simply called Poetry, a brief but ample title befitting the man himself. There were maybe eight in the class; we met once a week, sitting around a round table in the small seminar room of College V, one of Santa Cruz's half a dozen residential colleges.

That fall, I believe, was Ray's first term at Santa Cruz. He had distinctive yet classic teacher's instincts. He was intense, sensitive, inquisitive, patient, encouraging—all packaged with understatement, a temperament that I later realized matched well with the Zen masters. (Did he ever study Zen or visit Japan?) When Ray smiled, his eyes would disappear behind his black horn-rimmed glasses. He used to smile a lot.

I remember vividly one class in which he had strewn pictures from dozens of magazines on our discussion table. Our challenge was to select a few images and compose a poem. I chose one drawing of a man and woman standing in the hallway of a hotel, their heads and bodies turned in opposite directions. To this day there's one piece of personal verse that I'm willing to recite even among strangers—the piece I composed that day for Ray:

The end of the night
Your room or mine?
It matters not which for
Our legs won't obey
Our minds anyway.

Ray had me read this poem several times—calling for varied intonations and pacing—and listened carefully each time with his eyes closed. In Ray's class a student always felt appreciated, validated to the point of wanting to try again, to get it right! And isn't that the most one could ask for in an instructor—the honest encouragement to improve and to hone until achieving the desired effect? Given how arduous the craft of writing can be, particularly at Ray's level of perfection, the encouragement I received at that young age was the life-force itself. "Read it again, . . . Let me hear it again, . . ." and so on, relentlessly.

On another assignment he read out a series of unrelated words, maybe eight to twelve total, and had us write a poem with their inclusion. I'm sorry, but I can't recollect much about that effort—probably because my piece was pitiful.

One of the highlights of the year for me was the term-ending poetry reading that Ray organized. Held in the coffee lounge, the reading culled selected writers from the various prose and poetry courses to share recent work. Ray was kind enough to nominate me. This was my first-ever experience at public recitation and I found it exhilarating. A couple of days later I met Ray in his office and I still remember his warm words: "Thank you for your reading. You acquitted yourself very well. . . ."

He went on to ask me about my plans as a writer. What else did I want to do? I replied that I had no plans (being, as I was, entrenched in Santa Cruz's dominant milieu of *being,* not planning). But I conceded that his course had pushed me irrevocably out of the nest, stirring energies that would one day be reckoned with. Of course Ray reckoned with his energies unlike anyone else. Despite (because of?) that humble beginning at an obscure college in a remote setting, his later success never surprised me. He had the passion and the compassion to bring it all home.

A few years before he died, Ray visited New York and gave a

reading at my favorite bookstore, Shakespeare & Co. on Broadway. Though I had neither seen nor spoken to him since '72, I inexcusably missed the event. To this day each time I enter that shop I think of Ray Carver.

I hope this letter reaches you and finds you well and working. I also hope you've gained one more perspective on Ray, one that's nearly twenty years old. As I said, I once knew Raymond Carver; I wish I'd known him better, if only to hear him once more say, "Read it again."

Sincerely,
Kenneth Inadomi

HARUKI MURAKAMI

A Literary Comrade

It must have been around 1982 when I first came to know of the writer Raymond Carver. The first work of his I read was "So Much Water So Close to Home." It was printed in *West Coast Fiction,* an anthology edited by James D. Houston. There is a short and a long version of this story; I read the long version. (I think it is the more accomplished of the two.) Until then I had not only not read his work before, I had never even heard the name Raymond Carver. However, this story literally came as a shock to me. I felt just as if I had been out leisurely walking along on a sunny, cloudless afternoon when suddenly lightning struck. There was the almost breathtakingly compact world of his fiction, his strong but supple style, and his convincing story line. Although his style is fundamentally realistic, there is something penetrating and profound in his work that goes beyond simple realism. I felt as though I had come across an entirely new kind of fiction, the likes of which had never been before.

To be made to think, after reading only one short story, that you have encountered a true writer, that this writer is a genius—this kind of work is rare. It is something that does not happen often in a lifetime. In my experience, as far as I can recall, there has been Scott Fitzgerald's "The Rich Boy," Truman Capote's "The Headless Hawk," and finally this story by Raymond Carver. I was really bowled over by it. Shortly after that, I read his "Where I'm Calling From" in the *New Yorker.* This was also a brilliant short story, a story that left me with the impression that a door to a completely unknown world had been pushed open and a ray of light shone faintly through. I immediately began collecting and reading all his works I could find. I translated them and published them, first in a literary magazine and later in book form. At that point, I believe there was almost no one in Japan who knew Raymond Carver's name.

The publication of Carver's collected short fiction, however, elicited a response that can only be called extraordinary. The book sold well and most of the reviews were glowing with praise. Many readers wrote letters to me saying, "I don't know much about the writer Raymond Carver, but it has been a long time since I read anything so wonderful. Please, translate more of his work." Editors and other writers also exclaimed over what a brilliant writer he was. Although I am an author in my own right, this warm, even passionate, reception that Raymond Carver received from Japanese readers gave me almost as much pleasure as the reception of my own work.

Eventually, it was arranged that I would translate all of Raymond Carver's works into Japanese, using the time in between the writing of my own novels. *The Complete Works of Raymond Carver (Rei-mondo Kābā zenshū)* is being issued by Chuokoron-Sha Publishers in seven volumes, four of which are now in print. To date, this is the only complete edition of Raymond Carver in the world. Many people have asked me why I put so much energy into translating when I am a writer. The answer is simple. All rationalization aside, it is because I like translating Carver's work. It is because I would like to translate with my own hand everything he wrote.

As I translate what Ray has written, I can sense line by line the rhythm of his breathing, the warmth of his body, and the subtle wavering of his emotions. I can sense the feelings he experienced when writing certain lines. It is truly an extraordinary experience. Of course, you can probably get this kind of pleasure even from just reading his books. That is, after all, the sign of great fiction. But there are times when I am translating, painstakingly transforming one word after another into Japanese, that I sometimes feel just as though I have become one—body and soul—with the author. Through his words I can sense clearly the sadness or joy he experienced at the moment of writing them. Instead of translation, I prefer to call this "experiencing Raymond Carver." And there is nothing that can substitute for this experience.

Then again, this endeavor has been most rewarding for me as a writer as well, one that has borne much fruit. Until I encountered Raymond Carver, there had never been a person I could, as an author, call my mentor. After graduating from college, I managed a small jazz nightclub in Tokyo and did not write a single line until I reached the age of twenty-nine. I did not even have friends around me with whom I could discuss literature. I had only my own powers to fall back on when it came to learning how to write novels. Through reading books—and later through translation—I studied the art of writing fiction. Or rather, I learned to recognize what constitutes great fiction. And, in this sense, Raymond Carver was without question the most valuable teacher I had and also the greatest literary comrade. The novels I write tend, I believe, in a very different direction from the fiction Ray has written. But if he had never existed, or if I had never encountered his writings, the books I write (especially my short fiction) would probably have assumed a very different form.

The other day, when I met Jay McInerney, he suggested that the beginning of my story "The Windup Bird and Tuesday's Women" (the first work of mine to be published in the *New Yorker*) was reminiscent of the beginning of Ray Carver's "Put Yourself in My Shoes." At the time I thought that he might have a point and left it at that. But later, when I had a chance to think about it, it became clear to me that there was a decided similarity between the two beginnings. Carver's story begins with a scene where an unemployed man is vacuuming and receives a call from his wife. My short story begins with an unemployed man who is boiling noodles for spaghetti when he receives a call from a mysterious woman. I was certainly not conscious of this when I wrote it, but it can definitely be said that the two beginnings are quite similar in atmosphere. Until Jay mentioned this to me, I was not aware of it, but it is possible that I have absorbed the rhythm of Ray's phrasing and something like his view of the world much more deeply than I had suspected. Of course, he is not the only writer who has had an influence on me. But Ray Carver is after all the most significant writer for me. Otherwise, why would I want to translate all his work?

I only met Ray once in person. It was back in the summer of 1984 (the year of the Reagan and Mondale presidential race). By that time he had long stopped drinking. In the waning of that quiet afternoon, I remember with what distaste he was sipping black tea. Holding the teacup in his hand, he looked as though he was doing the wrong thing in the wrong place. Sometimes he would get up from his seat and go outside to smoke. From the window of Tess Gallagher's Sky House in Port Angeles I could make out a ferryboat on its way to Canada.

I spoke with Ray for only an hour at the time, but because I am not much of a conversationalist to begin with, plus the fact that it was my first visit to America and I could not speak English that well, I was unable to express to my satisfaction all that I felt. And then, Ray on his part spoke with that hesitant soft-spoken tone that I had heard was characteristic of him, so the tape I recorded of our conversation sounds like little more than a badly done wiretap.

When I met Ray the very first thing that struck me was his massive physical size; his shoulders were huge, his chest expansive, and his hands large. Until I met him in person, I had always secretly imagined him as being of rather small stature, thin and delicate in appearance. But after I actually met him, I came to think that everything about the writer of those works had to be larger than life. As we sat facing each other in the living room of Sky House, it seemed to me that he carried his huge frame almost as if he were ashamed of it. He sat on the sofa with his body crouched up as if to say that he had never intended to get so big, and he had an embarrassed expression on his face. Even the movements of his face were excessive; each time he laughed or became perplexed, his expression changed drastically and abruptly. It was not so much that his expressions were extreme as that the effort involved was so great that his movements became exaggerated as well. I had never until then met up with such a physically imposing writer. And it was also the first time I had met one with such an unassuming and gentle air. Later, when the news of Ray's death reached me, I was unable to believe it. I imagined what an ordeal it must have been for so large a person to die over such a long period of time. I thought it must be something like the slow fall of a giant tree.

I said to Ray, "Sometimes I experience your stories as though they were poems and your poems sometimes as though they were stories." He was so pleased by this observation that he got up from his seat and called out to Tess, "Hey, Tess, listen to this. Do you know what he said?" And he repeated my words to her.

Ray wrote a poem entitled "The Projectile" based on his impressions of his meeting with me. And this poem, hard as it is for me to believe, is dedicated to me. Of course, it has become one of my favorites. Every time I read it, I am filled with warm feelings. (Come to think of it, Tess also wrote a poem for me later on.)

When I am reading Ray's poetry, there are times when I become inspired to try my hand at writing poetry as well. Although I have personally never written a poem, when I read his poetry I immediately get the feeling that I could write poetry too. I think this is wonderful. Of course, it is unlikely that I could write poetry like Ray's. No matter how straightforward or how unadorned his writing may seem, it would probably be impossible for anyone to write poems the way he did. But when I read his poetry, I get the feeling that I, too, could write poetry. So many stories and poems in this world (many of them really uninteresting) seem to say, "How about it? I bet you couldn't do it if you tried." That's why I value so highly Ray's kind of poetry and fiction. It's almost as though I feel him turn to me and say, "If you try, you can do it."

My greatest regret when it comes to Ray is that he was never able to visit Japan. A visit was planned, and I was looking forward to meeting him and Tess again in Japan, but the trip was postponed because of his health, and it was never finally realized. If he had visited Japan he would doubtless have been able to feel the deep love that Japanese readers have for his work, and his Japanese audience would have been impressed by the warmth of his personality. I think it is unfortunate that this chance is forever lost.

But I can say with certainty that Japanese readers have taken the works of Raymond Carver into their hearts more readily and with more passion than readers anywhere else in the world—with the exception, of course, of Americans. And so it is that his works are being lovingly translated, one by one, by a writer who finds no greater joy than in translating them. There are, I am sure, many greater translators than I—strictly speaking, I am not a professional translator—but I think there cannot be many who love Ray Carver's works as deeply as I do. There are times when I think if only Ray were still living. There were so many things I wanted to discuss with him, so many things I wanted to ask him. And then, too, I would have enjoyed translating many more of his works. It is more distressing than I can bear to see that the number of works I have left to translate is steadily diminishing. But there is no point in saying this now that he is gone. I suppose there is nothing for us to do now besides carefully preserving each and every one of the works he did write and leave behind—nothing else for me to do, as a translator and as a literary comrade who happens to write novels in Japanese.

—translated by Tara Maja McGowan

JAY WOODRUFF

Laundroma

In the winter of 1983, browsing at a bookstore in Cambridge, Massachusetts, I picked up a thin collection of stories by a man named Raymond Carver. The name sounded vaguely familiar, though I realized I might have been thinking of Raymond Chandler. The cover and inside pages were full of rave reviews from other writers I'd never heard of. (I'd hardly heard of anyone then—I was a freshly graduated English major, and contemporary writers hadn't been a prominent feature of the college curriculum, nor had I logged too many free evenings, I must admit, in the periodical section of the school's libraries.) I turned to the first story in the book and read: "In the kitchen, he poured another drink and looked at the bedroom suite in his front yard." I was hooked and kept reading. I bought that book, and the next day returned to buy the only other collection of Carver's stories I could find, *Will You Please Be Quiet, Please?*

Those were days when it wasn't easy for me to buy books. I was unemployed and dead broke and sleeping in a friend's Somerville apartment, on the living room floor, next to the dog. In college I had wanted to emulate Jack Kerouac or the young Sam Shepard, Charles Bukowski or the Henry Miller who wrote, "I have no money, no resources, no hopes. I am the happiest man alive." It had been easier as a student to be drunk. But a few months after graduation I woke up one morning in a pile of peat before a strange building, in a city I wasn't sure I knew the name of and where I didn't speak the language, my shoes off my feet and thirty yards apart, my arms and face badly bruised and what little money I'd remembered having on me—nearly all the money I had in the world—nowhere in sight. I had by then been involved in a series of "incidents," each more violently stupid than the last, so that by the time I came across Carver's book *Fires* and discovered there his *Paris Review* interview, I was very receptive to what he had to say in response to the question of how bad his own drinking had gotten. "Let's just say, on occasion, the police were involved and emergency rooms and courtrooms," Carver told his interviewers. "I was dying from it, plain and simple, and I'm not exaggerating."

Raymond Carver had the unmistakable voice of a man who had been through some rough times and come out the other end. I don't mean to make too much of the bond I felt with him. Our lives were dramatically different. He was of my parents' generation and grew up poor in a working-class home in the Pacific Northwest, while I grew up in a comfortable midwestern suburb, the son of a physician, the grandson of a modestly affluent businessman on one side and an extremely successful physician on the other. By the time Carver was twenty, he was the father of two and still uncertain about how he'd ever manage to get himself through college, while by the time I reached that age I was halfway through Harvard.

Appearances, of course, are deceptive, and by the time I'd left St. Louis for Cambridge I was well acquainted with what sometimes lay beneath the veneer of the suburban middle class. My parents had divorced when I was twelve, and my father, an alcoholic, a psychiatrist, killed himself when I was fifteen. Many of my friends' parents were alcoholics and divorced as well. My friends and I knew more than we wanted to about drug abuse, not to mention other varieties of abuse. Two of my best friends had been locked into mental wards by the time I entered high school.

In short, my young friends and I, even within our relatively affluent and comfortable suburban community, had seen plenty of lives spin out of control and knew the insidious way in which things sometimes begin to unravel. Carver's people, often dazed by life's troubles, were familiar. Some of them had been my neighbors.

More than a few critics have attacked Carver for the dreary lives he often depicts, but the problems Carver chronicled are simply life's realities for too many Americans. It's hardly ironic that Carver (not to mention many other fine story writers of the 1980s who documented the struggles of working people) achieved prominence during the Reagan years. The Republican rise to power in that decade was due largely to that party's recognition of precisely the same widespread malaise Carver was depicting: Reagan's phony populism appealed to a profound yearning, not for pity but for stability and esteem, a new chance. "America is back," Reagan announced, "standing tall." People wanted to believe this so badly that most of Carver's characters voted Republican in 1980. As that Bull Decade unfolded, as Reagan's betrayal of working-class America became evident (scripted so skillfully that one might conclude the era's most influential writer of fiction was not Raymond Carver but Peggy Noonan), Carver continued to remind anyone who bothered to listen that much of America remained on its back, prone on a sofa, out of work, numbing itself with television and beer, cigarettes and dope, while the house fell apart and the repo men pounded on the front door.

Carver once said that "a good book is an honest book," and in his stories and poems and essays he almost always seems to be telling the plain truth. Writing of his former teacher, John Gardner, in the introduction to *On Becoming a Novelist,* Carver tells us, "It was [Gardner's] conviction that if the words in the story were blurred because of the author's insensitivity, carelessness, or sentimentality, then the story suffered from a tremendous handicap. But there was something even worse and something that must be avoided at all costs: if the words and the sentiments were dishonest, the author was faking it, writing about things he didn't care about or believe in, then nobody could ever care anything about it."

The commitment to a stripped-down, unflinchingly open-eyed storytelling is not without its own particular hazards. Hemingway's "iceberg theory" and dedication to *le mot juste* could result in a coy frigidity every bit as mannered and annoying as the distracting, nostril-flaring virtuosity of stylists who indulge in more pyrotechnic literary experiments. In "The Bath," for example, Carver describes a young boy's reaction to seeing his friend struck down by a car: "The other boy stood holding the potato chips. He was wondering if he should finish the rest or continue on to school." This reaction seems inhuman and false, designed more to serve an author's purposes of stoking a peculiar narrative tension than to do real justice to the perceptions of this young witness.

A tireless and consummate reviser, Carver of course later trans-formed "The Bath" from an exercise in muted terror to the more fully developed story he'd envisioned in the early drafts—one of his masterpieces, a story of such depth and redemptive tenderness that it's as good as any story has ever been: "A Small, Good Thing." Carver's revised description of the young boy's reaction is elegant and perfect: "His friend dropped his potato chips and started to cry."

In "On Writing," Carver wrote that he reminded himself often of Ezra Pound's dictum, "Fundamental accuracy of statement is the ONE sole morality of writing," to which Carver appended, with typical humor and straightforward honesty, "It is not everything, by ANY means, but if a writer has [that], he's at least on the right track." It was, I suppose, his commitment to this "fundamental accuracy" that led Carver back to stories that had already been published, to get them as right as they could be, to do justice to his people, even a little nameless boy who makes just a cameo appearance.

Carver's plain-spoken frankness is not intended to lull. In "Fires," his forthright ambivalence about the demands of parenthood con-tradicts some of the soothing pieties and amusing anecdotes we're accustomed to hearing about the wonders of young family life. He describes one afternoon in an Iowa City laundromat, when he was a student at the Iowa Writers' Workshop, trying to get his kids' clothes clean while his wife was at work, and all he wanted was to be somewhere else, writing:

> I remember thinking at that moment, amid the feelings of help-less frustration that had me close to tears, that nothing—and, brother, I mean nothing—that ever happened to me on this earth could come anywhere close, could possibly be as important to me, could make as much difference, as the fact that I had two children. And that I would always have them and always find myself in this position of unrelieved responsibility and perma-nent distraction.
>
> I'm talking about real *influence* now. I'm talking about the moon and the tide. But like that it came to me. Like a sharp

breeze when the window is thrown open. Up to that point in my life I'd gone along thinking, what exactly, I don't know, but that things would work out somehow—that everything in my life I'd hoped for or wanted to do, was possible. But at that moment, in the laundromat, I realized that this simply was not true. I realized—what had I been thinking before?—that my life was a small-change thing for the most part, chaotic, and without much light showing through.

In 1986, I got to meet Raymond Carver. He was visiting Iowa City with Tess Gallagher to attend a jubilee celebration of the Writers' Workshop's fiftieth anniversary. I remember his soft voice and the way he pronounced the word poem: "poim." I remember how he sat back in the stuffed chair at the Union, a man who seemed to know how to sit back and take it easy, his long legs sprawling out before him. He laughed easily and smoked nonstop, and when I asked if by any chance that laundromat he'd described in "Fires" was the one at the corner of Burlington and Gilbert, he nodded. "Yep," he said. "That's the one, all right." I told him that was where I did my laundry. The building had fallen into disrepair. The sign was now broken, and he seemed amused to learn that the place was now a LAUNDROMA.

Most of the students in town now did their laundry at one of the upscale Suds 'n Duds that featured a bar and a pool table and a wide-screen TV, but Carver's old laundromat was open twenty-four hours, and driving past it late at night, you could glance in at the fluorescent glare, and no matter the hour, there always seemed to be someone inside, sitting alone, staring at the window toward the street, waiting for another cycle to end.

TOM JENKS

Shameless

I first met Ray Carver in New York in early September 1984 at a publishing dinner to launch Gary Fisketjon's Vintage Contemporary paperback series. Many of the new VC authors and their friends were there: Richard Ford, Toby Wolff, Jay McInerney, Tom McGuane, Jim Crumley, and Ralph Beer—a distinctly male crowd, and what struck me most was that, as we geared up to move to a nightclub, Ray, amid teasing about running off somewhere to see a woman, put himself in a taxi and headed for his hotel room alone. By the ginger way he got himself into the cab and laughingly ducked the barbs all around him, there was no doubt he meant to keep himself out of trouble.

But he was fair game for the friendly taunts that followed him into the cab. We were witnessing the Good Ray, but we all knew about the Bad Ray, the one who used to be Lord Misrule himself.

Reformed, Ray was fast becoming the most famous short story writer in the world, and the facts of his life were well known, partly because they were often the stuff of his writing and because fame brings a peculiar public intimacy.

At the time, I was an editor of *Esquire* and had made Ray's acquaintance through the mail and on the phone. I had published some of his work and knew him somewhat, and as I watched him slip away in the cab, I imagined him going back to his hotel room (it was early yet—ten o'clock) and telephoning Tess Gallagher at their home in Syracuse. Each evening they set aside the hours beyond ten o'clock to spend with each other. He *was,* in a sense, running off to see a woman.

A year and a half later, I visited them in Syracuse. During the days, Ray and I read stories for a book we were working on and at night we watched TV. One night, we were watching a PBS version of *Wuthering Heights,* and Ray began tell about another night of TV: the night the blind man for whom Tess once worked had come to visit. Tess told her side, too—how Ray was uneasy about the man's visit, uncomfortable with his blindness and his familiarity with Tess, a mild jealousy rising in Ray. Their evening was slow and tedious, and ended with the three of them watching PBS, just as we were. But on the night the blind man was visiting, Tess had fallen asleep, and then a program about cathedrals came on. The blind man had no idea what a cathedral looked like, and, in the end, Ray sat on the floor with him, holding his hands, drawing a cathedral so the blind man could sense the miracle of the shape.

Ray had written this story and titled it "Cathedral." Tess, who with Ray's encouragement had recently begun writing stories, had her own version, titled "The Harvest." She gave me a copy, humor-ously telling Ray, "Watch out, I'm nipping at your heels." Their good-natured competition and openness was rare in my experi-ence of writers, many of whom are cagey about the intimate, personal connections in their work.

The more I got to know Ray, the more I saw his unreserved friendliness—the product of a decision to live each moment fully. I also saw other sides of him—the ghost feelings of pain from his bad years, his instant withdrawal from situations and people he didn't like, the obsessive craving that sometimes still touched him. Having given up alcohol, he never missed a meal, and if he had to wait to eat he became anxious.

Ray's generosity, his willing suspension of disbelief (even to the point of gullibility) made him a good listener. The other side of it was that he couldn't keep a secret if it meant not telling a good story. I discovered this the hard way.

In late 1985, I sent Ray the manuscript of a book I'd been editing, Hemingway's *The Garden of Eden.* The book would be a sensation when it came out, and I wanted Ray's reading to test the book's merit apart from commerce. I swore him to secrecy, not telling him that I was prepared to destroy my edit of the posthumous novel if his reading, with others, indicated the material was unworthy.

Ray phoned within a few days, and his first comment was rueful and humorous. "There sure is a lot of drinking in it, Tom."

As we laughed about it, I could see Ray gingerly ducking into the taxi away from the party. Hemingway had aroused a thirst in Ray. But the book, Ray said, had masterful stuff in it, great passages, a good story.

About a week later, I received a phone call from Toby Wolff, Ray's neighbor in Syracuse, who spoke in a kind of serious hushed tone. "Tom, I thought you ought to know there was a party at Ray's last night, and he stood up on a chair and announced he had a manuscript of the Hemingway book on the counter in his kitchen."

I could just see Ray grandly making the announcement, and I worried that he had let his guests read the book.

"No, I don't think so," Toby said. "But there were a lot of people there. I thought you ought to know. You can't tell Ray anything you don't want everybody else to know."

And sure enough, later the same day I received a phone call from John Blades, the *Book World* editor of the *Chicago Tribune* who had heard the story from someone at the party. And while I had to tell Blades at least a dozen lies to keep the book out of the news until it was ready to go, there was never any point in reproaching Ray. In some things, he was shameless.

MARVIN BELL

The Door

I see Ray's figure hugely framed by doorways
through which we had free passage
by looking past his big shoulders
at plain acres, at trailers and porches,
at kitchens, bedrooms, closets. Here was
a door through which we saw a man writing
at night in his car. And here a door to a house
that led to a door to another house and another
door and another house. A door to old
cars and a door into the showroom when it
came true that he could buy one for cash.
Not for travel, but for cash. And the houses:
not for safety, but for cash. But the boats—
that was different. He bought them,
not for cash but for fishing, and when he wasn't
fishing, he was writing but wanted to fish,
and when he was fishing, he wanted to fish again
and did, so that he had to sell the boat to get back
to writing so he could wish he were fishing.
Sent me a bookbag of smoked salmon
on my birthday. Said we'd go when we knew
we wouldn't. I haven't mentioned the door
to two jobs at once two thousand miles apart,
and I should mention that one because
that was Ray's life too, the hardworking part:

writing about bad luck brought him good luck
in the end, I guess, but in Carver country
good luck had a way of going bad, if you consider
the last of a life bad luck by any score.
If I get any money for this, I'll bury it
in Port Angeles near Ray so George Washington
can see the Strait, and Ray can hear the wind
fan the bills and know he's got a stake
and the price of admission, as if anyone
would keep a man like Ray waiting at the door.

PART V

Port Angeles, Washington

1984

MORRIS R. BOND

My Crony

Never, not once, not ever,
have I heard my friend and crony—
a term used by my wife—
pardner, I say, admit,
"You got it!"

Today started out no different—
except for the 200-yard belly crawl through
barbwire, three inches of water and
signs in the early morning light reading,
No Trespassing.
After the ducks were jumped and
the dead counted,
it was what I expected,
"I got 'em!"
How do you argue with a man, who
when you question this,
tells you to go ask the ducks?

Oh, if I could only tell them—
it was me who gave them that
last flight, that last chance at freedom—
how I'd had to threaten him that I'd tell
Richard if he'd gone ahead and ground-sluiced them as
planned.

But,
I let him get 'em
knowing I got 'em.
Not enough for him, though—
my own dear sister, my own blood,
she knew I got 'em—
yet she says, "He got 'em."

Now only you and I know who got 'em.

HENRY CARLILE

Fish Stories

Fishing formed the initial basis of my friendship with Raymond Carver. From August of 1984 until his death we corresponded regularly and fished whenever we could. His letters to me—there are forty-six—date from August 16, 1984, to June 26, 1988. In many of them he talks about fish he caught and even larger fish that got away. The following excerpt is from one of Ray's earliest letters:

> I lost another one this morning, a really good fish. Yesterday morning I lost two good fish. Three mornings ago I hooked something so big I thought for the longest while I'd hooked the bottom, and I was trying to break my line. Suddenly the line began to move off and I played this big fish for about twenty minutes, trying to follow him in the boat, in and out of the kelp, until he finally took all the line, every inch of it, and then broke off the hooks. I don't know whether it was a fifty pound king, or else a monster halibut. But some fishing adventures here of late.

In another letter, dated July 21, 1987, he writes,

> Henry, you are going to find this hard to believe, I did, but my French publisher, Olivier Cohen—a man who had *never* held a fishing rod in his hand before—well, he caught a *40 lb. king salmon*. (I have pictures to prove this.) We all divided up into two groups and went out one morning last week on 2 charter boats, and that's when Olivier caught his fish. I had one on about that size, perhaps larger.

All fishermen love to tell stories, and most fishermen violate, at least once in a while, Aristotle's rules of probability, combining truth with fiction in less than equal measure. And more than one writer has noted the similarities between writing and fishing. As I wrote once in an early poem about trout fishing: "It is like fishing for a line of poetry, / only in this case you already have the line."

I have never enjoyed fishing with anyone as much as I did with Ray. He was not an expert by any means, in fact he was often klutzy. But he caught his share of fish, sometimes more than his share. His enthusiasm was boyish, almost innocent. He became so excited at times his hands would shake, and once when Tess had caught five salmon and Ray and I had one between us, he tried repeatedly to steal her spot. Tess, however, was vigilant. "That's *my* pole holder, Ray," she would tell him. If you didn't watch him carefully, he'd steal the last bait, even after he already had his limit and you didn't. We forgave him these breaches of fishing etiquette even as we complained. Complaining was part of the fun.

But fishing, like everything else, has its dark side—a fact Ray was acutely aware of. A Jungian would say the water represents the unconscious and the fish the buried memories, dreams, and reflections, most of them appropriately phallic. Ray was never so analytical, at least in his writing he wasn't, but he nevertheless felt and wrote exactly, as in the following poem:

THE RIVER

I waded, deepening, into the dark water.
Evening, and the push
and swirl of the river as it closed
around my legs and held on.
Young grilse broke water.
Parr darted one way, smolt another.
Gravel turned under my boots as I edged out.
Watched by the furious eyes of king salmon.
Their immense heads turned slowly,
eyes burning with fury, as they hung
in the deep current.
They were there. I felt them there,

and my skin prickled. But
there was something else.
I braced with the wind on my neck.
Felt the hair rise
as something touched my boot.
Grew afraid of what I couldn't see.
Then of everything that filled my eyes—
that other shore heavy with branches,
the dark lip of the mountain range behind.
And this river that had suddenly
grown black and swift.
I drew breath and cast anyway.
Prayed nothing would strike.

In the original version of this poem which appeared in *Poetry* and a
limited edition broadside, Ray had misspelled the word "grilse" so
that phonetically, at least, it read "grisle." In an odd way, it still
makes sense, suggesting the toughness and resilience of that life
underwater. *Grilse* is an interesting word from the Middle English.
More commonly used on the East Coast, it refers to an immature
Atlantic salmon. An immature king or coho is called a *jack*.

When I first read the poem I thought immediately of Hemingway's "Big Two-Hearted River: Part II" and that scene where Nick
Adams fears the darker, deeper part of the river that flows through a
swamp:

Nick did not want to go in there now. He felt a reaction against
deep wading with the water deepening up under his armpits, to
hook big trout in places impossible to land them. In the swamp
the banks were bare, the big cedars came together overhead, the
sun did not come through, except in patches; in the fast deep
water, in the half light, the fishing would be tragic. In the swamp
fishing was a tragic adventure. Nick did not want it. He did not
want to go down the stream any further today.

When I mentioned this similarity to Ray, he seemed surprised.
The Hemingway story hadn't occurred to him. But every fisherman,
I think, has had this experience. There are rivers we never feel

comfortable with. We fish them warily. At night they flow through our dreams, and the fish they contain are the stuff of nightmares.

David Duncan, the author of *The River Why,* is another of my fishing partners. Years ago David studied with me at Portland State, and from that time on we began to fish together. Once, we were discussing Ray's story "Nobody Said Anything." I commented that the spawned-out steelhead and the fat green trout in that story were like the fish in one of my recurring river nightmares. David answered, like Bob Dylan in "Talking World War III Blues": "Hey, I've been having that same dream."

Not that the fish Ray wrote about couldn't exist in reality. They can and do. And Ray's description, as always, is precise. "Nobody Said Anything," originally published in the *Seneca Review* under the title "The Summer Steelhead," is an initiation story, a rite of passage toward, if not exactly into, manhood. But what an initiation!

To begin with, the adolescent narrator's homelife is a battleground: the parents fight with each other, and the narrator fights with his younger brother, George.

> "Stop gouging me, you bastard," he said. "I'm going to tell!"
> "You dumb chickenshit," I said. "Can't you wise up for once? They're fighting and Mom's crying. Listen."
> He listened with his head off the pillow. "I don't care," he said and turned over toward the wall and went back to sleep. George is a royal asshole.

The narrator feigns sickness in order to stay home and go fishing at Birch Creek. Soon the story begins to take on mythic undertones and comic hints of a "journey perilous," a feeling reinforced by the narrator's reading of *The Princess of Mars* and a chapter "where Tars Tarkas falls for a green woman, only to see her get her head chopped off the next morning by [a] jealous brother-in-law."

Ray often used what I call "subliminal connectors" in his stories, and the color green makes such a connection with the curious "green trout" the narrator catches later in the story, just as the mythic green woman makes a further connection with the real woman the narrator later hitches a ride with. The green woman's decapitation suggests the halved steelhead which becomes the object of the narrator's quest, though his quest is also erotic, as evidenced by his constant erections and compulsive need to masturbate. Initially, his quest takes him back to his parents' bedroom where earlier, searching for rubbers, he had discovered a jar of Vaseline.

> I studied the label and hoped it would reveal something, a description of what people did, or else about how you applied the Vaseline, that sort of thing. But it didn't. *Pure Petroleum Jelly,* that was all it said on the front label. But just reading that was enough to give you a boner.

The journey to Birch Creek is made comically perilous by the presence of orchards where "you can't hunt" because "you might get shot by a Greek named Matsos." At this point the narrator encounters a woman in a red car who offers him a lift. Any journey perilous has to have a woman, either as temptress or guide, and this one appears to be a little bit of both. But she is no princess. "She was thin and had little pimples around her mouth," the narrator tells us with typical adolescent attention to minute blemishes. "Her hair was done up in curlers. But she was sharp enough. She had a brown sweater with nice boobs inside."

The narrator begins to fantasize about taking the woman home "where she'll let [him] screw her all over the house." This produces the inevitable boner which the narrator hides beneath his baseball cap.

A more traditional initiation story might indeed have the woman initiating the hero into the mysteries of sex, but the boy is afraid to look at the woman, which underscores her perilous nature and his own painful shyness.

"Will this help you?" she asks, her function that of a guide who takes him only part way. After she lets him off, he cuts the air with his fly rod, and hollers "two or three times" in frustration, an action comically suggestive of the mythic hero cutting the air with his sword. Then he resumes his fantasy.

> Suddenly we are in my bedroom under the covers. She asks me if

she can keep her sweater on and I say it's okay with me. She keeps her pants on too. That's all right, I say. I don't mind.

No other passage in the story quite so effectively reveals the boy's sexual innocence, an innocence that contrasts sharply with his parents' lack of same. His initiation into the mysteries of adult sex frustrated, he unzips and shoots "off five feet over the creek," his visions of sexual conquest reduced to their adolescent equivalent: "It must have been a record," he says.

At this point the initiatory nature of the boy's quest is again hinted at. Just as earlier he examined the jar of Vaseline for some "description of what people did," he now wonders how to begin.

I tried to think where to start. I had fished here for three years, ever since we had moved. Dad used to bring George and me in the car and wait for us, smoking, baiting our hooks, tying up new rigs for us if we snagged.

But the narrator is on his own now and must find his way without his father. The father's apathy is evident in his disinclination to actually join his sons in fishing, and in any case, the strife between the mother and father, which provides the outer framework of the story, suggests the possibility, at least, of his eventual absence.

The perilous nature of the boy's journey is again hinted at by a KEEP OUT sign on a post where the airport runways start. While the airport represents flight and transcendence of a sort, the solo flight perhaps of the young initiate pilot, the reality is less uplifting. The narrator's attention is drawn to some "flowers growing in the cracks in the pavement" and the "oily skid marks all around the flowers" where the tires of landing aircraft have "smacked down." Moreover, the creek is now low, suggestive of near drought. When once again the narrator begins to fantasize about "the woman" his thoughts are interrupted by the "jiggling" tip of his fly rod. The trout he catches is green and strange looking and doesn't fight much. It is like a fish in a nightmare, enervated, impotent. The boy puts it out of its pain.

But he can't do the same for himself. He fishes awhile longer and decides to wait until night before he thinks about the woman again.

The labyrinthine nature of the boy's dilemma is evident in the very next line: "right away I got a boner thinking about the boner I would get that night."

In the traditional quest, the hero who has lost faith, like Dante lost in the dark wood, must regain it in order to accomplish his task. But Carver's approach is comically postmodernist:

> Then I thought I had better stop doing it so much. About a month back, a Saturday when they were all gone, I had picked up the Bible right after and promised and swore I wouldn't do it again. But I got jism on the Bible, and the promising and swearing lasted only a day or two, until I was by myself.

Religion is no help—it seldom is in Carver's stories—which illustrates the narrator's fallen state in a fallen world, especially that world which forms the outer framework of the story, a world divided by sibling rivalry and marital strife.

The hero of traditional mythologies often must kill some monster in order to acquire its magical powers and restore the world to its original vigorous state and so end the strife, drought, sterility, and pestilence that lay it waste.

In this instance the monster turns out to be a steelhead. The narrator encounters another boy—"a kid about George's size"—with buckteeth and skinny arms who looks "like a rat or something." The comparison with George, casually offered, is important, as we'll see later. The boy is dressed in a "ragged longsleeved shirt" that is "too small for him." He points out the fish to the narrator, and the two boys decide to collaborate in its capture.

The motley appearance of the other boy, and his obvious poverty, recall the appearance of a mythological trickster whose special powers are often required to help accomplish the hero's task, but whose mischievous spirit can also hinder him. Loki might be one example, from Scandanavian mythology. Another might be the classical Mercurius duplex who is both Hermes and poisonous dragon.

But there is nothing evil about the rat-faced boy. His clumsiness temporarily prevents capture of the frantic steelhead as it dashes through the shallows, and at one point the boy falls flat in the water. The narrator, exasperated with the boy's ineptness, twice calls him an "asshole," which recalls the narrator's earlier quarrel with his brother George. Eventually the boys succeed, however. The narrator corners the fish and scoops it out of the water.

The narrator doesn't say so, but it is clear from Carver's exact description that the fish is spawned out, dark, and fungally diseased. A passage in the original version of the story but deleted from the collected text makes this point explicit: "He was probably upstream spawning, and he's just late getting back to the river." The steelhead's battered appearance from fighting and banging into rocks on its spawning run suggests both a quest of another sort and the diseased state of the narrator's family life.

> His sides were scarred, whitish welts as big as quarters and kind of puffy. There were nicks out of his head around his eyes and on his snout where I guess he had banged into the rocks and been in fights. But he was so skinny, too skinny for how long he was, and you could hardly see the pink stripe down his sides, and his belly was gray and slack instead of white and solid like it should have been. But I thought he was something.

At this point the story takes an important turn. The boys must now decide what to do with their catch. At first they decide to flip for the fish, but neither boy has a coin. The narrator sizes up the other boy: "I could have taken him if it came to that. But I didn't want to fight." The narrator successfully resists the temptation to settle their dispute with violence, something he might readily have done with his brother George. The boys decide to halve the fish. As the narrator cuts down on the fish an airplane roars down the runway and lifts off right over their heads. The narrator hands the other boy the tail half but he refuses it: " 'No,' he said, shaking his head. 'I want that half.' "

Their disagreement is resolved when the narrator trades for the head of the fish; the other boy takes the green trout and the tail half. This negotiation, as I have already indicated, marks an important break from the narrator's combative family tradition. Significantly, the first person he sees on his return home is his brother George. But he makes no attempt to hail his brother and flaunt his triumph.

He has a more important objective: "I went to the back to take off my boots. I unslung the creel so I could raise the lid and get set to march into the house, grinning."

But the hero's return is ill-timed. Like a would-be Hercules bearing the cut-off head of the Hydra, he enters the kitchen filled with smoke from a pan on the burner. The implication is clear: he has reentered the hell of domestic strife. His parents are engaged in a full-scale argument: "What I'm telling you is the gospel truth," his father says. "What do kids know? You'll see." Since the story is told from the innocent narrator's point of view, the real issue of the argument remains unspecified. It perhaps relates to the father's infidelity, which the boy, in his sexual ignorance, is spared knowledge of. In any case, the narrator's mother has already told him that his father wants "to tear up the family." "I'll see nothing," his mother says. "If I thought that, I'd rather see them dead first."

The emphasis on seeing is important here, since insight is what is so sorely lacking. The mother's reaction brings us no closer to understanding the issue, but it does suggest her unwillingness to see her sons follow their father's example. When her husband calls her attention to the smoking pan she throws it against the wall.

The narrator chooses this inopportune moment to present his trophy. So excited he can barely stand, he holds the fish out to his mother, naively hoping it will please her. Instead, she is horrified: "Oh, oh, my God! What is it? A snake! What is it? Please, please take it out before I throw up."

Ray would have been aware that fishermen routinely call spawned-out steelhead *snakes*. But the reference here again has mythological undertones recalling the Hydra. The boy turns to his father, hoping *he* will understand, but the father is no better prepared to accept the gift of the nightmare fish.

I said, "It's a gigantic summer steelhead from Birch Creek. Look! Isn't he something? It's a monster! I chased him up and down the creek like a madman!" My voice was crazy. But I could not stop. "There was another one, too," I hurried on. "A green one. I swear! It was green! Have you ever seen a green one?"

He looked into the creel and his mouth fell open.

He screamed, "Take that goddamn thing out of here! What in

the hell is the matter with you? Take it the hell out of the kitchen and throw it in the goddamn garbage!"

The fish lacks the magical qualities that might establish the narrator's manhood and redeem the family from its fallen state. In the book *Understanding Raymond Carver,* Arthur M. Saltzman argues that the narrator is left "disqualified, holding garbage." From a pragmatic viewpoint, the narrator's quest has failed. But has it failed entirely?

A closer reading of the story's conclusion supports, I think, a more positive interpretation.

> I went back outside. I looked into the creel. What was there looked silver under the porch light. What was there filled the creel.
>
> I lifted him out. I held him. I held that half of him.

Like Jack, left holding his shoe at the end of "What's in Alaska?" and Bill and Arlene Miller clinging to each other at the end of "Neighbors," the narrator of "Nobody Said Anything" is left holding his mutilated fish. But the fish does, after all, have magical powers, if not on a grand mythological scale then at least on a smaller human one. Under the porch light it is transformed. The fish appears to be silver—the color of a bright steelhead fresh from the sea. The word *silver* also connotes treasure. And although the fish is of course dead, it is life the narrator clings to—his own. Somewhere else, the other boy is holding up his half—the fruits of compromise and sharing rather than of conquest. Something has been gained after all, and the narrator has made an important break from his destructive family. It is the parents who remain unredeemed by their failure to acknowledge the gift of the fish. What they have seen staring back at them out of the creel is the reflection of their own nightmare, one half of a spawned-out steelhead, like their relationship, impotent and dead.

Socrates said that the unexamined life is not worth living, but Ray might have disagreed with that. He would probably have argued that any life is better than no life—even a half life. In the classical sense of the tragic his characters suffer shocks, but without the usual accompanying recognition that would help them to understand the exact nature of the compulsions that harm them. In this respect their lives remain unexamined, or examined perhaps imperfectly. Their valor is that in a world without assurances, and without having much insight into their own characters, they persist.

The last time I fished with Ray we were trolling off Port Angeles about six miles out. The sun had set and we had just switched on the running lights. The water was flat and calm, the sky clear. Over the water we could see the lights of Port Angeles. We were in about ninety feet of water, but we had been fishing for silvers, running short lines near the surface. From time to time, while it was still light, we could see our plugged herring baits flashing astern. Now it was dark and we were getting ready to head in. At this moment Ray had a strike. "It's a big salmon! Henry!" he yelled. But it didn't fight like a salmon. Something dark and long wallowed off our stern and then we saw an eye glaring back at us reflecting our transom light. It was a huge dog shark. Usually you hook dog sharks whenever you get too close to the bottom. It is unusual to hook them near the surface. In a moment it was gone, the line bitten through. Ray was visibly upset. It was the last fish we hooked together.

OLIVIER COHEN

Lines of Force

Publishers rarely confide. With good reason. The need for reserve imposed by a job that is part spiritual director, part impresario, and part banker, and that also includes the secret delights of friendship and a deeply personal mistrust of false confidences, normally incites me to silence. Writing these pages, I am at least certain of betraying no one, unless perhaps myself. These are memories of a private nature. Their only interest, in my eyes, is to cast an intimate light on a man who has recently assumed a singular place in my life. In their oblique way, they reflect the questions—still unanswered—that the company of this man has evoked in me.

Five years ago, I was walking through the streets of New York when a shower, common at that time of year—it was April 1984, and the fog was coiled around the tops of the buildings, sketching complicated spirals in the sky—forced me to take refuge in a bookstore on Fifth Avenue. To pass the time, I picked up a volume by chance from one of the piles within reach of my hand and began reading. Very soon a feeling took hold of me to such a degree that I had to interrupt my reading several times to convince myself I wasn't dreaming. The author's name was not unknown to me. But I didn't know until that moment that it was he I had come looking for in crossing the Atlantic. Beyond the excitement of my discovery, I had the feeling that the adventure was just beginning. This feeling and the urgency that accompanied it would have been only a banal illustration of the reversibility of effects and causes—a paradox well known to lovers, one that leads them to look for reasons where others see only chance—if it had not brought about precisely what was going to follow.

Raymond Carver had found a publisher. It only remained for me to let him know. We exchanged a few letters. I assured him of my sincere interest. In that affable and precise tone of his, he responded by asking me about the details of publication. *Cathedral,* the volume I had begun reading in New York, was already scheduled for publication in France. Its appearance a few months later as *Les vitamines du bonheur* aroused the enthusiasm of a small circle of fans. It also marked the beginning of a misunderstanding. Carver's concise prose, and the subtlety of a style so stripped of ornamentation that it sometimes bordered on abstraction, created a trap for hasty critics who were blind to Anglo-Saxon understatement. (Hadn't Bill Buford, the fiery editor of *Granta* and an old hand at provocation, coined the term "dirty realism" to describe Carver's style?) True, Carver had never felt obliged to provide instructions on how to read his books. His favorite characters—the unemployed and shiftless, restaurant waitresses, traveling salesmen, and redneck lovers of hunting stories and beer—didn't resemble the yuppies who were already fashionable in the East Coast novel.

I invited him to Paris. Our first meeting, in the little reception room of the Saints-Pères hotel, left me with the memory of a rather ceremonious handshake. Such is often the case when words are inadequate to convey an emotion that has been restrained for too long, and bodies collide, embarrassed. Tess Gallagher, his companion, ignoring our bowing and scraping, good-humoredly inquired about the time for dinner. During the meal, at La Coupole, it was hard for me to keep my eyes off Carver's face. While he recounted the story of his life with complete indifference to conventional formalities and peppered me with indiscreet questions, I thought I could read in his expression all the nuances of a goodness tinged at once with irony and melancholy. During dessert, he invited me to go salmon fishing at his place in Port Angeles. This would be an opportunity, he said, to get to know each other better and for me to meet some of his oldest friends, who would also go on the trip. In response, I sketched on a paper napkin a ludicrous character armed with a fishing pole and pronouncing the ominous words "Where is the fish?"

Three months later, propped up in the stern of a boat doing fifteen knots in the swelling waters of the North Pacific, and having forgotten even the seasickness that was wrenching my guts, I was struggling to reel in a salmon whose weight could only have been legendary, considering the incredible pull it was making on the line. For how long had I been battling like this? It seemed I had been there forever, numbed with pain, tottering on the deck that the spray had made slippery, subjected to the temptation of calling it quits despite the encouragement of Richard Ford. I was not unaware that, had I succumbed to fatigue, discouragement, or what in my heart of hearts I could only call my cowardice, no one would have replaced me, and the giant salmon, given his freedom, would have made good use of it and never have come back. All sorts of strange ideas jostled one other on the surface of my mind, with a clarity all the more vivid because my mind remained calm in its depths, as if separated from the scene being played out. I saw my arrival all over again, in the little plane from Seattle, the column of smoke that rose up above the cannery, the mountains that suddenly tipped to meet us when the pilot dove down on the narrow landing strip. Tess's oceanside house, Sky House, never merited its name more than at sunrise when the waves of light made its glass walls iridescent. I recall having thought that the salmon and I were one and that the efforts he put forth to free himself actually strengthened our union a little more each moment. I also remember the absurd rose-framed plastic sunglasses that kept sliding down my nose, making my vision, already blurred by the mixture of sweat and salt water that burnt my eyes, still more unclear.

The salmon stopped zigzagging; the line fell slack. The skipper, who had gradually reduced speed, killed the motor. I climbed onto the deckhouse, followed by the bait boy who was ready to harness me if I toppled overboard. A great calm had set in. In the distance, a mountain range, its slopes covered with densely leaved trees, seemed to plunge directly into the ocean, whose surface was softly rising. The coast of British Columbia trembled under the sun in a kind of sparkling mist. He was there, somewhere under the hull, gathering his strength, I thought, in a final attempt to escape the trap he was caught in. The salmon emerged. I saw him rise in the air before realizing it was I who was drawing him out of the water, while the skipper, coming up on my right, landed him in full flight with a swipe of the net and fell over backwards under the impact.

As I learned later, the salmon weighed at least forty pounds. This arithmetic precision, far from reassuring me about the reality of the event I had just experienced, only augmented my perplexity. If I was the hero of the day, you have never seen a hero more troubled than that pale fellow with the hesitant smile, staring at the lens of the anonymous photographer responsible for immortalizing the scene. The salmon had bled before dying, staining my jeans and my shoes with blackish rings. I was groggy but I nonetheless perceived everything around me with an unusual sharpness. This lucid intoxication was accompanied by a curious feeling of respect and, as it were, compassion for the creature whose life I had just taken. I caught Raymond Carver's eye. He smiled. He knew.

At our next meeting, on May 16, 1988, it was again raining when I pushed the revolving door of the Saint Regis, where Carver and Tess awaited me. The disease that a few months later would take his life compelled him to undergo painful therapy. He gave no sign of his suffering and joked around as usual. Responding to an invitation from the American Academy and Institute of Arts and Letters, into which John Updike and others were to induct him with all due honor, he had agreed to come to New York, without concern for the fatigue that such a long trip would undoubtedly cause him. Moreover, he had promised to give a public reading in a bookstore on the Upper East Side and a book autographing session at Scribner's. I went with him. On both occasions, I witnessed the fervor his readers felt for him. They had come en masse to meet him, and the little group of disciples who surrounded him had all they could do to protect him from the overflow of emotion that was as sincere as it was overwhelming. It was there that I saw for the last time this man who wanted to be ordinary but whose greatness could not escape notice. "I wish I could be like everybody else in this neighborhood—your basic, normal, unaccomplished person," says one of his characters. Who was Raymond Carver?

Poverty and alcohol had marked him deeply. The written word saved him. At times, his craft seems a heroic asceticism. Nourished on Flaubert, Chekhov, and Babel, Carver composed elliptical stories in which the trace of an ancient fatality could be felt. "No cheap tricks," he said, before concluding, "No tricks." There was nothing tricky about him. How did it happen, then, that more than once I suspected him of playing a trick on us? If in his stories he accorded so much importance to apparently insignificant facts—minor setbacks, missed appointments, idle words—it was the better to convey the meaning he intended. He had written, "Influences are forces—circumstances, personalites, irresistible as the tide.... The influences I know something about have pressed on me in ways that were often mysterious at first glance, sometimes stopping just short of the miraculous." And he added, "But if the main influence on my life and writing has been a negative one, oppressive and often malevolent, as I believe is the case, what am I to make of this?"

By scrutinizing these invisible currents, by tirelessly examining the inflections of the human voice as those of his own destiny, Carver acquired the ability to trace on paper imaginary lives truer than nature. But his power didn't stop there. Without our knowing it, he had turned us into his characters.

What had I come to do in Port Angeles? I had followed a line of force at a moment in my life when everything seemed uncertain. I had no idea where this boat would take me, and that was reason enough for me to embark, without arms or baggage. To my great surprise, I was expected. And I can't help thinking today that Carver's art, in his life as in his books, was to give his contemporaries a helping hand, to show them, even if only for an instant, what they are blind to.

Man is a legend whose meaning has been lost. But the meaning is always there, deposited somewhere in the depths of language, in the stories we murmur at night when sleep eludes us.

Who is the author? Where is the fish?

—translated by Patrick Henry

DAVID CARPENTER

What We Talk About When We Talk About Carver

Thursday, September 23, 1986

"GETTIN KINDA dark out," says Robertson.

Honor leans toward me. "Bill says it's—"

"I heard."

"Oi," she says.

"How do we know these guys can shoot?" says Calder. "Maybe they're as rusty as we are."

"They can shoot."

"Hey, Carp, isn't it gettin kinda dark out?" Robertson asks again.

I mumble something and weave through the traffic on Eleventh Street, eyeing the dark gray horizon, then accelerate for an orange light. Honor clutches the dash. "Watch out," she says.

"It's okay."

In September, in Saskatoon, the evening light seems to vanish like a memory of August. Every fall this happens and every fall I get ambushed by this rapid change. You start thinking about winter for weeks before the Grey Cup or the World Series. It's unsettling. It makes me brood on the brevity of life.

"What if someone hears our shots in the dark?" Robertson asks. He can't quite believe what's going on.

"What if they call the cops?"

"There's still some light," I counter.

"Where?" Calder asks.

Honor starts to laugh. The other two join in.

Raymond Carver is coming to Saskatoon. He will arrive tomorrow with his friend Richard Ford. They are bringing their shotguns and expect to hunt with . . . well . . . hunters. I am determined that all of my hunters will make a good showing. They will act like Saskatchewanians. Bob Calder (a Somerset Maugham scholar) will rediscover that feeling of squinting down the barrel of a twelve gauge and Bill Robertson (a poet) will cease to wonder how to work his safety catch. He's just bought his first shotgun, an old twelve gauge double, for twenty dollars. Calder last hunted in 1963. I am the veteran here. I last fired a shotgun four years ago.

"Seriously though," says Calder, "It is pretty dark out."

"Maybe we can use the headlights," I offer. My determination is still strong, but my voice sounds limp.

My determination is strong because in 1982 I stumbled on Carver's stories and felt I just had to meet this guy. Bring him up here for a reading. The question was, how? Our English department is strapped for visiting speaker funds. Then I read "Distance," one of Carver's stories in *Fires,* and I began to see a way. In this story a young man is about to go goosehunting when his baby breaks out in a crying spell. His young wife suspects the baby is sick, but neither parent knows for sure. She prevails upon her husband to stay home and he misses out on his hunt. The baby stops crying and soon recovers. This story comes to us twenty years later when the marriage is long over.

An idea began to grow. I would invite Carver to read on campus (where I teach on alternate years). Art Sweet, a writer friend of mine, somehow dug up the address of Carver's agent. I wrote to Carver. Let the critics say what they will about "Distance" (. . . a poignant examination of lost bliss . . . a portrait of the raconteur as exile in time and space . . .), its ultimate meaning is a far more fundamental cry from the heart: Will somebody please take me goosehunting, please?

On January 19, 1986, Raymond Carver answered my letter and said yes, we might be able to work something out.

Honor turns to me. "Do you know the people who own the land?"

"Sort of."

"What are you going to say to them?" she asks.

"I'll just ask them if they mind us firing off a few shells behind their house."

"In the dark," Robertson adds.

"They probably won't even be home."

But the house in question has the lights on. It's a small cozy bungalow built among the aspens and willows. Through the front window I can see the man of the house helping his son with his homework, the woman and daughter kneeling by the fire. The man answers the door.

"Hi," I say, thrusting my hand forward. "I'm Dave Carpenter. I used to camp on that stretch next to you."

He shakes my hand, smiles, and holding his pipe, introduces me to his little foursome. I explain that Honor and I and a couple of friends want to try out our shotguns on a few clay pigeons, shooting into the dunes, of course. My neighbor, who has never seen me until this moment, glances nervously at something in the kitchen. He seems to be gauging the distance between his front porch, where we stand, and his telephone. He strokes his chin, peers at my car.

"Hmm," he says.

But sanity prevails, or something, and my neighbor shows us where to drive out to the dunes in the dark. I take my little Toyota to the top of a small sandhill and point the headlights at a dune about seventy-five feet away. We will release the clay pigeons with a little hand launcher that looks like a long slingshot, aiming these at the small hill in front of us. There is no dwelling in this direction for miles, so the setup seems safe, if a little unorthodox. I let fly with a few while my friends load up. The clay pigeons are black and yellow discs about the size of a small dessert bowl. They glide like accelerated Frisbees into the beams of light and out again. For about three seconds they are visible.

"Gotta be kind of quick," says Robertson dubiously.

He goes first.

"Ready?" I call out.

"Ready."

I send one out a bit high. It skirts the very edge of the headlights' beams.

"Try again."

"Ready?"

"Ready."

I send one across the beam and this time Robertson manages to get his gun to his shoulder.

"Little low?"

"Yeah, try one medium height, straightaway."

"Okay, ready?"

"Ready."

This one wobbles in flight, but it's just where Robertson wants it. He fires and misses.

Calder tries. The same thing happens. Robertson tries again. The night reverberates with shotgun blasts followed by "Shit" or "Next time send er higher." Honor tries and nicks one. I try, but no luck. Then Calder, then Robertson. The little yellow saucers pass in and out of the headlights, untouched, safe as UFOs. No one scores a direct hit, but after half an hour of this, we all have a feel for the gun's recoil, and where our safety catches are, and what not to do with a shotgun among friends, so we head back to town. When I've dropped everyone off I discover that my car doorjambs are sticky with dozens of rose hips.

September 24

Raymond Carver is inspecting a hunting license in my kitchen. "I am Lee Henchbaw," he says, "and I am from Sass-katchewan."

"No," says Honor, "S's-katchew'n. You don't pronounce the first 'a'."

Carver looks up from the license. "My name is Lee Henchbaw and I am from Skatchewan."

"S's-katchew'n," says Honor.

"S's-katchew'n," says Carver. "I am Lee Henchbaw and I am from S's-katchew'n." He smiles. "Eh?"

This is the first time I've participated in giving lessons in spoken Canadian: the interrogative "eh" at the end of declarative sentences, the tightlipped "ou" sound that rings Scottish to American ears, the clipped syllables through a puckered mouth, the irresolute shift of the eyeballs as if to ask if life were a federal or a provincial responsibility.

"Have the geese come south?" asks Richard Ford. His south sounds like *sowth* to my ears. There is a trace of Mississippi in his voice.

"South," says Honor, "with the mouth contracted. Pretend you're ashamed of your teeth."

"Sewth," says Ford.

"Sewth," says Carver.

"No, south. Don't open your mouth so wide."

"Mewth so wide," says Ford.

"My name is . . ." Carver peeks. "My name is Lee Henchbaw and I am from Sass-katchewan."

"Fantastic," says Ford.

"Oi," says Honor.

A lot of geese are down, I tell them. Honor and I have heard them going over for the last three nights, wave after wave.

"Now, Dave, how is this going to happen?" Carver asks. He and Ford are very keen. The thing that makes a springer spaniel strain at his choke collar is in these guys.

"Pits," says Peter Nash. "A guy named Jake will dig them for us." Nash is a bearded physician I have known since I was six or seven. Like Richard Ford, he is in astonishingly good shape. At every birthday party, Nash was the kid who had twenty-five percent more laughs than anyone else. He is still that way. Becoming a father and an ophthalmologist have not visibly altered him. His preparation for this trip meant buying and reading all the books by Carver and Ford he could find in Vancouver. He's as keen as they are. There is an excitement here among us that keeps building. I know that I will scarcely sleep tonight.

"You guys call em?"

"Jake does. He knows what he's doing."

Even though she isn't coming on the hunt, Honor's face is all aglow. She has lived in six states and it seems to me she has missed the sound of American voices. As most Canadians know, Americans are anything but ashamed of their teeth.

The deal is this: I will take Ford and Carver goosehunting if they will give a joint reading at the University of Saskatchewan for a drastically low fee, what you might call the best kind of free trade arrangement. I have written to the Saskatchewan Minister of Fish and Wildlife to waive Carver and Ford's alien status so that they can hunt in this area right after their joint reading, rather than wait around for six days with nothing to do. The reading is slated for

September 25, but around Crocus, Saskatchewan, Americans aren't allowed to hunt until October 1. Duke Pike, the minister in question, is a circumspect man who believes the universities and intellectuals are out to get him, or so people have told me. Predictably, our request is denied. He suggests we reschedule the whole damn event, which at this point is impossible.

I had to get two extra hunting licenses. Enter Art Sweet and Lee Henchbaw, both writers. They haven't hunted a day in their lives, but for the cause of literature, they put their asses on the line. Art Sweet, among other things, is a very fine one-armed guitarist. Emergencies seem to be his stock in trade. Lee Henchbaw is a possessed poet; he seems perpetually astonished by life. He handed me his hunting license and announced his intention to write a Raymond Carver poem. Perhaps Carver will write a Lee Henchbaw poem. Lee is beset by verbal overload. He may burst before he jumps on his motorcycle.

"I am Lee Henchbaw, and I am from Sass-katchewan," says Carver, all night long, through a bout of insomnia.

That's the part I remember from Wednesday night. What Honor remembers is quite different. None of this talk about goosehunting. She remembers Nash at the stove frying a large batch of fresh-caught smelts in egg and breadcrumb batter. She remembers a series of confessions during our meal. Ford was first: "You know the last words my mother ever said to me? She was on her death-bed. She said, 'Richard, will you please stop asking me all those questions?'" This remark inspired other confessions about pain, death, and worry. Carver talked about how terrified he was when Tess Gallagher had to have an operation. Nash told us about his fears upon discovering an advanced melanoma on his right arm. I'm sure I put in my two cents worth. In my youth I was very enthusiastic about pain.

Just before we fell asleep, Honor marveled about the evening's talk. "Here's four guys, none of them trying to sound liberated, talking about their *feelings*." She was still all aglow. "I've gotta tell Lorna."

September 25
From B.C. to western Saskatchewan there is a hurricane warning,

rare for these parts. In Lethbridge it has rained four inches; in Calgary it has snowed twelve. In Saskatoon the wind buckles the elm trees near the campus and dismantles election campaign signs. For the first time in Saskatchewan history, there are New Democratic Party signs on the lawns of the wealthy. The rain has turned to sleet, but not yet snow. Carver and Ford are having lunch down the street from my house, Nash and I making sandwiches for the road, when the phone rings.

It's Honor at her studio. Jake's been trying to get hold of me. He thinks we should cancel the trip. I tell Nash. He can see I'm very worried; I've got that why-me look.

"Let's not phone Jake," he suggests. "Let's pretend we never got the message. Let's just go."

"Yeah." Desperate dilemmas require desperate solutions.

We stare at each other. The reading is two hours away. Perhaps more than a hundred students, writers, profs, and book lovers will be getting ready to brave the storm for this event. I am holding my head in my hands, moaning something about the unfairness of life. In Saskatchewan that often means weather. I rail for a while, and Nash, undaunted, counters with his own philosophy: that life is random, not fair or unfair. "The test is always how well we deal with the randomness!" he cries. He is in a state of furious inspiration, like the wind outside. We seem to be caught in the plot of a Russian novel here.

We decide to phone Jake. Jake says exactly what I had feared: "Yiz guys better call the whole thing off, eh. I mean my brother an I we can't even get a four-wheel drive into the field, dig the pits. You can't get no vehicle nowheres near there."

"Jake, I can't call this whole thing off. These guys have come a long way."

"Well, I dunno what I can do. We got two inches a rain down here in the past twenty-four hours. Fields an roads solid gumbo."

"Are the geese down?"

"Yeah."

"Could you show us where they're flying?"

"Yeah, but yiz'll all have t'walk some."

"What's the forecast?"

"Pissin."

I look at Nash, who holds a knife heaped with mayonnaise in one hand, a slice of bread in the other. He does not seem rattled. "Well, Jake, we're coming."

This is one of those days when you simply worry your way from one decision to another. I will worry about the reading till it's happening, worry about not telling Carver and Ford that Jake wanted to cancel, worry about the condition of the highway, worry about the sufficiency of everyone's rain gear, hit the sack and worry about how to get to sleep. I will worry about setting back Canada/ U.S. literary relations by twenty years and giving Saskatchewan a bad name. In my dreams my parents will tell me that they told me so, and I will worry about where they went wrong with me. I am leading five guys to their death. I will really worry about that one. Outside, the wind howls, the rain lashes, and life's randomness proclaims itself all day long.

The classroom is full, hushed. People's foreheads, hair, and coats are streaked with rain. The linoleum is splattered with mud and yellow elm leaves. We can hear the wind outside, and this sound precipitates, it seems to me, a cozy smug feeling. The best writers and some of the best artists in the province are here. A contingent of twelve people has driven all the way from Regina against this wind and into the sleet. The classroom seems to bristle and glow. People are still gasping from that last dash across the quad.

"Ladies and Gentlemen," I begin. My voice seems to be talking and I'm helpless to do anything with it. "I suppose I was hired on here because I am a regionalist. That means I'm interested in the writing that has been done around here. Well, angling for Raymond Carver and Richard Ford has been a very good exercise for me, because I'm now willing to admit that, yes, some very good writing is going on outside of Saskatchewan."

Polite laughter.

Get on with it, Carpenter.

Carpenter gets on with it. A warm applause, at long last, for Richard Ford. He is lean, pale; his face flickers with sensitivity. (Elizabeth Brewster confides later to me that he certainly is "cute.") His voice has gathered the intonations of all his wanderings, from the Deep South to the industrial Northeast, to the Midwest, and to the Old West, where he now lives.

> I was standing in the kitchen while Arlene was in the living room
> saying good-bye to her ex-husband, Bobby. I had already been
> out to the store for groceries and come back and made coffee,
> and was drinking it and staring out the window while the two of
> them said whatever they had to say. It was a quarter to six in the
> morning.
>   This was not going to be a good day in Bobby's life, that was
> clear, because he was headed to jail.

Thus begins "Sweethearts," Richard Ford's latest story in *Esquire*.
For half an hour, the audience wraps itself up in Richard's story and
wears his voice like a comforter as the wind buffets the win-
dowpanes. It occurs to me that being read to is a great luxury,
especially on a stormy day. The audience responds warmly, and I
wonder if the public Carver can be half as captivating. On the page,
of course, he is, but this is show biz.
    Raymond Carver stands six feet two, a big-bodied man appar-
ently comfortable with his size. He has a way of going quiet and
quizzical and at such times reminds me of that awkward brainy kid
in grade six. Or as an undergraduate, he would be the shy, dishev-
eled guy in the corner, lost in thought. A bit like Lee Henchbaw.
They both have an abundance of curly hair which I envy, and it
seems to announce something luxuriant in their minds that cannot
stop growing. They are working-class men right down to their
cigarettes. Both recall hard times and domestic strife all the way
back to childhood. But the man at the lectern has now become
Raymond Carver, and Lee is perhaps fifteen years away from becoming Lee Henchbaw. His first poems have just appeared, but he
is still young enough to ride a motorcycle. In a few years, he will be
up there at the lectern, launching one of his books. In a few more,
if he remains devout and disciplined, he will become a small part of
literary history. Then fade with the rest of us. We are clay pigeons
flashing through the headlights of the Cosmos. The critics take their
potshots in the dark, and usually miss, and then we all die. I
wonder if Nash would agree with this. The weather breeds such
ruminations.

Carver is absolutely unhistrionic, soft-spoken, humble by disposition rather than design. He begins by asking the people at the back of the room if they can hear. But perhaps they can't hear him yet, so they just stare back at him. He asks again. They stare back again. Carver is in Saskatchewan, where seldom is heard an extrovert's word. People in readings don't raise their voices if they are in the audience. That would be showing off. So Carver begins, plainly worried. He reads from one of his recent *New Yorker* stories, "Whoever Was Using This Bed." In about one minute, with the line, "What in God's name do they want, Jack? I can't take any more!" he has us. Soon, more than a hundred sodden people are howling with laughter. The characters grope through the night for words to put on their fears and their despair, but throughout the story there is this laughter. The applause continues for a long, long time.

The crowd ascends to the tenth-floor coffee lounge and descends upon the Americans. They have to clutch their styrofoam cups close to their chins, and guard them with the other hand. Saskatchewan has come to pay court to them. The mood is suddenly effusive.

In fact, for this place at least, it is wildly effusive. I feel like one of those Broadway producers who chews on cigars and shouts at the last minute replacement for the leading lady, "Go out there, Mabel, and break their hearts!" My God, I keep thinking, I've got a hit on my hands.

An hour later it occurs to me that I have a hit and no pits. No pits, no geese. No geese, no reciprocity from us to them. Carver and Ford have waived a considerable sum in fees and expenses to come here and shoot. Which makes me (in collusion with the weather) one of the all-time welchers in Canadian literary history.

"Say, ah, David," says Carver in the front seat, "that's a heavy rain coming down. Is that normal for here?"

"Well, no, Ray. Actually it's a real heavy one."

He looks out at the countryside flashing by in the fading light. Ford is silent. Perhaps he is looking for geese. So far we have seen none.

A minute later, Carver says, "Say, ah, David, that's a heck of a wind out there. Is that normal?"

"Well, no, Ray. Actually it's quite unusual for up here." I've said nothing about the absence of goose pits or Jake's phone call. I've said nothing about the hurricane warning. The one blessing is that this pummeling wind is coming from the rear..

"About these pits," says Ford. "Aren't they likely to be a bit on the wet side?"

I tell a censored version of the grim facts. There may be no pits at all. There can't be any digging in the farmers' fields until they've managed to take in their crops. And in this weather, digging is impossible, walking "a bit dicey." I suppose my nervousness has begun to show through.

"David," says Carver, "I'm excited. Richard here is excited. I feel I'm on some sort of adventure. If I even see some geese tomorrow and get a bit of walking in, that'll be fine. I'll have had my fun. So don't worry. Hell, we're all on an adventure here."

I nod, very much relieved, and repeat Nash's words on contending with the randomness of life. This view, the kind of advice an ophthalmologist may have to give to a patient on occasion, rides well with us all the way through the storm and down to Crocus. Nash is no doubt spreading his gospel of adventure in Calder's vehicle. The six of us have become soldiers of fortune. We face the howling infinite together. This last statement probably sounds self-dramatizing. Such is the language of epic.

Robertson goes from room to room in his underwear. Rallying the troops. "Five thirty tamorra mornin," he growls. He sits on anyone's bed, at home wherever he goes. "Hell," he says after a pause, "it'll be just like summer camp, first night. We'll all stay awake an talk about sex."

The wind shakes the basement windows as we sit around, the rain seeps in and sprays anyone beneath the screens. We lay out our rain gear, our long-range magnum shells. The geese will be flying high, spotting us easily. Carver and Ford, both insomniacs, will room together, Calder with Robertson, and I with Nash. Carver wants to be roused by five. He has a little coffeemaker and wants to get it going so we can all have a shot. Nash warns me of his snoring, claims he can shake a building with it. He tosses me some earplugs.

Maybe Robertson is right. It is a bit like summer camp. Nash sleeps like a baby, but I review the day, try to think about lying in mud, revel in the success of Ford and Carver's reading, blink and ruminate all night long. Perhaps I doze for half an hour, but when the alarm goes off at five, I'm as galvanic as an electric owl.

September 26

Five o'clock in the morning. Ford mumbles, "Why the fuck do we have to get up so early?" He sounds very much like a boy in Mississippi embarking on his first hunt. He will demonstrate later that he is anything but a greenhorn.

Ray makes pot after pot of strong filter coffee. Each pot is a cup. Each cup gets passed from room to room, from bed to bed. The empty cups come back to Ray and he has another to send down the line. Breakfast is doughnuts, several kinds. This is our gift to Ray, because apparently he is addicted to them in the morning. Our rooms are littered with crumbs and spattered with coffee. We drag on our clothes, layer after layer. I start with long johns, then thick pants and T-shirt, then K-ways top and bottom, then thick wool sweater, then canvas hunting coat and hat. Most of what I wear is what I've worn for decades on these trips. My pants are torn, my coat stained and stiff with goose and duck blood. Calder looks about the same to me, and Nash and Robertson. We reek of barley and odd prairie smells. An old fellowship seems to reemerge with the donning of this brown canvas coat.

Carver and Ford have newer waterproof clothes, and Ford actually looks dapper in his. We'll have to do something about that, I think, but I can't imagine what. Guns in hand, we lurch and waddle through the rain and mud to Jake's house. He meets us with a friend in his garage. It is brilliantly lit inside. He too has doughnuts and coffee, knowing of Carver's addiction.

"She's colder'n a sonofabitch out there," says Jake. "Sock er down, eh? It's a long time till dinner."

The garage is huge, full of duck-hunting equipment and all-terrain vehicles. The lighting is so intense that we stand around in embarrassed silence, yawning, savoring the last dry surfaces we will feel for many hours.

Four of us go in Jake's jeep, three follow in Calder's truck. We take the highway about ten miles south past the town of Horizon, and Jake pulls over and parks on the shoulder. "Far as she goes," he says, knowing full well that nothing with wheels could get a hundred yards on the side roads.

The sun makes faint gray streaks on the eastern horizon, but it's still dark where we sit in the jeep. Suddenly we stumble out onto the road, Jake in the lead, swearing. "Timed er wrong," he says. "Shit."

I hear choruses of falsetto barking, and then I see them: wave after wave of geese lifting off the slough and pouring over the road, low but out of range. The sky is exploding with them: greater Canadas, lesser Canadas, specklebellies, snows, and many ducks.

We lurch down the road in single file. We are almost at the edge of the flight path, but it's getting lighter and there is no place to hide. The mud builds up around our boots until each foot wears ten pounds of Saskatchewan gumbo. Our breath comes hard. The wind and rain lash into our faces. My glasses need windshield wipers.

Jake and Ford and I manage to reach a point on the road about a half a mile down from the vehicles. Jake and Richard begin to blaze away, standing on the road. I have only a sixteen gauge, so I keep on trudging into the middle of the flight path, Nash right behind me. I hear guns going off but I keep on going till I reach a culvert I can hide behind. Nash and Ford fire down the road and double on their first goose. A lone duck tries his luck swinging low over the culvert, and I bag him. He falls on the road with a squelch and he's dead before I stuff him into my coat pouch. This is how you always want it to happen, a clean kill.

Calder and Robertson are nowhere in sight. Jake has headed back into town. Carver and Ford lie in the ditch back down the road two hundred yards from me. Nash trudges slowly out into the north field and disappears over the edge of the world. It is every man for himself, and the birds are wise to our plan, such as it is. They spot us a mile off and fly high over our heads. We blast away and they keep on flying. This is called pass shooting. The geese pass, the hunters fail.

By nine o'clock we still have only a duck and a goose, apparently dispatched by Calder as it tried to escape. This I learned later; Calder and Robertson are still missing in action.

The wind has been playing with us as we lie in the mud. By ten o'clock it rises up like a windigo and blasts sleet and rain into our faces. To remain as innocuous as possible, Ford and Carver lie face down in the mud, and when the geese fly over, they leap up and try to fire as their feet slide beneath them. I shoot occasionally, but it's clay pigeons in the dark again, so I huddle down by the culvert to try and keep my back to the wind, checking every minute or so for new flights of geese. Nash reappears over the northern horizon like a perambulating scarecrow, then disappears. He moves to keep warm.

At last the wind and sleet are unbearable, so I head for a clutter of grain bins out in the field. Crouching behind these bins is a bit better, but I'm still so cold my teeth chatter. One of the bins is actually an old wooden granary. I peek inside. It is empty, which surprises me. But because of this weather, half the farmers haven't been able to harvest their grain, thus the empty bins. I turn the lock and go inside, and at last, with the wind shrieking all around the bins, I begin to warm up. From time to time I can hear geese flying over the bins but my gun leans against the wall. This soldier has bid good-bye to the wars.

Then I smell something, an offering from below, sour and rotten. *Skunk.* I'm out of there in about four seconds and back to my culvert.

By eleven Nash returns, three large geese and a duck hanging over his shoulder. He is tired, happy, and very wet. We push on down the road. Carver and Ford get up out of the mud, and I see now what they are made of. From lying face down in the mud, Richard has acquired a carapace of bluish clay over his face. His clothes are filthy. Carver is just as muddy and he is bleeding rather badly from two cuts in his left hand. We look each other over for a while. We are the remnants of a defeated army, trench warfare, *circa* 1916 when the Americans entered the fray.

And the Americans haven't yet admitted defeat. First Carver, then Ford, then I, begin to build a large duckblind out of chaff. I gather the chaff, hand it to Richard, who gives it to Carver. Back and forth we go, the geese flying cautiously high. By noon we have what resembles a huge bird's nest, big enough for three hunters. Ford and I are puffing, Carver close to exhaustion.

It's time for lunch. We shoulder our guns and slowly trudge the long mile to the vehicles. Robertson and Calder greet us by the truck. They've had no luck at all and seem discouraged, especially Calder. When he had to dispatch the wounded goose by wringing its neck, he discovered something about himself. Over the twenty-three years between this hunt and his last one, he had acquired a conscience about killing things. We discussed this later. We all shared a real affection for those geese we hunted—apart from their value as food or quarry. This affection is what Faulkner refers to as loving the creatures you kill. But Calder's conscience took him one step further. The killing felt unbearable to him and he had lost the hunter's instinct.

On our last fishing trip, Calder had always been the driving force, the keener, the strongest courier over the last portage. I had been the one to lose sleep worrying about bears and the first to tire after a portage.

"Can't cut er," says Calder, plainly discouraged.

"But Calder, you've been an administrator. You've been in the dean's office, for God's sake. You're not supposed to have a conscience anymore."

He gives me a sardonic grin. There is nothing more to be done. Like prehistoric creatures who dimly feel the end of their epoch, we slither into Calder's camper and head home for lunch. Some of them curse Jake, though it's not his fault. We curse the weather and dream of showers and more hot coffee.

While the others shower, I head over to Jake's garage and find him in the grease pit. Four other guys stand around talking with Jake as he works. I'm carrying the four geese and two ducks. "Where can I get them cleaned?"

"Goose plucker's daughter," says an old fellow. "Over at Horizon."

"Does she work fast?" I ask.

Jake sticks his head out of the grease pit and smiles. "Oh, she's fast, all right."

The men chuckle.

"You go t'Horizon, Dave. Doris'll take care of ya."

Again, tribal chuckling from deep in the belly.

"No crap, Dave, you're gonna meet a real pretty girl, eh?"

By the time I get back to the motel, some of the guys are eating, some showering. When it's my turn, I simply hold my K-ways and canvas coat under the shower until the clay peels off and down the drain. The bottom of the shower is plugged with three inches of mud. Changing into dry clothes is a pleasure worthy of a voluptuary.

Finally, after lunch, as the others rest, I load up the birds and take along Robertson for protection. This Doris woman sounds very threatening to me. I've turned her into a monster of Gothic proportions in my own mind, and Bill is very curious. He assumes she is merely old and disfigured.

Horizon is a ghost town. Two families remain. It used to have hundreds, but bad crops and large farm corporations seem to have driven out the residents. Doris's place is a one-story frame shack next to a demolished house and barn on the edge of town. Her back yard is the endless prairie.

I think of Mrs. Bentley from Sinclair Ross's classic novel *As for Me and My House,* how each day she would listen to the wind and dust sift through her house. At one point she calls the wind "liplessly mournful." I don't understand this phrase, but it haunts me.

I knock on the door.

Doris answers. She is about five foot two, ash blond, twenty-five, her makeup a bit on the heavy side, barefoot, and gorgeous. "Hi," she says with a bright smile.

At three o'clock, fed and rested, we cram into Calder's camper and try our luck again. Someone has told us we aren't supposed to shoot geese after twelve, but we assume sufferers' rights and plow onward. We will pretend we are shooting ducks only. Every goose within sixty yards will become a mallard.

We park the truck by the road again and off go Nash, Ford, and Robertson. Nash will stick to his perambulating; Ford and Robertson will crouch in the duck blind.

Carver tries the muddy road again, but it's no go. He has a torn muscle or a charley horse in his left groin, a bum right leg, a swollen left toe, and from compensating all day long, a bleeding blister on his right foot. We've helped him bandage up his hand and his foot, but the man is on his last legs, sweating and hobbling in the mud. "You know, Dave, I think if I try this road again I'm just not gonna make it. I think maybe I'll stick by the highway."

We stop and look around. The other three have gone on ahead and disappeared. The rain has almost stopped but the wind persists. "I think I'll stick by the highway," he says again. "I think I'll try my luck here." A while later he says, "I tell you, Dave, I could sure use a Coca Cola. Where do you think we could get one?"

I have the keys to Calder's truck. There is Horizon and Bean Coulee just a few miles down the road, and of course Crocus in the other direction. We head for the truck.

"If I could have a Coca Cola," says Carver, smiling painfully, "I think I could maybe make it through the afternoon." Perhaps this is how Carver talked about booze in the bad old days before he took the pledge. I too am thirsty. Before us looms a huge frosty bottle of Coke. The prairie has become a desert, and that ultimate American symbol, the Coke machine, our oasis. By five o'clock or so, we are beat but we simply will not acknowledge this. Like I say, Horizon is a ghost town. We discover it has no store. Bean Coulee hasn't even a Coke machine. We head back toward the muddy road, thirsty as hell. But before we reach it, Carver spots a huge wedge of geese flapping over a gravel road. A *gravel* road. This means it can be driven. We try it out. The truck moves slowly down the road; wet though it is, the tires grip. We drive beneath another large flock of honkers. Carver clambers out and checks the ditch. It is almost too dark to shoot, but we have tomorrow morning. Carver and I discover ample patches of weeds and standing grass, deep patches where we can hide in the morning. There is a light in Carver's eyes, a youthful look. "Goddam, David, this is it. We can come here tomorrow morning. Five o'clock. This is the place. Would you like to join me here tomorrow morning?"

"You bet," I say. "If they're flying low, I'm with you." My gun is built for close range stuff, so we seem destined to try our hand at this new road. To the north are several huge fields of swath. To the south across the road is a large slough, and string after string of geese pouring into it from the fields. The whole dark sky is honking.

"You bet," says Ray. "This is it. This is the place. You know what? I'm comin here tomorrow morning. Would you like to come?"

We arrive at dark on the mud road to pick up Nash, Robertson, and Ford. The latter two are waiting with big smiles on their faces. They each have four geese. Ford has been coaching Bill. These are his first geese ever. Robertson is the most talkative man I've ever hunted with, but as he loads his geese in and helps with the others, a strange aura of silence has fallen over him. Like his little two-year-old boy, Jesse, he just grins a lot as though the world has come to honor him.

Nash is a mile in again, and I have to go and get him in the dark. The more the mud balls up around my boots, the more tired I get. It's dark out now, but at least the rain is gone and the stars are out. We meet on the road where Nash has been listening to the geese. He has long since given up shooting. The flocks are pretty much all back on their water. Nash has been counting strings of geese. He figures there may be as many as fifteen thousand in a slough of scarcely more than a dozen acres. Goose shit surrounds the slough like cigarette butts at a race track. And the falsetto cackling is incredible. When I yell to Nash across the road, he can't even hear me.

That night in the bar we have a pizza supper. We're all sleepy, so the talk has hit the drowsy stage by the time we reach the presentations. Calder and Robertson present Carver and Ford with official Crocus tractor caps. Nash presents them with Wayne Gretzky tractor caps. I toss them each a bag of Saskatchewan books and deliver a little speech. The idea is, if one of their literary colleagues says, "What? Serious writing in Saskatchewan?" they are to respond either with violence or one of the abovementioned books. Ford and Carver are visibly touched by these presentations but even more moved by their need for sleep.

We all hit the sack before ten o'clock. By this time Doris has done twelve geese and two ducks for us. They've all met her and been smitten. She sits in a shack in a ghost town and flies through our dreams. Not too long from now, we will read each other's stories or poems with Doris as the muse. All through the storm, I imagine, she is listening to the wind. All day long we've been lying in the mud or shooting off boxes of shells at the indifferent gods, unaware that the muse was waiting for us. . . . Amused by the muse . . . abused by the muse ... but none too clever to ... refuse the muse? These things dribble from my lips as I fall asleep to the thunderous applause of Nash's adenoids.

September 27

Five o'clock, still pitch black out. I knock on everyone's door. Carver makes coffee, but this time there are only a few crumpled two-day-old doughnuts for breakfast. Calder is going to give it one more go. He heads out in the truck with Nash and Robertson. Ford and Carver come with me. Ford managed to bring down five geese, and he feels Carver should try his gun. Richard has generously decided to sit this one out. Neither Carver nor I have managed to bring down a goose, and Ford is eager that we do well this time. We drive out to the gravel road; the others return to the mud road. The stars are out and the dawn lifts slowly like a warm cup of tea. There is not a trace of a cloud. Ford coaches Carver on the handling of his gun and leaves in my car to pick up our plucked birds. Just as I'm settling into the ditch behind a telephone pole, the first wave comes over Carver's head two hundred yards down the road. He fires twice and two geese fall. One is only winged and takes off across the field flapping frantically over the swath. Carver leaps out of the ditch and gives chase. I race over to help him—after all, he has become one of the walking wounded—but Carver has suddenly regained his youthful legs. When I get there he sports two large specklebellies and an enormous grin. "Boy, isn't that something," he says.

We hurry back to our separate positions in the ditch, and over they come again. Carver knocks another goose down, this time a young Canada. A pair of specklebellies come at me from the sunrise, just in range. I stand up so that my body is shielded by the old telephone pole, lead the bird on the left, and fire. It seems to stop in midair and climb straight up. I fire again and down it comes, my first goose in four years. Carver waves. Minutes later a large chevron of honkers passes over our heads out of range, then another flock, this time lower. Carver fires first, knocks one down, and then I fire and down comes my first lesser Canada. We chase our birds into opposite fields, bag them, and lurch back into the ditch. It's about nine thirty; the sun is climbing and hangs in a blue sky over a stubble field filled with thousands of specklebellies, Canadas, and snow geese. The geese tend to feed with their own kind, and so the snow geese stand out among the darker specimens in blotches of white. Thousands of geese are still in the slough to our west, and all day they will cross in waves of a hundred or more from slough to stubble, from stubble to slough. They fly high now, and Ray and I are extremely visible. What the hell.

Ford returns in my car, and with our instinct for show biz still proclaiming itself, we manage to meet him carrying our geese. He is ecstatic. He wants to shake our hands but of course they are filled with goosenecks.

"Oh boy!" he yells to Carver. "You liked it?" he asks, pointing to his gun. That one gun has accounted for nine geese so far this trip. "And you shot two of these?" he says to me. "You got two geese?"

I say, "Aw."

The six of us have brunch in Crocus and gas up for the long ride home. The woman at the pump asks us how we did and we tell her twenty geese, two ducks. The weather has been so bad that hardly anyone else has been able to get to where the geese are. The woman at the pumps tells us another group of five hunters picked up six geese, but we apparently were the only ones to do half decently. This for me is a source of enormous pride. I'll be telling this story for a long time to come. The sleet will become snow, eventually a blizzard; the edge of a hurricane will become the eye of a hurricane; the bag will grow from twenty-two to forty-four; Carver's cuts on his left hand will become an ugly gash on his left arm. . . .

"Doris took care of yiz, did she?" says the young woman at the pump.

"Yep," says Calder.

"Oh, the hunters really appreciate Doris," she goes on.

Calder's ears perk up. All of our ears perk up.

"Oh, Doris really pulls in some extra money in huntin season," says the woman with all the innuendo she can muster.

"No kiddin," says Robertson.

I can see a poem flapping across the ditch as Robertson gets back into the truck: "The Gooseplucker's Daughter" by William B. Robertson. How will Carver handle this one? Will Ford beat him to the punch? Will I?

"There's a dance on tonight," says the woman. "You guys should come along."

"We have planes to catch," says Nash.

"Too bad," she sings. "Doris'll be there."

Carver has a coffee and cigarette at the Crocus Hotel cafe while the other guys get their gear together. He's in his reading duds again, surprisingly dapper: a beige raincoat he bought in London, brown turtleneck and tweed jacket, civilized shoes and slacks that seem out of place in Crocus. He looks pleasantly tired, a lot like that author whose pictures are on his dust jackets.

"You look like Raymond Carver," I tell him.

I can now confess to him that Jake had phoned just before his reading to cancel the trip. He likes that: the fact that we risked our hides against strong odds to come down here and be boys again. And what an adventure we had. Six guys wallowing in the mud and struggling with other things as well: Carver with physical pain, Ford with the unusual cold, Calder with his feelings about killing things, Robertson with his old/new gun, and on it goes. It was six guys unaccustomed to mud and hurricanes trying (metaphorically at least) to shoot pigeons in the dark. Above all, trying to help each other get through the day. Ford coached Robertson in the duck blind; Nash and Carver bolstered my courage when it looked bad for the trip; Calder wired on a muffler by lying under his truck in a mud puddle so we could all go in the first place; I ran around being host for several days and worried for everyone; Carver made something like twenty cups of coffee from his tiny pot at 5:00 A.M.

At the airport, Carver tries to thank me for a great hunt and gets choked up. I try to tell him that such rewards are his due because he happens to write well, but my words come stumbling out for want of sleep. Carver and Ford both want to come back and stay longer. We're already dreaming of next fall when great cackling legions of geese in flocks as wide as Saskatoon will once more descend from the north to fatten up on the grain fields, reminding us (who shoot at clay pigeons in the dark) that we were once Lee Henchbaw and we are from Sass-katchewan.

CHARLES WRIGHT

Twice-Touched

Port Angeles, 6 a.m.: saw mill
And boat swell, sea water thick with oil shine,
                                        the bay's back
Pockmarked with milk jugs and styrofoam,
Logs stacked for the lumber ships,
Ice chests and chum buckets,
                        old tires, Bud cans, release springs
Loose in the wind chop,
White stroke of a sail, daub and blister of power boats
Under horizon line,
Pink bill, sun's burn, shore front falling away
                        as we enter the ribbed straits . . .

All morning we trolled the bay
                        with deep lures and skip jacks,
All morning as under us
The sea in its great indifference rumpled its shoulders,
Crossing and crisscrossing our own wakes.
It's hard to write about
                        what we want to write about:
I should have been otherwise,
                                pure-pitched and golden-stroked:
I should have been born to sing.
As it is, the wakes fade, the images drift and fade
And only the joy remains,
                        unspoken, untold of.

———————

Always we ask ourselves, "What matters,
What counts in the true design?"
What matters is what we expiate,

                         what grace and affection
We bring to our daily lives.
Simple enough, we think, and easy to exercise.
Not so. It's almost impossible
Except for the twice-touched,

                        the unsanctimonious
Who have saved themselves by their own hand.
Simplicity factors out

             as the hardest thing to come by.

You never mentioned the great questions.
You never talked about the blank unanswerables.
You never needed to,

              for everything that you wrote about
Was something we had to know,
And had to relearn each time you wrote it:
There is a decency,
A love of things as they are,

                  not as they might become,
A real acceptance of dailiness,
You taught us,

        life in a human way.

———————

How to proceed?

        After the last *no* is a new *no,*
Empirical, out of breath:
Like landscape in late Cézanne,
Such distance from life and humanity, such brushwork,
Devolve from infinitude
Into something important,

              a bend in the road, an aside.
Always the same motif, but a different idiom.
Always the same tune,

        but a different dance,

Gospel and hillside restructured and given the devil's words.

You know how it is,
                    a verb here, a smudge there, and then
Everything comes together,
Everything hooked up and screwed down in its single place,
An object, an acolyte
Of exit's devotional—
For someone who saved his own life more times than once,
                                    surely you've got a leg up
Now on the tide's slip and salmon run.
Your words, if the devil's words they are, give him his due and
                                            then some.
                    Their book of you is not yet finished . . .

PART VI

Port Angeles, Washington

1988

JANE KENYON

The Letter

Bad news arrives in her distinctive hand.
The cancer has returned, this time
to his brain. Surgery impossible,
treatments under way. Hair loss, bouts
of sleeplessness and agitation at night,
exhaustion during the day.

I snap the blue leash onto the D-ring
of the dog's collar, and we cross
Route 4, then cut through the hayfield
to the pond road, where I let him run
along with my morbidity.

The trees have leafed out—only just—
and the air is misty with sap.
So green, so brightly, richly succulent,
this arbor over the road . . .
Sunlight penetrates in golden drops.

We come to the place where a neighbor
is taking timber from his land.
There's a smell of lacerated earth
and pine. Hardwood smells different.
His truck is gone.

Now you can see well up the slope,
see ledges of rock and ferns breaking forth
among the stumps and cast-aside limbs
and branches.

The place will heal itself in time, first
with weeds—goldenrod, cinquefoil, moth
mullein—then blackberries, sapling
pine, deciduous trees ... But for now
the dog rolls, jovial, in the pungent
disturbance of wood and earth.

I summon him with a word, turn back,
and we go the long way home.

DOROTHY CATLETT

Do You Like It?

I met Raymond Carver in July of 1984. He had mentioned to the lady in Port Angeles who was doing some picture framing for him that he needed to find someone to type for him. She and I had known each other for years, and she knew that I did typing, but evidently at the time she could not remember my last name. So, she told Ray that my husband worked at Brown's Sporting Goods store in town. He drove straight to Brown's and found Dick behind the counter. He asked him if his wife did typing, and Dick confirmed that I did and then called to make sure I was home. Ray was here within five minutes of the phone call.

When I answered the door, I saw this tall man, slightly stooped, and with a wonderful smile on his face. He was carrying a manila folder, and he wore casual clothes (a baggy sweater that zipped up the front, with his shirt collar poking out at the top). He came into the room, and we both sat on the sofa so that he could show me the work he wanted typed—several pages of poems in the folder he carried. To begin with, Ray introduced himself and told me some about who he was. He told me about the five-year grant he had been awarded, about having his books published, some translated into other languages, and about having recently been interviewed by *Life* magazine. (I heard later it was never published.) He briefly mentioned his relationship with Tess Gallagher, and the fact that she was a poet. I'm embarrassed now to say that I had never heard of either Raymond Carver or Tess Gallagher. I was somewhat taken by surprise. I had never imagined that a well-known author would come to my door, in this small town, and ask me to type for him. I liked him immediately. My first impression (which never changed in the years to come) was that he was a big, gentle, soft-spoken cuddly bear of a man.

I went right to work on Ray's poetry manuscript, which consisted of ninety poems at the time. This manuscript eventually became *Where Water Comes Together with Other Water.* Over the next several days Ray and I were handing work back and forth as he revised the poems and I made the changes, then ran new copies. One thing that always impressed me about Ray was the fact that when I called him and told him that the work was ready, he was here in a matter of minutes. (In my business, this seldom happens, even when people tell me they are "in a hurry." Often when I call them, they tell me they'll pick it up the next day.) I realized immediately how important it was to Ray to see a smooth, clean copy of his work. He was always so appreciative of my quick response, I found myself working long hours in order to get his work back to him in the shortest time possible. Often, he would have the next revision back to me in a matter of hours. Once he was working on something, there appeared to be a continual drive to complete it.

Ray seemed genuinely interested in what I thought about his work. When he would pick up work, he would ask, "Do you like it?" And when he would pick up something he had revised, he would ask, "Do you like it better now? Did you like the changes?" It didn't matter that I did not know that much about fiction or poetry and, in fact, had had very little exposure to poetry before meeting Ray and Tess. Since I had read it, I qualified as a reader and, as such, he wanted to know what *I* thought of what he had written. He made me feel that my opinion was important to him. He always seemed so excited about his work. It was contagious.

Having gotten a taste of Ray's poetry, and liking it, I wanted to read some of his stories. I bought a copy of *What We Talk About When We Talk About Love.* I had never before read stories such as these. They seemed to be hard slices of life, without the glamour, optimism, and "happy endings" that were usually evident in most of the short stories I had read before. These were the stories of people with hard lives and difficult relationships. I have to admit that I didn't like some of the stories the first time I read them. I think maybe I just didn't like the sad circumstances and hopelessness they seemed to depict. But as I began to reread some of those stories, I saw them in a different light. I realized Ray had a unique way of telling a story. I found I could actually visualize the people and the events through Ray's descriptions. And the dialogue was wonderful. I can't explain it, but I no longer found them depressing, just good stories.

From time to time Ray and I would talk about the subject matter in some of his poems and stories, specifically those that involved problems caused by drinking. I told him my first husband had been an alcoholic and that I recognized many of the circumstances and actions that he captured so vividly in the poems about his own life. I can never remember Ray talking to me directly about his having been an alcoholic. (I had learned that he was a recovering alcoholic from the information accompanying one of his stories in an issue of *Esquire* a friend had loaned me.) However, he always seemed genuinely interested in my observations and the comparisons to some of the alcoholic scenes I had witnessed.

The work Ray brought to me was generally in the form of a draft that he had typed on his Smith-Corona. It would be a pretty fair copy, but chopped up a bit with typos and lines crossed out here and there. Occasionally there would be some words inserted by hand on this first typed draft. The revisions, however, contained numerous handwritten inserts with writing spilling onto the backs of pages sometimes when the margins had given out. We both laughed about his handwriting. What a challenge it could be to read that inscrutable small scribble of his! I did, however, have strangely little trouble deciphering it. As the revision process continued, a different hard-to-read handwriting would be threaded into the typing along with Ray's own handwriting. That handwriting, I was to learn, belonged to Tess. Ray explained to me that he and Tess were each other's best critic. (When typing for Tess, I would also see a word or phrase here and there written in Ray's handwriting.) There was an occasional time when he would misspell a word. It seems to me now that it was generally someone's name. I would look it up and put in the proper spelling. The next revision would come back with the word crossed out and the improper spelling written in. When I'd tell Ray, we'd both laugh about it. I soon learned to tell him, when he picked up the work, that *my* spelling was the *correct* spelling for a certain word, "SO DON'T CHANGE IT!"

Over the next three years, I typed for Ray when he was in Port Angeles. My records show that the last time was in August of 1987. In addition to the manuscript for *Where Water Comes Together with Other Water,* I had the pleasure of typing his poetry manuscript for *Ultramarine,* an essay entitled "Friends," and several of his short stories, including "Boxes" (which was called "Son" the first time I got it), "Menudo," and a story I truly enjoyed working on, "Errand" (which started out as "The Mortician" and went to "The Errand" before finally becoming "Errand"). Ray was really excited about this last story. He told me it was the first time in his writing he had brought together historically true incidents with fictionalized happenings. It was fascinating to me to see how the emphasis of the story changed along with the title.

Ray had a way of really *listening,* of showing genuine interest, of making me feel what I had to say and my opinion were important to him. He sincerely wanted to know what I thought each time he revised something. So I did more than type his work; I read it. As he listened, he would look me directly in the eyes and, although I sensed he was intuitively aware of all that surrounded him, I felt I had his full attention and that he heard everything I said. I was never conscious of his own thoughts interfering or his concentration wandering. This rare quality, of being able to truly listen, is one that I seldom witness in as developed a form in others.

During the period I was typing for Ray, I also typed for Tess, and they both became good friends of mine, and also of Dick and myself as a couple. When I heard of Ray's cancer, it was devastating news. I was angry at his cigarette smoking. Angry at him for not having given it up long ago and possibly saving himself from this suffering. As much as I loved Ray, I have a great physical and probably emotional intolerance to cigarette smoke and, most often, when he brought me work, his clothes and his manuscript would reek of cigarette smoke. That part was difficult for me. He was such a wonderful person in every respect, and I kept wishing with all my heart that the cigarette habit would one day be overcome. I did not want to lose this wonderful friend.

One of the most distinct memories I have of Ray was when he

and Tess came back from New York after his lung surgery, early in 1988. They came to see me in the law office where I was working at the time. Ray gave me a big hug, and as my nose was buried in his winter coat, there was such a fresh, clean smell—no stale cigarette smoke! Tess had told me on the phone that Ray had quit smoking, but this made the fact real to me. It made me smile all over. It still makes me smile when I think of it today.

Dick and I were fortunate enough to be invited to Ray and Tess's wedding reception at their home in late June of 1988. They were both glowing with happiness. The small diverse group that attended this celebration included a few close friends in the area, family, and a couple of close neighbors. It was a pleasant day, and at times we wandered out on the deck to view the Strait of Juan de Fuca and hear the birds singing in the trees. The dining room table was filled with delicious food to snack on. It was fun for us, meeting new friends and visiting with old ones. Ray and Tess played a tape recording of their wedding ceremony. To watch them relive the moment as they listened to the tape, laughing at the Reno-style ceremony, filling in some of the sidelights not captured on the tape, made it obvious that they were very much in love and that they intended to make the most of every precious moment they had. It was such a festive and happy event. I really thought right then that Ray just might beat the odds.

I also saw Ray on August 1, the afternoon before he died. In my heart, I knew when I left him that I was really saying good-bye to him. I held his hand, and he squeezed mine. It was one of the saddest times of my life, but I'm so glad I had a chance to see him that last day. Tess called me the next morning to tell me he had died. I felt the loss of a very dear friend.

My most vivid memories of Ray are his smile, his wonderful laugh, those eyes that didn't look at you, or through you, but "into" you, his ability to listen with genuine interest in what you had to say, his almost boyish enthusiasm for his work, his delight in his successes, his love for Tess, and that wonderful bear hug without the odor of cigarette smoke. I feel so very fortunate to have known Raymond Carver and to have played some small part in his life and his work.

TED SOLOTAROFF

Going Through the Pain

For days after I learned that Raymond Carver had died an image of his face would appear in my mind each time I thought about him. The face was not that of the stricken man I had seen for the last time two months before, but of Ray in his prime—boyishly spruce and expectant, his face slightly averted, listening in that cocked way of his. It was strange to think of him as dead and to see him so alive, like studying the sealed photograph of a particularly striking face attached to a tombstone, as I had done in the Novodevichy cemetery in Moscow after visiting Chekhov's grave.

It was also strange to be so haunted by his presence since I hadn't known him that well. We were together probably ten or twelve times, always in professional or social situations. The closest we had come to a personal conversation were the few occasions in recent years when he and Tess Gallagher, my wife Virginia and I had gotten together during their visits to New York, or once when we had met up in London and gone to the British Museum together.

Ray recalled that sweet time in London in a letter he wrote to Virginia toward the end of his life. He said that the four of us were "lucky people, all things considered." Virginia and I took this to mean that he had sensed that we, like Tess and himself, had lucked out in finding each other in middle age. We also took his words as another outcropping of the courage and gratitude with which he had come to terms with dying in one of his last poems, the extraordinary one called "Gravy."

GRAVY

No other word will do. For that's what it was. Gravy.
Gravy these past ten years.

Alive, sober, working, loving and
being loved by a good woman. Eleven years
ago he was told he had six months to live
at the rate he was going. And he was going
nowhere but down. So he changed his ways
somehow. He quit drinking! And the rest?
After that it was *all* gravy, every minute
of it, up to and including when he was told about,
well, some things that were breaking down and
building up inside his head. "Don't weep for me,"
he said to his friends. "I'm a lucky man.
I've had ten years longer than I or anyone
expected. Pure gravy. And don't forget it."

So, at first I thought that my image of him was honoring his wish
to be remembered for what he had been given rather than for what
had been taken away. With that explanation, I figured that the
image would fade. But it didn't: it continued to recur, its vividness
still filling the hole that his death had punched out in my sense of
rightness. His face wasn't lodged there in the soft way of grief but in
a firm one, as though its vitality was a kind of message—something
being given to me or possibly being asked of me.

The third day or so the image changed: his face was no longer in
its listening mode but had turned to me, his eyes looking to make
contact. He was less the literary figure and more the person, whom
I felt I had known less well. I sensed that I was being visited and
perhaps instructed by the gift of his friendship, that he had meant
more to me than I had recognized or acted on when I'd decided not
to fly across the country to his funeral. His eyes had his open,
welcoming, sincere (there's no other word for it) look that brought
out one's own sincerity, what was left of it. They also had his
gentleness: unlike most of the writers I've known from working-
class backgrounds, there had been little, besides his passion for
fishing, that was macho about him. His smile was that of a boy who
was close to his mother, and he carried himself and attended to
people in a careful way that made him seem more like a minister
than a writer, particularly a famous one. As for his reputation, he
wore it with a kind of naive pride, like the beautiful tweed jacket he

had bought during his reading tour in England, and this too was endearing, particularly when one remembered from his fiction and his autobiographical essays how far he had come and what he had overcome on the way.

I began to believe that this imaging of Ray was coming from the soul, telling me that I had been privileged to know a rare person, a *mensch,* as we Jews say, a real sweetheart, as Ray would have said—a brave man with a highly developed feminine side, the type of man I most cherished and wanted to be. This brought to mind Chekhov, another of my models of conduct, and Tolstoy's famous remarks to Gorky about Chekhov: "What a beautiful, magnificent man: modest and quiet, like a girl. He even walks like a girl."

Ray had picked up Tolstoy's words and used them in his final published story, "Errand." An account of Chekhov's end, it has a documentary character that makes it unlike any of Ray's other stories; yet it becomes a Carver story all the same by the laconic yet brooding way it deals with the dark, oncoming facts of the event and its aftermath (". . . the injection didn't help—nothing, of course, could have helped") and from the expressive power with which he endows a commonplace object—in this case an errant champagne cork—to concentrate both the chill and poignancy of death. There is also, of course, another chilling and poignant story that is telling itself between the lines, a story based on implicit similarities, beginning with the detail that Chekhov had "peasant's blood in his veins."

A few weeks later Tess asked me to speak at the memorial for Ray in New York. This meant the writer as well as the man, so I stayed up one night reading his stories. The fact was that I hadn't read many of them until then. Except for "Errand," I had respected his fiction rather than cottoned to it. His typically small-town isolates were of marginal interest to me; they didn't seem to see or feel or learn much beyond their insecurities, the bleakness of their prospects, the force of their streaks of envy, jealousy, cruelty, shame, dishonesty, or some other twisted energy that flared up like a chronic fever in a meager, congested life: the unemployed salesman who pressures his wife to lose weight so that he can watch men ogling her; the drinker and adulterer who drives himself to begin to put his family's life in order by secretly getting rid of their messy dog; the baker who torments the couple whose child has been run over about the birthday cake they had ordered. I admired the integrity of Carver's work—his firm grasp of damaged lives for which there was little help or hope and his bluff style that conceded nothing to literary entertainment. But his vision was too limiting, to my taste: the world seen from the barstool, the forsaken marriage bed, the car rubbernecking the traffic accident.

That was my superficial response. What I remembered best was his astonishing essay "Fires," in which he said flat out that the main influence on his fiction had been his long subjection to the needs and caprices of his children. He and his wife had been teenage parents, uneducated and unskilled, working at one "crap job" after another, subsisting, stretched thin, losing hope and heart until "everything my wife and I held sacred, or considered worthy of respect, every spiritual value, crumbled away. Something terrible had happened to us. . . . It was erosion and we couldn't stop it. Somehow, when we weren't looking, the children had got into the driver's seat. As crazy as it sounds now, they held the reins, and the whip." That kind of rockbottom honesty was electrifying: it generated the power and light of his stories. But it didn't make me a fan of the stories. It mostly made me wonder how the sweetness of the man had survived the bitter erosions and defeats the writer kept recounting and imagining.

That night and on into the early morning I read through most of *Where I'm Calling From,* his new and selected stories. I found myself giving up my dismissive respect or, rather, having it pushed aside by assent. At first it took a literary form, a fascination with the exactness of the writing—common language that "hit all the notes" as Carver put it, and with the subtle variations of the emotional burden that I'd read too glibly as an obsessive gray doom that fogged in his people's world. What I had taken to be a grim reductiveness was, when seen in the round, a finely calibrated ruefulness: a more tender and interesting and philosophical kind of understanding. As one of his characters, in the grip of an unwarranted but intractable jealousy, comes to see: "Yes, there was a great evil pushing at the world, . . . and it only needed a little slipway, a little opening."

Those rusted-out marriages and stalled affairs and misfiring bar seductions and sprung friendships: each testified in its own distinctive tone to the erosion at the heart of things that he spoke about in "Fires." I also began to see that his understanding of it had widened and become more nuanced: the blue-collar ruts of the earlier stories branched out, as it were, into the mazes of better-educated people, the undercurrent of menace or risk was giving way to more uncanny and strange threats, like the blind friend of the narrator's wife in "Cathedral" or the good-bye letter from the wife in "Blackbird Pie" that is not in her handwriting or style. But he still refused to brighten or soften the testimony of his narrators about their secret meannesses, screw-ups, losses, and the prose remained homely and unsparing, as though a naked lightbulb were burning in their minds. The ruefulness was built into the "unique and exact way of looking at things" he recommended, just as it was built into the lives he trained it upon, . . . just as it was built into my own. The pity was in the telling itself and it began to get to me, to chasten my way of reading him.

The last story I read was a late one called "Menudo" about a man who can't sleep, who is on the verge of breaking up two marriages and is thinking about his previous one:

> When Molly and I were growing up together, she was a part of me and, sure, I was a part of her, too. We loved each other. It *was* our destiny. I believed in it then myself. But now I don't know what to believe in. I'm not complaining, simply stating a fact. I'm down to nothing. And I have to go on like this. No destiny. Just the next thing meaning whatever you think it does. Compulsion and error, just like everybody else.

I read those words again. They could have been my own words through much of my adult life. Like Carver, I had married too young, had held the same kind of high hopes and values along with the same low jobs, had also tried to raise two children with more despair and panic than care and money, had witnessed the same terrible slow entailment and foreclosure of that striving first love. Though my ordeal hadn't gone on as long and as hopelessly as his, and though I had been spared the grimmer consequences he had known as an alcoholic, it had left some of the same scars and kinks of error and compulsion that he wrote about. For most of my adult life that passage in "Menudo" could have served as the "unspoken meditation of my heart" (a phrase from the Yom Kippur liturgy), which I usually managed to evade or gloss over.

I finally went to bed, fell asleep, and had a dream. I was driving my new Honda Accord, the first quality car I've owned. One of the warning lights came on, the one that tells you to head for the nearest repair shop. It was a dark, cold, snowy night with no traffic, no pedestrians. A Ray Carver night in the sticks, except that I was in New York. I drove past a couple of garages, the kind that are inside buildings. I found a place to park in the street and went back to the first garage. A surprisingly friendly mechanic there told me to bring the car in, he'd work on it. Much relieved I went outside and walked to where my car was. It was gone. I couldn't believe that even in New York a car could be stolen that fast and I walked up the street looking for it, thinking I'd gotten its location wrong. But though there were other cars that looked like mine, none of them was, and when I got to the end of the block I knew that it was gone for good. I began to panic, to go crazy in my lifelong way. When I'd calmed down a bit I remembered that I'd parked the car near a second garage and thought that perhaps they had taken the car in. But no, they hadn't seen or heard of it.

I woke up then and lay in a daze of revelation. The dream seemed like a Ray Carver story about losing him. It was also about the panic and craziness of suddenly losing one's assurances, of once again being down to nothing. It was about the permanent ruefulness that the passage in "Menudo" had led me to recognize in myself.

Much of what is written here, including the dream, comes from what I said at the memorial. Since then the image of Ray's vitality and the dream have taken on a further meaning.

A month or two before his death I had abandoned a long piece of writing that dealt with a surrogate version of those desperate years. I'd adopted a jaunty style to make it less depressing, livened it up with a romantic relationship from a later period, provided a strong therapist to lead my persona out of the wilderness, and modified or left out most of my actual mistakes and pain and, most of all, harmfulness. For several years it had been fun to write, off and on, but just as it was heading into the crisis I had suddenly lost interest and conviction. Its liveliness now seemed willed, a smiling whine, its issues psychologically precious, its narrator ungrounded in an actual life and hence increasingly arbitrary, and the way ahead tedious. I thought I'd been writing a novel that went deep into the process of psychotherapy but now saw that I had been seduced by a facile first-person voice, had managed to ignore most of what I had learned about fiction from editing, teaching, and criticizing it, and was writing still another narcissistic first novel, possibly quite like the one I would have written thirty years ago if I'd had the freedom.

All of which was disappointing but not heartbreaking. I told myself that I had only postponed an apprenticeship, that like most novelists I worked with I'd written an unpublishable first novel, had gotten a lot of vanity out of my system, had learned about certain pitfalls by occupying them. Perhaps I'd rewrite it in the third person and let more of the world come into it. In any case, my experience with the process would be useful, one way and another. Asked to speak at a writing program last summer, I quickly recycled the main lessons into a lecture entitled "The Pits of Fiction."

But my "mature" response to the failure has proved to be facile too. Hidden and defended by egotism, the real cause began to reveal itself as I was revising this essay. For I'm as sure as one can be about such matters that Ray's image in my mind and the dream, whatever else they're about, have to do with that abandoned manuscript, that the opportunity was taken away because I finally got bored with kidding myself. To write with any sustained energy and interest about those years of losing my way, of anguished trial and error, I would have had to go back into how I came to be down to nothing and tell about the force of error and compulsion in my life. For that's the bedrock of what I've been given to know and am still learning about thirty years later, since all too often the knowledge slides into obliviousness. To establish that bedrock I would have had to tell about the bitter, crazy side of premature marriage and child-rearing; those Medusa truths that even shielded by time and forgetting can still make my heart as heavy as stone.

In his *Paris Review* interview Carver speaks of turning one's life's stories into fiction. "You have to be immensely daring, very skilled and imaginative and willing to tell everything on yourself. . . . What do you know better than your own secrets?" He's not saying that telling them guarantees anything, for fiction is more likely to fail from lack of skill and imagination than from evasiveness. What he is saying is that if you want the energy and authority that comes from telling your secrets, they had better be the real ones: the ones that make you go through their pain again. Otherwise the writing will be coming not from the secrets but from the defenses against them and the fiction will not be the bread of experience earned in the sweat of your brow but rather the cake of fantasies that you can have and eat too.

I think I see now why the image of Ray in my mind had so much vigor—the vigor that comes from honesty—and why my dream was a secret told in a Carveresque way. As I read him now and write about him he has come to seem less like a dead friend than a vital ally. I imagine that when Chekhov died many Russian writers felt the same way: that his fiction was itself a friendship. What one wants most in a friend is both candor and empathy—qualities rarely found together. Chekhov's vision was less relentless than Carver's and he had more social range, but they started from and came back to the same ruefulness: a radical honesty and empathy about ordinary lives and how they go wrong.

Gorky wrote that in Chekhov's presence "everyone felt an involuntary desire to be simpler, more truthful, more oneself." This was also Ray Carver's gift as a person, as I've said earlier, and one that is literally conveyed by his stories and poems as it was by Chekhov's stories and plays. It explains, I think, much better than does the fashionable talk about "minimalism" and "rural chic" why Carver has been the most influential writer of his generation. He had the kind of gift that travels: the common touch raised to the next power, the power of art, that can be conveyed intact to his readers and brings out, as my dream did, the giftedness in them, the possibility of getting down to the charged and freighted roots of our lives. To God's honest truth, as he would have said, and as he did.

LIGGETT TAYLOR

Reunion in Yakima

It wouldn't be accurate to say I really knew Raymond Carver. We were in the same high school class—with about 460 other kids. I can't recall whether we had any classes together. I'm not even sure whether I knew of Ray from having seen him around school or from having seen his name and picture in the 1956 Yakima High School yearbook. I learned he had achieved some degree of fame in the spring of 1986 when we were organizing our thirtieth-year class reunion.

I was on the phone with a reunion committee member when she asked me if I'd heard about him. She said Ray was included in a feature story in *Pacific,* the Sunday magazine of the *Seattle Times.* The issue had come out a couple of weeks earlier, on March 9. I still had a copy in the house, so I dug it out. The article was about five Northwest poets, including Raymond Carver and Tess Gallagher. It said Ray was "practically famous" and was "among the best-known American short story writers." It also indicated that Ray and Tess were living together.

I called the reporter who had written the story to find out how to contact Ray. The man was pretty guarded, as I recall. He wouldn't give me Ray's address so I could send him a copy of the reunion announcement and a questionnaire for the memory book. I had to mail the information to the reporter. He promised he'd send it along.

I was pleasantly surprised when Ray returned the completed questionnaire within a few days. As far as I know, he hadn't attended our tenth- or twentieth-year reunions. The only information we had on him for the '66 memory book was his name and a Sacramento address. For the '76 memory book all we had besides his name was a Cupertino address: nothing on occupation, marital status, or children.

I thought the fact that Ray had become a successful writer might make a "local-boy-makes-good" story for the *Yakima Herald-Republic,* the newspaper where I'm employed as a copy editor. So, early in April I took the *Pacific* article to work and gave it to the city editor. Later, when I found out Ray would attend the mid-August reunion, I suggested this might be a good time for an interview. The city editor passed the article to the night-shift reporter. If the night man had time, the editor said, he'd drop by.

The main event of the reunion was on Saturday night, when we had a cocktail hour followed by dinner, a short program, and dancing. On Friday evening, we had a social session at the big motel-convention facility where we were to have the Saturday banquet.

The Friday thing was an outdoors stand-around-by-the-motel-pool-and-visit-and-drink session. I think my wife and I were about the first people to visit with Ray and Tess. When I saw them, they were standing by themselves on the lawn, Ray looking a little tentative. I don't recall much of what Ray or Tess said, except that Ray didn't talk much. Tess told us about a deal Ray had with the *New Yorker* and that he was featured in the latest *Esquire.*

I asked Ray about the picture of him in *Pacific.* He'd had one hand up by his chin with the middle finger extended slightly in front of the others. I wondered whether the gesture was intentional. Ray said he hadn't noticed the finger's position. My wife and I chatted with Ray and Tess awhile, but I don't recall talking to them again that evening.

Saturday morning I bought a copy of the August *Esquire,* the summer reading issue. It included Ray's story "Intimacy," about a man's meeting with his ex-wife. A nice color picture of Ray standing behind a picket fence accompanied the story. I'm not much of a recreational reader, but I liked that story. I'm kind of a "just the facts, ma'am" sort of a reader. I took the copy of *Esquire* to the reunion Saturday night to show Ray's story to anyone who might be interested.

Ray and Tess didn't arrive until the end of the cocktail hour, when everyone was heading in for dinner. I told Ray I'd read his story, that I liked it, and why I liked it. I asked him whether "Intimacy" was an account of something that had actually happened. He smiled a little and was noncommittal.

Some of the reunion organizers had put together a trivia quiz. Copies were included in the packets classmates received when they checked in that evening. One of the questions was "Which classmate has become an internationally known poet?" As the master of ceremonies proceeded through the quiz, answers were shouted out all around the room. But when he got to Ray's question, as I recall, the m.c. had to give the answer.

Ray and Tess left the reunion fairly early. As we were saying good night, Tess said something about a teacher's having invited Ray to come back sometime and talk to a class at the high school. Tess indicated he might do that. Since Ray had supplied the reunion committee with his address, I asked whether if my wife and I ever drove up to Port Angeles, some bookstore personnel might be able to direct us to Ray and Tess's house. Tess said such folks were pretty careful about local people's privacy. She gave me a telephone number. Then she spotted the *Esquire* I'd been carrying. She said, "Would you like Ray to sign it for you?" I hadn't thought of that, but I said sure, and he did.

Over the next two years I contacted Ray and Tess several times. I wanted to know when Ray might get back to Yakima. Would he be willing to meet one of our reporters for an interview?

During this time, Ray was getting more and more public notice. There was a story about him and Tess (with beautiful color photos) in the October 1986 *Vanity Fair*. Then there was a big piece about him in the magazine section of the Sunday *Portland Oregonian* on January 11, 1987. And there was a nice story about him and Tess in the November 23, 1987, issue of *People*.

Whenever I read something about Ray I mentioned it to the city editor. Sometimes I brought in articles to show him. And I passed along any other news of Ray I heard. I had to be careful, though.

The city editor didn't seem much interested. At times, he seemed a little irritated at my mentioning Ray's name.

One day when I was at my desk one of our young reporters came up to me. "You went to school with Raymond Carver?" he said. I explained that although Ray and I were in the same high school class, I really hadn't known him. The reporter told me he was a big fan of Ray's writing, had been for about five years. "I'd love to do a feature on him," the reporter said. He added that he had a friend in Port Angeles who knew Ray. He talked about getting up there on his own time to do an interview.

In maintaining contact with Ray and Tess, I called Port Angeles about three times. Only once did I talk to Ray. (The address I had was for Ray's house, and the phone number Tess had given me was for her Sky House on the other side of town.) Each time I telephoned, I was nervous. After all, these were fairly famous people. They might not like my bothering them. But I fretted for nothing. When I mentioned that my wife and I still hoped to visit Port Angeles, Tess said, "Just let us know when. We'll all go out for dinner."

One day at work we received a wire story about a shake-up at the *New Yorker.* I remembered Tess's saying that Ray had a deal with the magazine, so I ran a copy of the story on the line printer and mailed it to him. Ray sent me back a thank-you note in which he commented on the situation. He said, "It is front page stuff in the *New York Times,* and there is still a lot going on. Please feel free to send me more AP wire stories, as I can't get the *Times* out here." He added a p.s.: "I hope we'll see each other again, some time or another. Tess said you called and you had a nice talk."

In the summer of 1987 we received a news service item that mentioned Ray's position at the "red-hot center" of *Esquire*'s literary universe. I inserted a note about Ray's Yakima connections and sent the story to an electronic file. When it wasn't used in the paper after a couple of weeks, I retrieved it. I worked it into a sketch about Ray and routed it to the file where we store items for our "Upbeat" column. When the column finally appeared, I sent Ray a clipping.

The one time I talked to Ray on the telephone was in the first week of January 1988. He told me he'd had most of a lung removed the previous fall because of cancer. Then he mentioned a book project. A photographer was going to take pictures of the Yakima valley, and Ray was going to write about growing up there. To refresh his memory, he wanted to visit some of the neighborhoods he'd lived in, places where he'd hunted and fished. He hoped to stop by in the near future, maybe on his way back east. "I'm doing pretty well," he said, "but I get tired."

A few months later I wrote Ray again, hoping to confirm the interview with our reporter. As with the phone calls, I was afraid that as a famous person Ray might consider me a pest. His reply was dated June 1:

Thanks for your letter. This is simply a little note. . . .

I wish I could meet up w/your reporter for an interview, but the truth is my health is none too good right now, and I am having—and wanting—to stay quiet as much as is possible these days. You may recall that I told you or at least I *think* I told you that I had lung cancer surgery last fall in Syracuse. Well, I've had a recurrence of that so I've been taking radiation therapy treatments over in Seattle.

We rented ourselves an apartment, I took treatment five days a week, and we came here on weekends. It was a hard seven weeks, but it is over now, and I am on the road to recovery. But I did have to make an eight-day trip back east to pick up a doctor of humane letters degree—an honorary doctoral degree—at U. of Hartford and go on to N.Y.C. for induction into the American Academy, a couple of book signings, three interviews, and a reading. And I had asked that everything be kept to a minimum. Anyway I'm tired right now, Liggett, and don't have anything new to say. A profile did appear on me in the May 23 issue of *Publishers Weekly* and another profile with photo and talk of my upbringing . . . in the 31 May issue of the daily *NY Times* (yesterday). I will do an interview but I don't think this summer is the best time.

Best wishes,
Ray

On June 15, the Knight-Ridder news service sent out a long piece on Ray by Gail Caldwell of the *Boston Globe*. The next day I wrote him. I told him that two days after our phone conversation and mostly as a result of hearing about his surgery, I'd quit smoking (again). And I told him my doctor's wife was a big fan of his.

After consulting with the city editor, I made a suggestion. I told Ray that since it looked like it would be some time before he could get to Yakima, we could run the Caldwell piece in the meantime. To add some local flavor, we could accompany the article with a "First Person" column on him. I enclosed a "First Person" question-naire with my letter.

Ray sent back only one sheet of the three-page questionnaire. And he didn't answer all the questions on that sheet. For "first job" he wrote "picking hops, cherries, apples in the Yakima Valley." For "worst job," he wrote "the above." "Favorite childhood memory" and "favorite music" were left blank. For "favorite movie" and "favorite TV show" he just made a more or less horizontal mark with his pen. "Last book I read" was *Love in the Time of Cholera* by Gabriel García Marquez. Ray did write out his address, which surprised me, since this was for publication. In the space after "marital and family status" he wrote "married to Tess Gallagher (6-17-88) (!)." With the questionnaire came a letter dated June 21:

> Thanks for your good letter.... This is just a few quick lines.... I'd be pleased if you wanted to use the Gail Caldwell piece from the *Boston Globe;* I think it's a good piece.
>
> The book of photos by Bob Adelman & text by RC has pretty much fallen by the wayside.... Right now I'm under a three-book contract for poems, stories, and a novel or a book of memoirs, so I will stay with that....
>
> My health is more or less okay—stable—but I don't plan to do any moving around this summer....
>
> The book of stories is doing very well and is now into a second printing. The reviews have all been quite good, though of course I expect a sorehead to weigh in one of these days. But, in the meanwhile, I'll enjoy this while it's happening.
>
> Thanks again for your interest in doing something; I hope

something or another will work out.

If and when we get over to Yakima I'll look forward to seeing you. (I'll let you know when, if time.) If you don't hear further from me, it simply means I've disappeared into my work, or I/we didn't go anywhere.

In any event, this is with my good wishes.

Yours—
Ray C.

About this time the paper got a letter (also dated June 21) from a reader who sent along a clipping from the May 31 *New York Times*. The letter said, "I have never read anything in our local paper about Raymond Carver, who evidently spent his childhood in Yakima. This might make an interesting feature. He is well known in New York and his latest book is on the best-seller list." The managing editor brought the letter and clipping into the news room. When I heard him talking to the city editor about them, I mentioned our efforts to set up an interview.

We wondered why Ray hadn't completed the questionnaire, but we decided not to trouble him about it. We inserted into the Caldwell piece the facts that Ray was from Yakima and that he and Tess had gotten married.

The story appeared in our Sunday edition of July 10. I sent Ray a clipping with a note saying "At last!" or "Finally!" He answered with a postcard:

Many thanks! I'm very, very pleased that the paper ran the Caldwell piece. Good, good, good. And all thanks are due to you and your persistence. Thanks again. My health is still not so good so I can't make plans to come over, but I do hope we can get a trip on the books sometime or another & look forward to seeing you then. / Warmly, Ray

The card was dated July 15. Ray died on August 2. The reporter who had wanted to interview Ray wrote the story of his death for our paper. Some time after that, the city editor said he'd read some of *Where I'm Calling From* and allowed as how Raymond Carver was a pretty good writer.

When I got Ray's card I was pleased that he'd taken the time to send it, even though it wasn't necessary. And I thought he was a bit too generous with his credit for my persistence. I know now that Ray had more important things to do with the precious little time he had than to write me a postcard. But I guess that says a lot about the kind of person Ray was.

ROBERT COLES

American Light

During the past decade I have been calling upon novelists, short story writers, poets in the teaching I do at Harvard University. I am a physician, trained in pediatrics, child psychiatry, psychoanalysis. For twenty years my wife and I, with our children, lived as wandering "field-workers"—an effort to understand how children of various backgrounds grow up: black and white, southern and northern, those who live on Indian reservations, or in the Eskimo villages of Alaska, or up the hollows of Appalachia, or indeed, nowhere and everywhere, as boys and girls whose parents are migrant farm workers. Eventually, we worked with children abroad, in the *favelas* of Brazil, the various townships of South Africa, and the strife-ridden neighborhoods of Belfast, for example—in hopes of learning how young people caught in third world poverty, or in a kind of racial or religious conflict that dominates a country's political life, manage to figure out their loyalties, their aspirations, their values and ideals.

More recently, for about ten years, I have made a major commitment to teaching, a real pleasure and challenge. When I came back from the South to Boston (in 1966), after an eight-year spell of studying school desegregation and working in the sit-in movement, I studied with Erik H. Erikson, who had in his late middle age begun teaching at Harvard College. Erikson asked me to be one of his teaching assistants, and I gladly accepted the offer. He was interested in the relationship between psychoanalysis (his profession) and history—how our thoughts and interests are shaped not only by our early experiences but by the world we happen to inherit: our class and race and nationality and, not least, the time in which we live. He used much of his own writing, and that of other social scientists; but he did assign Ralph Ellison's *Invisible Man,* and he did allow each of us who taught the course's sections to come up with a book or two of our own as something for the students to read and discuss.

I still remember some of those sections, the way a story by Flannery O'Connor, say, or William Carlos Williams, caught the attention of the young readers, prompted in them a kind of discussion all its own: less attention, by far, to generalizations with respect to the psychology of "human development" or "psychohistory," and much time given to a contemplation of life's ironies, complexities, ambiguities, inconsistencies, paradoxes—the terrain of fiction, with its modest interest in rendering the concrete as faithfully and suggestively as possible. I still remember the braking influence of those stories on our conceptual energies, our desire to tuck into this or that generalization all we could grab in our hands. "The task of the novelist," Miss O'Connor had told us, "is to deepen mystery," and thereupon she added, pointedly: "But mystery is a great embarrassment to the modern mind." An embarrassment, for sure, to some of us eager, ambitious social and psychological theorists: as in "The Artificial Nigger," whose character, Mr. Head, is quite readily able to betray his own grandson for the pettiest of reasons (so much for all of our heady, self-important lives); and as in "The Lame Shall Enter First," which offers a psychologist of sorts who can't see how hurt and vulnerable his own son is, even as he seeks to work with a youth who has no use for him. In such stories the old adage that "pride goeth before the fall" gets worked into a narrative that turns out to be disturbing, indeed, to those late twentieth-century secular students, many of whom had never laid eyes on the Bible, even as they knew a lot about psychology and sociology not only through courses taken, but as one student told me, a memorable moment: "My folks brought us up on psychoanalysis and politics—that's what they believe in: you should have your head shrunk and you should try to change the world!" I was obviously not one to disagree—and yet: after the hundreds of analytic hours, and the various legislative victories (or the struggles on the streets that preceded and enabled them) there remains our rock-bottom humanity, with all the warts and larger that make us, always, less than perfect in the way we present ourselves to others.

By the early 1970s Erik H. Erikson had retired, and my wife and three sons and I were living in New Mexico, where I was talking with Spanish-speaking children and with children who lived on the Pueblo reservations north of Albuquerque. In 1975 we returned to New England, and it was then that I was offered a job at Harvard by the president, Derek Bok—to teach, as he put it in a letter to me, "what you want, where [in the university] you want." I knew I did not want to teach psychoanalytic psychiatry, no matter my respect for what it can offer particular individuals (in the right physician's hands, one wants to add immediately). I knew, actually, that I wanted to use fiction and poetry in my work with medical students and young doctors learning to be pediatricians or child psychiatrists; and I knew, too, that I wanted to teach undergraduates. Soon enough, then, I was offering a college lecture course, a freshman seminar, a "medicine and literature" course, and "supervisory seminars," as they are called, to psychiatric and pediatric residents. Across the board, I called upon William Carlos Williams: I had written my college thesis on the first two books of *Paterson,* had come to know him, and respect him, and seek his advice—and yes, follow his example by choosing a career in medicine. I called upon Chekhov and Tolstoy, old loves, and Tillie Olsen, whose stories meant a lot to me, and Flannery O'Connor, who had done so well as a disturber of the peace when I had taught for Professor Erikson. I called upon Walker Percy and Ralph Ellison and Zora Neale Hurston (then, in the middle seventies, far less well known than she is today). I called upon *Middlemarch* and *Great Expectations* and *Jude the Obscure*—and Simone Weil and Dorothy Day and James Agee and George Orwell; and I often added a poem of Philip Levine, whose work I have long much admired, a "son," in certain respects, of Dr. Williams—a big, generous heart that has been notably responsive to the lives of "ordinary" (so-called "working-class") American people.

I've tried hard not to grow old with those authors, those books alone. I've tried to meet others, get close to their writing, feel able to teach their stories, their poems—most recently, the work of Raymond Carver, who has been a mainstay of my teaching life, now, for over five years, to the point that I don't frankly know how

I did without him back in the seventies. I had read an occasional story of Carver's on my own, but I was introduced to his full range and power by a one-time student of mine, Jay Woodruff, who went on to attend the Iowa Writers' Workshop, become a short story writer, and also (for four years) work with me, help teach (and run) my college course. Jay knew how much time I'd spent talking with factory workers, with men and women who barely get by, who are nurses or automobile mechanics, who work in restaurants or hotels, who are struggling hard and long to pay their bills, to hold onto what they have, no matter the odds against them. He brought to my attention one Carver story after another, and soon I was exploring every square mile of Carver country, and eager to take with me my students.

I began by connecting Carver to one of his own heroes, William Carlos Williams. I asked students in my college lecture course to read Williams's "Doctor Stories" and his novel *White Mule,* then read Carver's stories, such as "Cathedral," "Vitamins," "What's in Alaska?", "Fat." The students really took to those stories—asked a lot of questions not only about them, but their author. We have about twenty-five sections (each with twenty members) in the course and we who teach found ourselves in our weekly discussions spending more and more time on Carver—on the way Carver gets so much going among all of us who read him. He became more than yet another author for us; he became the heart and soul of the course—an important writer, indeed, for a number of students, and their section leaders (not to mention me, who gives two lectures a week). When I read passages from the stories, in a lecture, or read from the personal essays, such as "My Father's Life" or "On Writing" or "Fires," I sometimes hear my voice crack; and I learn, afterwards, that a number of students had teared up, or had gone back to their rooms and read those passages again and again—and had wanted to talk and talk about them with their roommates and friends, or in the sections they attended. When I visit those sections (and I do so throughout the term), Carver is more on the minds of many of these young men and women than the other writers: he touches them, gives them pause, stays with them in a powerful way.

Moreover, he prompts those youths (so many of them lucky all their lives, at least with respect to the money and social position they can take for granted, or in hopes, soon enough, of being lucky) to stop and think about others, and not only a distant "them," living in another city, but men and women and children who live only a few blocks from important university buildings—indeed, even nearer than that, as one student reminded himself in an essay he wrote, and later, me, in a discussion we held during my office hours: "The people who keep this place running—they're out of Carver's stories. I worked a summer for 'buildings and grounds,' and we'd be raking or sweeping, and I'd hear them talk, and I realized, after a while, that they were really on the edge, those guys. They were up to their ears in debt, and there'd always be some trouble, it seemed—something that was about to pull the rug out from under them. There I was, making a few bucks for the summer, in between my sophomore and junior year at Harvard; and there they were, fighting disaster all the time, or just 'keeping even.' There was a guy who kept knocking on wood any time he talked about his life, his family, and himself, and if there wasn't any wood nearby, he'd go walk to find it—and he kept saying 'things are OK,' and 'we're keeping even, so far,' and he'd knock on wood, and I could see in his eyes that he was glad, but he didn't know how long his luck would hold out, and he was always expecting the worst. I kept thinking of him when I read Carver's stories—and when I'd see him, sometimes, I felt a little closer to him. I mean, he wasn't this stranger, who seemed to be a big worrier—that's how I first saw him. He was a guy who I understood a little now: he was trying to steer clear of trouble, but he sure didn't have much leverage on life, and so he was running scared!"

Somehow, for that student, as for others, Carver's stories enabled a leap out of one world, into another—not an immersion, but a sense of how it goes, walking in other shoes as a result of such conversations. I decided three years ago to offer a freshman seminar devoted to Carver alone, so far as reading goes. I titled the seminar "American Light," with this subtitle: "Raymond Carver's Writing and Edward Hopper's Paintings." I gave this description of what we'd try to do: "Members of the seminar will examine these [books and paintings] separately and together as a means of thinking about the lives of America's twentieth-century working-class people. All of Carver's fiction and essays, and much of his poetry, will be read. The seminar will look closely at selected Hopper paintings and drawings. Members of the seminar will discuss contemporary American working-class culture, its characteristics and its values, as narrated by a master American storyteller and as glimpsed by a master American artist. The tradition of documentary observation and research will be discussed to provide a context for the lessons Carver and Hopper offer with respect to the lives of ordinary working-class Americans—their routines and habits, their goals and aspirations, their values, the moral complexities and ambiguities of their lives."

Such flat, stilted academic language notwithstanding, the ten or so students and I have had quite a time each autumn, once a week for several hours, reading those stories, talking about them, sharing with one another what they have caused us to think about, remember, notice, ask of ourselves and others. I'm no great one for "deconstruction"—I share Carver's bold suggestion that it may be a kind of lunacy. But I love reading him carefully, closely—noticing moments, scenes, images, words I'd missed the first or second time around. I love imagining the people he has created—their looks, their surroundings. In my thoughts, I start with Carver's descriptions, then amplify, sometimes out of clear memories I have of others: people I've gotten to know doing my "fieldwork"—meaning fellow human beings I've visited in their homes, sat with, the television on, now and then my tape recorder also on, or people I've heard talking in offices or stores or factories or hotels or bars, people who have spoken of how it goes for them in this life. (When such "fieldwork" ends and "life" begins might be described in the pompous literature of social science as a "methodological issue"!) So with the students—I encourage them to make friends with Carver's stories, read them for pleasure, for the education about the world to be had, for the wisdom they offer. I encourage them to meet his longtime companion, Tess Gallagher, to read her poems and stories, and to meet his two friends, Richard Ford and Tobias Wolff, to read their stories. I encourage them to learn to be as watchful as Carver was, and to enjoy his plain yet magically suggestive language. I encourage them to let his cast of mind inform what used to be called their "sensibility"—the shrewd and knowing clarity of vision that helps us comprehend the confusions, the mix-ups, the perplexities that present themselves to us during this time spent here called "life." I encourage them to stick fast to those stories, to take them on as companions or friends, as warnings, as reminders, as teachers. Needless to say, what I urge of them, I try hard to keep in mind for myself. I know we are all getting some-place when a student will say (it keeps happening, repeatedly, each year): "This Carver, he's really something." What follows is not an outburst of cleverness, a "text" analyzed, words and more words devoted to big-deal abstractions, but silence, and the nods of us who have also begun to know just that, and to talk in moments as this guy who has become a presence of sorts in our lives used to talk, and maybe even, to think as he used to think.

I've gone elsewhere with Carver—to medical students at Harvard and at Dartmouth medical schools. In those places I teach some-thing called "medical humanities"; that is, my old hero and friend Doc Williams, and Tillie Olsen and Tolstoy and Walker Percy and Carver's hero Chekhov, and Carver himself: "A Small, Good Thing," obviously, and "Errand" and "Cathedral," and his last poems, such as "What the Doctor Said" and "Gravy" and "After-Glow" and "No Need," but also some others, such as "Poem for Hemingway and W.C. Williams" (I love it) and "The Mailman as Cancer Patient" and "Alcohol" and "Your Dog Dies"—as many of them as I can work into the time I have. I get excited, really turned on, trying to figure out how to introduce a particular poem, how to bring it to those soon-to-be doctors in such a way that the language, the sights and sounds, will stick fast and long to minds filled to the brim with the fearful or foreboding factuality of those big fat medical textbooks.

So many of Carver's stories tell of the trouble people have in understanding one another: remarks that are heard the wrong way; silences that won't yield to a reasonably pleasant exchange; out-right battles that are, really, in their sum, the last straw, the final good-bye for people supposedly so close by virtue of blood, or the past intimacy of sex, or marriage. Again and again, misunderstand-ings are evoked, small and large, and we become sad, or we shudder, aware that we run our own risks along similar lines. Doctors, especially, in their work, struggle to make themselves clear—and so often, fail miserably, out of their own fear and anxiety, out of callousness, out of simple human error, out of the limitations imposed by their inevitably flawed humanity. Still, we ought keep trying to reach out, to connect with those others who get called patients in such a way that we have a good idea what we intend to convey, and then offer our words in a manner that enables the person addressed to get our intended message. If the immediately foregoing is a bit didactic or hectoring, the reason may have to do with the precariousness of a doctor's situation, not to mention that of patients: they are desperately seeking clues, not to mention reassurance, hope; and they will, often enough, take what they've heard and tailor it to their urgent needs, their craving, even as some of us physicians are tempted to appease at all costs those we fear to disappoint, or, too, are tempted to hide from them with inscrutable phrases or the inscrutability of our manner, our mien. Our arrogance can measure fear or the apprehension of a coming defeat, even as a patient's pleadings, become importunate demands, can measure a hunch that soon it may well be over for good—all of which Carver knew to work into some of his poems and stories: a wonderfully thought-provoking gift to a profession he, alas, like Chekhov, came to know too well, as a patient, far too early in life. Speaking of Chekhov, my medical students find "Errand" especially stirring—and some wonder whether a glass of champagne might be exactly what certain patients and their close kin need to share with their physicians at a certain point in time— even as those students, too, wonder how they, as future doctors, might somehow become the kind of baker who sat with the heartbroken father and mother in "A Small, Good Thing," fed them, helped drain their anger, their bitterness, their rage: a communion, a taking of "bread and wine."

I've brought Carver to other students, to a class I gave, one spring, at Duke University's Center for Documentary Studies— those stories, again, as a way of seeing the world, taking note of dozens and dozens of social variations: the subtleties of class and region that inform our lives, given shape by someone with a keen ear for language, a wide-eyed responsiveness to a broad segment of America's people. I've brought Carver, also, to the psychiatric residents I get to teach. Sometimes, as I listen to them talking about their patients, I ask them to read one of Carver's stories, such as "What We Talk About When We Talk About Love" or "Elephant" or "Neighbors" or "Why Don't You Dance?"—and we have quite a time of it. These young psychiatrists, occasionally, are all too condescending. At first, how "intuitive" the writer is, I hear them say to one another, to me—as if he has almost approached *their* level of psychological savvy. After a while, though, such gratuitous compliments (a masquerade for a put-down) yield to a growing respect, and in turn, a sense of awe, of enormous admiration. I have sat with these psychiatrists, at moments, in a hushed silence, watched them as they shake their heads: an acknowledgment of a particular writer's extraordinary grasp of the mind's life—its capacity for aspiration, for survival, and its more than occasional moments of self-deception, meanness, despair.

Not rarely I work with graduate students, some of whom teach in my course. I ask them (I ask myself) to pick up "The Student's Wife" now and then, reflect upon all it has to say. When I read it, I remember Doc Williams giving me lectures on the distinction between "big-shot learning," as he put it, and "our daily conduct." Throughout *Paterson* he reminds us (sometimes confessionally) that one can be learned, indeed, gifted with the muse, a great success, and not necessarily a kind and thoughtful person. That story of Carver's, for me, belongs with Chekhov's "Anyuta," with his "Two Tragedies," with Williams's moments of Augustinian self-scrutiny in *Paterson,* with Tolstoy's *Confession,* with Walker Percy's observations in *Lost in the Cosmos* as well as *The Moviegoer* and *The Last Gentleman.* To read Rilke and be unable to meet the challenge a marriage presents is to be yet another bright failure, and so it can go for any of us.

Teaching Raymond Carver, for me, has meant calling upon a great storyteller in order to bestir both my students and myself: that we look inward and outward, both; that we try to extend the range of our social vision, but also, our moral empathy; that we try to understand how pitiable any of us can be, how isolated and lonely (as in many of Hopper's paintings—such a strange congruence, their vision and Carver's), but that we also remember those daily, unheralded breakthroughs which, finally, give us human beings what dignity we can achieve, as in those closing moments of

"Cathedral," moments worth textbooks of psychology and philoso-phy. Teaching Raymond Carver has meant, I now realize, learning about how to teach, and yes, how to be: we all, so often, as in "Cathedral," are the blind leading the blind, yet we can and do enable sight, even elicit the visionary in one another—our only hope, one another. Teaching Raymond Carver has meant glimpsing lots of flaws in myself, yet feeling stronger for partaking of the wonderful feast this exceptionally talented twentieth-century writer has left us: a large and great thing, his books, their astonishing, compelling wisdom as it slowly, modestly unfolds, nourishes and sustains and inspires us fragile, thirsty, hungry, ever so needy readers.

STEPHEN HUNT

Stories Change You

I decided to camp, and started walking uphill out of Port Angeles, headed for Black Rock. I wore sandals that day. The big Mexican lunch and mug of draft bogged me down.

It was uphill, away from the water, all the way up Seventh Street. The day was bright and breezy.

A walking day, on any other day.

I passed a Salvation Army Thrift Shop. Might be runners in there. It was a salvage mission, but it beat walking uphill in sandals. I went in.

I found a pair of used hiking boots that fit. They were wrecks, really, mud-caked and stiff. One was split open at the toe. They had been worn to work, to somebody's job. They were a dollar. I could squeeze two more days out of them.

I bought them.

I sat on the sidewalk outside the Sally Ann lacing up those worthless boots. It was maybe three in the afternoon. With no lantern, I was looking at an early night, but that was fine. I'd been up, on the road and then on water, since before dawn.

I felt lunatic, a little life-is-wild. What I had done wasn't explainable, not in the way many things are. The dead man was someone I didn't know; I had traveled to bury a stranger.

Now I was lacing on someone else's boots.

This was lunatic too, wasn't it?

This was crazy talk.

Watching me from the driver's side of a nondescript silver sedan, a blonde in Ray-Bans munched a nectarine.

A babe.

She smiled.

She got out of the car, walked around to the trunk and flipped it open.

She wore a T-shirt and khaki dungarees. The kind of clothes you can sleep in and still wear the next day.

She took a second look.

The voice-over narrator that accompanies me everywhere on my travels cranked itself up for some hard-boiled remarks about the way her legs looked in the Port Angeles sunshine.

I stuffed it back where it came from. Voice-over narrators were for later, when you see all the scenes and they don't add up.

This was life in the present tense.

"Know the way to Black Rock?" I asked.

"No, but I've got a map," she said. "We could look it up."

She found the map in the glove compartment and opened it onto the passenger seat. Using her index finger, she scanned the area around Port Angeles.

I noticed she'd had some trouble with her skin. It had a pock-marked texture to it. She had a jaw like a quarterback.

She was OK.

"It doesn't have to be Black Rock," I said.

The day before, I was eating a salmon sandwich and reading the paper when I saw in a one-inch-by-one-inch box that he died.

I finished the sandwich, packed the suit, some shoes, and a sleeping bag.

I planned on hitching from Vancouver to Seattle, then seeing about catching something to Port Angeles. I was short of money that summer.

I rode city buses for over an hour, past Burnaby, past Surrey, past White Rock.

"Camping trip?" the bus driver asked, seeing my pack.

"Funeral, actually," I said. "One of my favorite writers died."

"One of mine just died too," the bus driver said. "Louis L'Amour?"

"The Western writer," I said.

I walked through the Peace gardens and into America. I found the interstate entrance out of Blaine. It said no walking or hitching on the interstate. I set up shop there, waiting to hook a lift to Seattle.

I'd done it before. I'd done LA to Vancouver. Hell, I'd done Laredo to Winnipeg, Montreal to New York, Athens to Hamburg through the Eastern European countries.

I had faith in myself to get lucky when I needed to.

An hour and a half later, it was getting dark.

I couldn't get a ride.

I went into a saloon and drank a beer.

I went back out and stood by the interstate, talking to my voice-over narrator.

It wasn't supposed to be this way.

This wasn't the script.

Then I remembered the ferry.

There was ferry service from Vancouver Island to Port Angeles.

I phoned up Black Bart's in Victoria and asked for information. There were all kinds of boats.

"I remember Black Rock," she said. "I used to live around here, but not for a while."

"Black Rock," she said, tapping the map for emphasis.

"I was going to camp there," I said.

"Straight up Seventh," she said. "Gets you there."

"Give me a lift?"

"I was going to take a look," she said, indicating the Sally Ann.

"I'm here for a funeral," I said.

"That's at four, right?"

"It's over. It was at one. I was late myself. But I caught the last twenty minutes."

"Shit, you're kidding me," she said. "I tried renting a car all morning in Seattle and couldn't get one. Don't tell me I missed it. How was it?"

Now it was time for the voice-over narrator.

You arrive on the morning ferry. You walk the streets, looking for a dry cleaner, or at least lunch. You see a bookstore and go in. You find a paperback copy of *What We Talk About When We Talk About Love*. You decide to buy it. You take it to the counter, your

voice-over narrator congratulating you on your ability to act sym-
bolically.

You make a mental note to ask about a dry cleaner.

"His funeral starts in ten minutes," the clerk says.

ASSHOLE, your voice-over narrative hisses.

"Where?"

The funeral is out of town, up the hill. The only way to get there
is by cab.

You rush out of the bookstore, looking for a cab.

There are no cabs in Port Angeles.

There is no time to consider the options. The funeral is about to
start. You came without asking. You either make it or you don't.

You run around downtown Port Angeles in sandals, motioning
for people to roll down their windows.

It is a small town. People roll down their windows.

"Can you give me a ride to the cemetery?" you ask. "I'm late."

Everyone says they are going the other way, as if that were the
only thing preventing them from helping you.

A cab arrives and drives you up the hill. The cabdriver says he
knew of the man, that he understood he was a good man, but
private.

"His people protected him," he says.

You wish he would drive faster.

The cab arrives up the mountainside. You pay the driver. He
points across the cemetery, over by the bluff, on the edge of the
cliffs. A tiny crowd has gathered.

"There it is," he says.

We drove downtown to a coffee shop. One of those quaint places,
with doilies everywhere and many kinds of soup.

Her name was Rocky. She was substitute teaching in LA, but
decided to head back to Nantucket, where she'd spent some time.
She was visiting friends in Seattle when she read about his death.
She'd been meaning to get over to Port Angeles anyway, to clear
something up—sounded like some boyfriend issue—and this happened.

She knew it was time, then, to drive over.

"Did you know him?" she asked. "Did you study with him?"

"No."

"So, do you want to go up to Black Rock?" she asked again. "I'll drive you."

"Actually, I'd rather do something with you," I said.

We bought a six-pack of Extra Old Stock at a supermarket, some pistachios, grapes, and yogurt.

The Pacific Northwest is religious in its beauty. The scale of everything is at a level that surpasses anything human. It's not like the Northeast, where the rolling gradients, the climate—it all fits nicely within a real estate developer's framework of how nature should work.

In the Northwest you go for a drive and almost die seven times.

We stopped at a small campground. I kept referring to the tent I had, remarking that we had everything we needed. I didn't know if I was implying seduction or not.

I suspect I was.

There were no campsites available. Families were set up, barbecues hot. A fair amount of beer was being drunk. It was August; half the nation was perched on the western edge of the country, hoping to catch a breeze. There was nothing remote about that place, not in August.

Rocky didn't seem concerned. "Can always sleep in the car," she said. "Do it all the time." She did not seem to imply seduction. She acted as though my presence there was somewhat accidental, a happy coincidence.

We climbed down a cliff and sat right out on an inlet, where you caught spray when a wave crashed into rock.

Rocky was half-Mexican, half-Swedish. She grew up in Bonsall, on the Mexico-California border. Her dad was long gone. Her mom lived with her brother, who was agoraphobic. He wouldn't leave the house. He just lived in the basement.

Her mom grew rhubarb.

"Hey, we used to have rhubarb in our backyard," I said. I was searching for a connection. Anything would do.

I put my arm around her.

Her body stiffened, holding out against my attempt at intimacy. She didn't say anything, but you could tell I'd made a mistake.

Another mistake.

I acted as if everything was perfectly normal.

You run across the cemetery, towards the funeral of someone you've never met.

It is a small gathering, friends and family. There will be no blending in with the crowd today.

You walk the final few steps up to the group. It is bizarre, this collision of slapstick and tragedy. From wishing the cabdriver would go faster to wishing someone wasn't dead. It trips you up.

You wait for them to look up, to question you with their eyes, but no one does.

You want to explain this, to make it right. You want them to know what it meant to read his stories.

If it was closer to town, you'd walk back now.

But town is ten miles down a mountain.

Maybe you can get a ride, save the fare.

Tess reads "Gravy," one of the last poems he was working on. Years earlier, he thought he was dead. He'd drank so much and smoked thousands of smokes. The doctors told him he was done.

He quit drinking. He was allowed ten more years. Ten years of work, a great love, the bonus of recognition.

After what he'd been expecting, everything was extra.

It was all gravy.

They lower the box into the ground.

An announcement is made that everyone is welcome to come to Tess's place.

You don't belong there.

In Vancouver, you considered calling a friend, to drive down together on a motorcycle. But you didn't. It seemed wrong, somehow. Turning it into a road trip like that held the threat of turning the story into an anecdote. Like Ouisa said in *Six Degrees of Separation:* "How do we fit what happened to us into life without turning it into an anecdote? . . . We become these human jukeboxes spilling out these anecdotes. But it was an experience. How do we *keep* the experience?"

You can't share your experience of someone's stories. Stories change you. They're one-on-one. You hear them, and the world you knew tilts in some new way. How do you explain that to your bus driver?

In the same way, there is no point going to Tess's house, drinking her drinks and eating her crackers and cold cuts.

A reporter for the local paper asks who you are.

You offer to tell him on the drive back to town.

We returned to the car. I thought about asking some campers if I could set up the tent, but didn't ask. Truth was, I'd never set that tent up before. I wanted to be the man who went off and camped alone, but I was useless that way. I liked a coffee shop in the morning. I liked getting the scores from the paper.

Rocky said it was no problem for me to sleep in the car.

We drank the rest of the Old Stock and ate pistachio nuts. I told her about the television show I'd been developing in Canada. I was on the verge of landing a series pilot. The problem with me, I said, was that I was a television writer *at heart*. It's one thing for TV writing to rob you of your soul, I said. It's another sad situation altogether when it *is* your soul.

She talked in a more literary mode. She airbrushed her stories with melancholy. She was a drifter.

I was a drifter too but felt this to be less an honorable status—the status of Kerouac, Bowles, Bukowski, Burroughs, Corso, and Carver—than a failure of character.

Something I should get over.

I waited for her to suggest I accompany her to Nantucket.

I wanted to accompany her to Nantucket.

"Well," she said, staring out into the swing sets rattling in the night wind. "I'm just gonna pee."

"Me too," I said.

Rocky got in the backseat. I stayed in front. I'd just done a road trip—Winnipeg-Chicago-Montreal-Winnipeg—with my buddy Larry. Our routine was that he slept in back and I in front. I was the shorter of the two, so the steering wheel wasn't such a hassle.

"Good night," I said.

No response.

"You should come back here," she said. "You might gouge yourself."

The difference between men and women: women take longer to decide. They don't necessarily think different thoughts.

I thought she wanted to switch seats.

"That's OK," I said. "I'm used to sleeping in front."

The next morning, after we'd gotten lost on those back roads looking for a fine breakfast and ended up in a diner; after she'd made a joke about me driving with her to Nantucket and I'd let the comment hang there like a fat lob, waiting to see what she'd do with it (she changed the subject); after I'd decided to be sensible and return to Vancouver to write my thesis and meet sensible, rooted women (and Rocky muttered about her need "to clear a few things up"; otherwise she'd love to spend more time with me); after all this, we stood on the road by the ferry, ten minutes before departure.

I felt relieved.

Things were a little out of control. This death, this trip, this woman—I couldn't have planned any of it. It unnerved me that life could spin away from you like that.

The first time I read one of his stories, I was up in the library of the University of Winnipeg, leafing through *Best of the Small Presses,* when a siren sounded. There'd been a bomb threat.

A door flew open and we evacuated onto the mall below. It was a beautiful spring afternoon. The speculation was that it was a prank to disrupt the exam schedule.

Rather than return the book to the library, I took it. I never took a book before.

I read the stories sequentially, starting with the first one. I didn't recognize the names of the authors.

One stood out. The voice I recognized.

The story was about the Memorial Day fishing trip three old friends take every year. They discover the dead body of a girl down by the river. Rather than report the accident right away, they wait, so as not to spoil the weekend. The one man's wife learns of this, and it ruins her view of her husband.

It changes everything.

It was so unsettling.

"Well, I'll see you, Rocky," I said. "I'm sure, somewhere I'll see you."

The weather had deteriorated since the previous day. It was a dark and stormy morning. She wore a V-necked sweater, I remember. A kind of khaki or brown thing.

She held me against that sweater and I pulled on her ribs and kissed her. I kissed her with a passion. I wanted, through that kiss, to make up for the mishaps and half-efforts that seemed to plague me. You drift because you lack an anchor. My kiss was my offering, my flowers, my poem, my condolence.

How do you grieve?

How do you say you miss someone?

You miss the stories they used to tell?

The kiss came out of nowhere, it held, and we felt no urgency to cut it short.

We just kept kissing.

GARY FISKETJON

Salt Water and Fresh

"Hope this finds you well and all" is how Raymond Carver began so many of his letters to his friends, and by saying, "All's well here," or "We're fine." For the last decade of his life we mostly were, as were he and the poet Tess Gallagher, his boon companion and then wife. This was something of a miracle, of course, and none of us is willing to admit that it has ended. "Meanwhile," as a woman says in one of Ray's early stories, "the people around you continue to talk and act as if you were the same person as yesterday, or last night, or five minutes before, but you are really undergoing a crisis, your heart feels damaged. . . ."

I first heard his voice in 1978. In his first letter to me Ray wrote, "I must say I don't feel I've even begun to hit my stride yet, and the next two years are going to be extraordinary for me; and I mean that." Ray was wrong about not yet hitting his stride, but the next *ten* years were even more extraordinary for him. If only I'd been closer to right in 1987, when as his publisher I wrote that his career should reach as far into the future as it already extended into the past. That it now cannot is an incalculable sorrow, although it is equally obvious to those who knew him or read him that Ray Carver will be around far longer than any reckoning in years.

Much has been written about his two lives—one comprised of alcohol and bitter frustration, the next of joyful sobriety and mounting acclaim. And indeed Ray often remarked on this, even on the date, June 2, 1977, when his sea-change began. But such a commemoration is just that, a marker of sorts, and I suspect his lives mingled together like salt water and fresh where the river meets the sea. Excitement and disappointment and accomplishment moved in either direction; one life could not have existed without the other, and neither was without the acts of courage that eventually made so much possible for him. I knew Ray only after his great personal triumph, but like anyone who reads his work I know those earlier times as vividly as a trance or a nightmare.

"Beats all I saw or heard of, this life," he said in the early eighties, after things were going his way, and specifically on a rainy, cabless Manhattan evening when heading home after midnight we'd hailed and were taken up in a decrepit limousine. The driver's irrepressible nature and simple kindness made us feel that *anything* was possible and that the two of us were as far from Oregon, where we both came from, as Dorothy ever was from Kansas. Thereafter we frequently referred to this Mr. Walker, an unwitting personification of wonders randomly available, almost as a character in a story we couldn't believe was happening to us.

And whatever wonders were offered—to himself, his friends, those he admired—Ray willingly, delightedly received, including some that most of us would have called cold comfort. He was an enthusiast. As he told the *Paris Review,* when as a boy he'd mistakenly submitted his first story to the circulation department of an outdoors magazine, "The piece came back, finally, but that was fine. It had gone out into the world, that manuscript—it had been places." And later, when his work was first accepted for publication, a poem and a story on the same day: "It was a terrific day! Maybe one of the best days ever."

Throughout his first forty years there were also many black days, when the temptation to give in to despair must have been overwhelming. His father before him, toward the end of *his* life, broke down utterly, reduced for a time to mute silence and an empty room. Having stepped into such a place, one can never leave it entirely behind. This is the room where many of Ray's characters find themselves, and doubtless where he imagined finding himself too many times to even think about. In fact, when told that Richard Brautigan was reported to have shot himself, Ray wrote me, "Even if he did it, it was the booze thing, sure. I entertained that same way out myself on many occasions, back in those dark days."

But he saved himself, never forgetting what it's like to have no prospects whatever. For that matter, how many of his characters fold at this point? This is the moment of truth, and it's where his work puts us. He didn't flinch, and his characters stare without blinking. The challenge, then, is what to make of diminished things and intolerable events. What are we, any of us, going to do about that? What Ray did about it was to write, which he lived to do. "Working, praise be," was a refrain in his letters. "At my station." He took more pride in his work than in how it was received, and he suffered no illusions about his calling. "Nobody ever asked me to be a writer," he said.

He also filled a room with a spirit to match his considerable size. Giving someone a leg up or a kind word, congratulations or consolation, loyalty and kindredness ... these acts and qualities *were* Ray, and he showed them countless times—in a letter, a phone call, a packet of smoked salmon sent through the mail. Which is not to suggest he was always merry and bright, or that he didn't worry, even brood, over what might go wrong for him, his friends, those he admired. "It can't be good," he'd say. Around 1983 he wrote me, "There's so much to do, and I wasted so many years." After that, death was more frequently the subject of his fiction and poetry, and of course of "Errand," the last story he published.

"A light can go out in the heart"—a line from a story by his best friend. And it has. But Raymond Carver seized so many hearts that this is hardly surprising. As the epigraph for his last book of stories, Ray chose the following lines from Milan Kundera's *The Unbearable Lightness of Being*: "We can never know what to want, because, living only one life, we can neither compare it with our previous lives nor perfect it in our lives to come." In fact, I think he came as close as humanly possible to proving Kundera wrong. Ray was able to compare, to re-create, and to damn near perfect.

BIBHU PADHI

Something Else
Remembering Raymond Carver

There's always something else to these lines,
always someone behind you, watching.

You, and the women and men who're elsewhere, sharing
our children's request to be near them, always.

The things that you use every day
without prior thought, the bed on which

every night you await your sleep,
your very own hours of the night,

your ill-timed sleep, desired rest of a lifetime—
there's always something else to these,

something other than ourselves
or objects we pretend to possess.

There're times when we feel something else
slowly coming to its fruition and flourish

through us, accomplishing its greenness
in the leaves' abandon, smiling

through the lean dead branches of an old
banyan tree, now waiting for its conclusion.

At the end of a period of defiant cheer, when
we lie exhausted, thinking what other line

might return us our plain human pride,
it hangs above us, smiling at our absences.

Who are we to think of others, anyway,
or even about ourselves, our children and friends,

our days and nights? It seems
all of them belong elsewhere, only

faintly nurturing that place's true character,
maturing into nothing beyond their own frail forms.

Something is always missing in the things
we use, the persons we care for—

something that teases us to believe
that we've come to the very end of things

in its absence, amid its withdrawing ways.
Something which caused these lines,

pushed every word to a place that was
a lie long before it took its stanzaic place.

At this moment, elsewhere, a lone house sparrow
is calling out for someone who isn't

anywhere around, a slight voice speaking to
itself, consuming each moment of its mistaken time.

We know, it's always something else,
something other than the words in these lines.

PART VII

Syracuse, New York

1989

BARRY SPACKS

Carver's Medallion

An ax hacks a dumbhead block
and a blade makes shape, the way old friends talk
for the talk's sake, no thought obscure,
the chisels quibbling *so . . . so . . .*
their fine points smoothing the hard wood's flow
till the inborn turn of the grain runs sure
contour into contour.

TOBIAS WOLFF

Appetite

Raymond Carver was my dear friend, and I still feel his presence in my life. I hope and trust I always will. It was Ray who gave me the news that my first son was born, and Ray and Tess Gallagher who sat up all night with that boy while the second was coming into the world. We taught together for years. He brought me to Syracuse, found us our house, helped me with my work. Many of my friends were Ray's friends too, and I hear him sometimes in their voices as they must hear him in mine.

I haven't been eager to write about Ray. Writing about him involves a sustained recognition, which I've been pretty good at avoiding, that he's gone. And there is no way of containing him in words—he was too big, too various, there was too much of him. But I knew Ray at a good time, by his own reckoning the best of times, when he had broken free of a life that almost destroyed him and was making a life of dignity, honor, and joy. What I want to do here is remember a few moments of that time, without any wish to represent them as the whole. This is not a summing up, nor a eulogy. Ray never said good-bye to me and I'm not ready to say good-bye to him.

We first crossed paths in Palo Alto in 1976, though later on he had no memory of it. That was natural enough—my reason for remembering the occasion was better than his. *Will You Please Be Quiet, Please?* had just come out. I'd read some of the stories before, and admired them, but reading them ensemble was a different experience, both humbling and exhilarating. Taken together, these stories gave a new picture of America, in a voice never heard before. Their

humanity and exactitude and elusive humor, the music they found
in ordinary speech—in the very failures of ordinary speech—
moved me powerfully. He was clearly a master. Moreover, he was a
master of the form that was my own passion, and in which I had
just begun to do work I liked well enough even to put in the
mailbox.

I was teaching at Stanford then, and Ray was living somewhere
nearby. We'd turned up at a few of the same parties but had never
actually spoken. Even if we had he probably wouldn't have remembered, because these were serious, take-no-prisoners parties
that often went on for days if the police didn't shut them down first,
and he was in the darkest hours of his drinking then. Liquor had a
grip on Ray, and you could almost feel the strength of that grip from
the look of him. He seemed restless, queasy. His skin was chalky,
his eyes deep-sunk and watchful, not with the bright Chekhovian
alertness of later years but in a nervous, narrow way—a narrow-
ness emphasized by thick sideburns that obscured the natural
openness of his face. He bore his great size with an air of discom-
fort, even apology. His friends called him Running Dog.

When I think of Ray, I think of appetite. Even then, before I knew
him, I was struck by it. He always had something going—a drink, a
cigarette, a piece of food. At a particularly wild birthday party, a
party where a childless woman was discovered trying to nurse
someone else's baby, Ray and a friend of his stole the cake and ate
the whole thing by themselves, in a car outside. The birthday girl
shared an office with me. She complained bitterly for weeks afterward. After all, she had thrown this party and bought the cake
herself. She wanted to give Ray a piece of her mind. For some very
compelling reasons, one of them being the IRS, Ray was hard to get
in touch with then, but eventually she ran into him somewhere and
said, "We have to talk. We have to talk about the cake."

"There's nothing to talk about," Ray told her. "We already ate it."

Anyway, we didn't meet until later that year, when Grace Paley
and I were walking across the Stanford campus to a hall where she
was to read. Ray came up to us from a group of people waiting
outside. He was holding a cigarette and a Styrofoam cup. He
approached hesitantly. In a soft voice he said, "Grace? I'm Raymond Carver," and she immediately opened her arms and pulled

him close while I looked on from the infinite remove of my apprentice condition. Then we shook hands and exchanged names.

I have always been happy to remember that I met Ray in the presence of a conjurer named Grace.

I didn't see Ray again until January of 1978 when we were hired to teach at Goddard College in Plainfield, Vermont. The deal was, we'd spend two weeks on campus then and in July, and correspond with our students betweentimes. We lived in dormitories left vacant by students on their winter break. Goddard was an experimental college. It had a Marxist-Leninist dorm, a vegetarian dorm, a nudist dorm, a primal-scream dorm. Our dorm appeared to have been occupied by people whose therapy was to pour beer on rugs and steal lampshades. They were bleak quarters, and our suspicion that Plainfield was the coldest place in the world was confirmed one night, no kidding, by none other than Walter Cronkite.

Ray was pathetically equipped for this arctic expedition. He had no boots and no coat, only a thin leather safari jacket. His shoes were pinch-toed and flimsy and kept skidding on the ice. But he made it plain that he was glad to be there. He had stopped drinking some months earlier after a binge that nearly finished him off—a doctor told him his next drink would probably do the trick—and Goddard was his first job since, his first chance to prove himself as a sober man. After what Ray had just been through, this gig was a vacation, a trip to camp, and aside from the seriousness of his teaching, that was how he treated it, smuggling desserts out of the mess hall and sitting up all night spinning yarns.

We had plenty of other writers at Goddard with us: Stephen Dobyns, Robert Hass, Donald Hall, Louise Glück, Michael Ryan, Lisel Mueller, Heather McHugh, and Ellen Bryant Voigt. John Irving came through for a while, and Ray's great friend Richard Ford. My brother, Geoffrey, dropped by from his place in Warren. At night we gathered in the almost-comical squalor of the dorm lounge to try to make sense of the world, giddy as snowbound children. Ray and I generally stayed up after the others went to bed, Ray because of all the coffee he was drinking and I because of chronic insomnia. We talked about everything, no holds barred. For all the toughness Ray had needed to endure as a writer and a man, he was still boyish and fragile and alert to the fragility of others. He was also very, very funny. By the end of the residency we were friends.

But it wasn't staying up all night that made us friends, or being thrown together in peculiar circumstances. It was stories. Stories and storytelling. I don't mean only written stories, though that was certainly part of it. He responded generously to my work, and I still remember the excitement I felt hearing Ray read his own most recent stories, "Viewfinder" and "Why Don't You Dance?"—I still remember the conviction of being in the presence of something that was both fresh and certain to last, news that would stay news. As good as Ray's first book had been, these stories, both written since he'd stopped drinking, were even better—more luminous, mysterious, striking deep into the spirit.

But our friendship took root and afterward refreshed itself in the act of telling stories. Ray was a great storyteller. He spoke in a hushed voice that made you lean forward. Sometimes he stopped and glanced around, as if there might be spies present. He had the manner of one imparting confidences, as he sometimes did, his own and others'—but only after getting a strict promise that you keep them to yourself. His timing was flawless, his presence as comforting as the fire he and Tess kept burning in their living room from early September to late May.

And he was a great listener. His curiosity was almost predatory. He listened with his head cocked and a slight squint in one eye, like a man taking aim. There was a vibrancy to his listening, a quality of breathlessness, as if everything depended on what you might say next. He let his surprise show, and his enthusiasm, and his shock. "No!" he'd cry, "No!" and "Jesus!" and "You don't say!" At the moment of a particularly horrific revelation, he would shake his head and say, "It's a jungle out there, Toby, it's a jungle out there!"

Part of his achievement as a listener was to make you feel as if you could tell him anything without fear of judgment. He accomplished this by continually acknowledging his own complicity in this fallen creation, by refusing ever to take the moral high ground. He was entirely without pretense. The writer Jim Heynen once told Ray a story about something strange that had happened to him. As Jim was coming out of a bank, a bald eagle dropped a salmon bang on the hood of his car, which salmon Jim took home and ate. Not long after Jim told Ray this story he read a poem of Ray's in which an eagle drops a salmon at the poet's feet while he's out taking a walk. The poet cooks it up. Later Jim asked Ray about it, asked if by chance Ray had made use of his story. "Well, Jim," he said, "I guess I must have, because I don't take walks."

Ray had this bedrock honesty about himself, and the effect was that you could be equally honest. He took you as you were, with as little sanctity or heroism as you owned, so long as you did not pretend to more than you owned. I felt absolute freedom in his company. I could, and did, reveal anything—Ray had an insatiable hunger for stories on the human scale, stories about the endless losing war our good intentions wage against our circumstances and our nature. It was another aspect of the appetite that governed him. In fact, he was so greedy for these stories and so liberal in telling them on himself that one day I found myself confessing to something I hadn't done, just to keep up with him.

It happened like this. We were both living in Arizona then, Ray and Tess in Tucson, I and my wife, Catherine, in Phoenix. We used to visit back and forth. One night Ray and I were driving around somewhere, trading misdeeds from the past. Ray told some stories from his drinking days, and crowned them with an episode that happened when he was teaching at the University of Iowa some years earlier. John Cheever had been there at the same time, and they started drinking together. The writers and students in the program were concerned for them, to the point of regularly inviting them over for dinner to make sure they were getting something to eat. By the end of the year they had accrued some considerable debts of hospitality, which they proposed to mitigate by throwing a big party together. To this end they reserved a banquet room in the local Ramada Inn and sent out scores of invitations. As it happened, though, both of them had to leave town for a few days before the party, Cheever to the East Coast and Ray to California. They agreed to meet back in Iowa City the day of the party to make the final arrangements, but both of them got drunk and missed their planes, and that night the guests arrived in a room devoid not only of their hosts but also of food, drink, and music—a great Gobi Desert of a room.

He shook his head after telling me this and clucked in ritual disapproval of his old self, "Bad Ray," as he called him. I shook my head, too, while I tried to think of a topper—there was a competitive element in our storytelling, and where tales of former malfeasance were concerned I wasn't ready to take a backseat to anyone.

"Now, Ray, you've got to keep this to yourself," I said, not really knowing what I was going to tell him.

"Jesus, Toby, of course. Of course!" He leaned forward. "What? What is it?"

"This isn't something I want people to know about."

He nodded. He understood, but he was getting impatient for the product.

There's that old excuse we give for saying what we shouldn't, *The words walked right out of my mouth.* Well, these were the words that walked out of my mouth, and I watched them with complete surprise and horror: "Ray, I used to be a heroin addict."

"No! No, Toby!"

I couldn't stop myself. Ray's surprise and horror were even greater than my own, and I found them bracing, inspirational. Now, what I know about the ins and outs of heroin addiction can be engraved on the head of a pin. So I improvised. I let my invention run riot over Ray's credulity until I was satisfied that I had indeed topped him, and then I thought, My God, what am I doing? and clammed up, leaving Ray itching for more. But I kept quiet and made him promise once again not to tell anyone.

I brooded for weeks, until the next time I saw Ray. As soon as we were alone I told him there was something he should know.

"What's that, Toby?" He looked eager—possibly in expectation of further insider trading about "horse" and "nodding out" and "cold turkey."

When I told him that I had never been a heroin addict he just stared at me. I said that I was sorry, that I didn't know what had come over me to say such a thing.

He looked stricken. "Jesus," he said.

I started to apologize again, but he waved it away. He was silent for a time, mulling things over. Then he said he had a little confession of his own to make.

"What's that?"

He had told a few people. Actually, he said, he had told quite a few people. But he had pledged them all to secrecy, he added.

"No, Ray. You didn't."

He nodded. He was mortified with embarrassment, so much so that he couldn't take his eyes off the floor. I looked at the floor myself. "How many people?" I asked.

He shrugged.

We sat there for a while.

Then we started to laugh. I don't know which of us laughed first, but in a moment we were helpless with it, Ray bent double in his chair, pounding the floor with his feet, me howling and staggering and careening off the walls. I laughed until my cheeks were wet and every breath drew pain.

From that day on we never spoke of it, but now and then other people, some of them strangers, have given me cryptic words of sympathy and encouragement.

When Fitzgerald said there are no second acts in American life he was thinking about success, and a particular kind of success, the celebrity that arises not from talent alone but also from glamour and youth, and is therefore fated to pass and impossible to recover. In that sense he was right. But otherwise he was wrong. If we keep our eyes open we will all witness astonishing second acts, maybe even have one of our own. I've seen more than a few, and Ray's was among them.

He used to love to tell the story of Dostoevsky's last-minute reprieve from the firing squad: the condemned men weeping and embracing as the soldiers took up their positions, the officer calling out the last orders just as the czar's messenger rode up with the pardon. How one of the men was beyond the reach of mercy, having gone hopelessly mad under the strain. This episode later became the central moment in a movie script Ray wrote with Tess Gallagher. It interested him so much, I think, for the simple reason that he had been there himself, and in more ways than one. He had come very close to suffering not only physical death but also moral and spiritual annihilation. As he wrote in *Fires*: "The time came and went when everything my wife and I considered sacred, or considered worthy of respect . . . crumbled away."

Ray had been to the brink, and he had been spared. His consciousness of that release, and of its provisional nature, inclined him to view his life with amazement. He took nothing for granted. Every moment with friends, every fresh story and poem was a gift he hadn't counted on. The loving life he shared with Tess Gallagher, the respect his work inspired in all kinds of people—to Ray, these were miracles. He wore his honors more lightly than anyone I've known, and not by pretending they weren't there, or that they didn't matter to him. They did, very much; his appetite for praise was as uproarious as the rest of his appetites. (When I ran across a good review of his work that he hadn't yet seen he would ask me to come right over with it, then tear it from my hands. If he was out of town he would beg me to "Fed-Ex" it to him.) He wasn't particularly modest about his work either; he knew he was something special, had to have known it or he couldn't have survived all those years of almost nobody else knowing it. What made Ray's success so easy for others to take was the kindness it inspired in him. He was always trying to help someone find a job, or win a fellowship, or get a book into print. I never knew him to do a mean thing. Not once.

Ray was an artist, not a careerist, but he observed his own heady rise in the world with undisguised pleasure. He was too smart to be defined by the opinions of others, but smart enough to be glad when those opinions were good. At moments of particular happiness he would look around with pure wonder. "Things could be worse," he'd say.

He was right. Things could have been worse. And they got worse. But as bad as they got, he did not lose his sense of privilege at finding himself alive at all, and not only alive but blessed. The last poem in his last book, *A New Path to the Waterfall,* is an act of insistence on his right not to be pitied.

LATE FRAGMENT

And did you get what
you wanted from this life, even so?
I did.
And what did you want?

To call myself beloved, to feel myself
beloved on the earth.

Ray did not get smaller as he suffered; he got bigger. He wouldn't like being described in heroic terms, that kind of language bored him, but the truth is that in the last months, as his cancer grew worse, he did what heroes do. He went into the shadowlands— "reached through to the other side," as he says in his poem "Another Mystery"—and brought back to the rest of us what he had learned there. Ray's work had always been conditioned by his sense of mortality, most often felt as an atmosphere of malign possibility, but in his last stories and poems he dragged the beast out of the corner and stared it in the face. And the result of these encounters was not cynicism or despair but increase of appetite— appetite for love, for adventure, for friendship, for knowledge, for work, for more life. In *A New Path to the Waterfall* he's grabbing everything in sight, stories told him by local workmen, passages from Chekhov's stories and letters, poems by other writers, all disposed through the book in such a way that his own poems become a part of a conversation, a community of voices. Through his customary greedy alertness he is making his world bigger by finding more of it to wonder at.

That was how he responded to fear.

I'd seen this before, during a trip we took to Rhode Island, to go sailing with Richard Ford and my brother, Geoffrey, on Geoffrey's new boat, *Blackwing*. This venture had been planned as a kind of piratical excursion. There was a lot of bravura threat and swagger about coming into Block Island under the Jolly Roger, sacking the town, generally demonstrating what rakehell fellows we were. As it happened, there was no wind at all except what came out of our mouths, and we limped into the harbor with sails furled, in a cloud of exhaust. As for making the locals tremble, we did throw rocks at a water fountain—for which we were scolded—and Richard sent back his dinner that night. Otherwise we didn't make much of an impression. In fact, we might have been mistaken for a bunch of rollicking burghers too happy to be dangerous, satisfied just to be with good friends on a sunny weekend.

Ray and I headed back on Sunday afternoon. When we hit the

Mohawk Valley that evening a dense fog was rising up off the fields and the river, pouring out of the ditches and across the road. The sky turned black. The air was clammy and still. Then it began to hail, and the hail turned to blinding rain, and lightning struck all around us. It was close; the thunder followed almost without pause. I felt a stinging freshness when I breathed. I pulled the car onto the shoulder. I couldn't see a thing except when the lightning struck. Then the whole world seemed to jump.

"Jesus," Ray said. "Think we're okay, Toby?"

I said I thought we were probably fine. Ray said that with four rubber tires under us we had to be safe. But he didn't sound convinced, and I wasn't, either. Shave my hairy chest, but lightning scares the hell out of me. Ray was scared, too, at first, but he distracted himself by shouting his admiration whenever a big one landed nearby. He was like someone paying tribute to a great performance.

"Isn't it *something?*" he kept saying—"Isn't it *something?*"

HAYDEN CARRUTH

Ray

How many guys are sitting at their kitchen tables
    right now, one-thirty in the morning, this same
time, eating a piece of pie?—that's what I
    wondered, a big piece of pie because I'd just
finished reading Ray's last book. Not good pie,
    not like my mother or my wife could've
made, but an ordinary pie I'd just bought, being
    alone, at the Tops Market two hours ago. And how
many had water in their eyes? Because of Ray's
    book, and especially those last poems written
after he knew: the one about the doctor telling
    him, the one where he and Tess go down to
Reno to get married before it happens and shoot
    some craps on the dark baize tables, the one
called "After-Glow" about the little light in the
    sky after the sun sets. I can just hear him,
if he were still here and this were somebody
    else's book, saying, "Jesus," saying, "This
is the saddest son of a bitch of a book I've
    read in a long time," saying, "A real long time."
And the thing is, he knew we'd be saying this
    about his book, he could just hear us saying it,
and in some part of him he was glad! He
    really was. What crazies we writers are,
our heads full of language like buckets of minnows
    standing in the moonlight on a dock. Ray

was a good writer, a wonderful writer, and his
    poems are good, most of them, and they made me
cry, there at my kitchen table with my head down,
    me, a sixty-seven-year-old galoot, an old fool
because all old men are fools, they have to be,
    shoveling big jagged chunks of that ordinary pie
into my mouth, and the water falling from my eyes
    onto the pie, the plate, my hand, little speckles
shining in the light, brightening the colors, and I
    ate that goddamn pie, and it tasted good to me.

Contributors

MARVIN BELL's eleven collections of poetry include *New and Selected Poems, Iris of Creation,* and *The Book of the Dead Man.* A teacher and essayist also, he divides his time between Iowa City and Port Townsend, Washington.

MORRIS R. BOND is, like his sister Tess Gallagher, a native of Port Angeles, Washington. A writer and outdoorsman, he has published poems in *Ploughshares* and *Island of Rivers,* an anthology celebrating fifty years of the Olympic National Park.

LEWIS BUZBEE is the author of a novel, *Fliegelman's Desire.* His interviews with Raymond Carver have appeared in the *Paris Review* and the *Bloomsbury Review.* He lives in San Francisco.

HENRY CARLILE has published three collections of poetry: *The Rough-Hewn Table, Running Lights,* and, most recently, *Rain.* He teaches at Portland State University.

DAVID CARPENTER is a writer from Saskatoon, Saskatchewan. His works of fiction include *Jewels, Jokes for the Apocalypse,* and *God's Bedfellows.*

HAYDEN CARRUTH taught for many years in the Graduate Creative Writing Program at Syracuse University. He has published some thirty books, the most recent of which are *Suicides and Jazzers* and *Collected Shorter Poems, 1946–1991.*

DOROTHY CATLETT operates a home-based secretarial service in Port Angeles, Washington. She was Raymond Carver's typist when he was in Port Angeles, and since his death has been Tess Gallagher's personal secretary.

OLIVIER COHEN is Raymond Carver's French publisher. He has published French editions of many U.S. and British writers, including Richard Ford, Jay McInerney, and Shiva Naipaul.

ROBERT COLES is a child psychiatrist who teaches at Harvard and uses Raymond Carver's stories in classes of undergraduates and medical students. He is the author of the *Children of Crisis* series and biographies of William Carlos Williams and Walker Percy.

RICHARD CORTEZ DAY is professor of English at Humboldt State University in Arcata, California. He is author of *When in Florence,* a collection of short stories set in Italy.

PATRICIA DOBLER's first writing teacher was Raymond Carver. She has published two books of poems, *Talking to Strangers* and *UXB,* and is Director of the Women's Creative Writing Center at Carlow College in Pittsburgh, Pennsylvania.

STEPHEN DOBYNS has published eight books of poetry and fifteen novels, most recently *Velocities: New and Selected Poems* and *The Wrestler's Cruel Study*. He is Director of the Creative Writing Program at Syracuse University.

GEOFFREY DUNN, an award-winning writer and filmmaker, grew up in an Italian fishing colony in Santa Cruz, California. His films include *Voyage of the Heart (Madalena Z), Miss . . . or Myth?* and *Dollar a Day, Ten Cents a Dance.*

RICCARDO DURANTI teaches English literature at the University of Rome "La Sapienza." He has translated Raymond Carver's *Fires* and *Elephant* into Italian. His own books of poetry include *Bivio di Voce* and *The Archer's Paradox.*

GARY FISKETJON is an editor at Alfred A. Knopf in New York City.

TESS GALLAGHER's most recent books of poetry are *Moon Crossing Bridge* and *Portable Kisses*. She is also the author of a volume of literary essays, *A Concert of Tenses;* a screenplay, *Dostoevsky* (with Raymond Carver); and a collection of short stories, *The Lover of Horses.*

WILLIAM HARMON, professor of English at the University of North Carolina at Chapel Hill, has published five books of poetry and a study of Ezra Pound's work. He has edited anthologies for Oxford and Columbia, as well as the Macmillan *Handbook to Literature.*

PATRICK HENRY (translator) teaches French at Whitman College in Walla Walla, Washington, where he also fly fishes for steelhead and coedits *Philosophy and Literature*. Recently he has edited *An Inimitable Example: The Case for the Princesse de Clèves* and *Approaches to Teaching Montaigne's Essays.*

WILLIAM HEYEN teaches at the State University of New York at Brockport. His recent books of poetry include *Pterodactyl Rose* and *Ribbons: The Gulf War. The Host: Selected Poems, 1965–1990* will appear from Time Being Books in 1994.

JAMES D. HOUSTON has written a dozen works of fiction and nonfiction, including the novels *Gig, Continental Drift,* and *Love Life.* A former

Wallace Stegner Fellow at Stanford, he is currently a visiting professor at the University of California, Santa Cruz.

STEPHEN HUNT has had several plays produced off-Broadway, including *Eye Spy* and *Insomnia*. He recently performed his comic monologue *The White Guy* at the West Bank Theatre in New York City.

KENNETH INADOMI, an aspiring writer, is the president and CEO of CIS Factual Data, a credit reporting firm in New Jersey. He and his wife, Melinda, live with their daughter in Manhattan.

DAVID RAPHAEL ISRAEL began reading Carver in a Walnut Creek A-frame. He has covered music for the *East Bay Express;* helped edit *Ear Magazine;* and dabbled with paint and film. He recently completed a first book of poetry, *Orison.*

TOM JENKS is the author of *Our Happiness,* a novel. He is a contributing editor of the *Paris Review* and a former senior editor at Scribner's. He and Raymond Carver coedited the anthology *American Short Story Masterpieces.*

JAY KARR graduated from the Iowa Writers' Workshop. In 1965 he came to Westminster College in Fulton, Missouri, and started the creative writing program which he heads. He has published fiction and poetry and is the founder of a publishing firm, Kingdom House.

JANE KENYON has published five books of poems and translations, the most recent of which is *Constance.* Her work appears frequently in magazines. She is a past fellow of the National Endowment for the Arts and the Guggenheim Foundation.

WILLIAM KITTREDGE has published a collection of short stories, *The Van Gogh Field;* a book of essays, *Owning It All;* and a memoir, *Hole in the Sky.* He teaches creative writing at the University of Montana.

MORTON MARCUS has published a novel and six books of poetry, including *Pages from a Scrapbook of Immigrants* and *The Santa Cruz Mountain Poems.* His work has appeared in over fifty anthologies. He teaches at Cabrillo College in Aptos, California.

TARA MAJA McGOWAN (translator) is a graduate of Princeton University, where she majored in comparative literature and East Asian studies. She works as a free-lance writer and translator in Princeton, New Jersey.

JAY McINERNEY is the author of four novels: *Bright Lights, Big City; Ransom; Story of My Life;* and *Brightness Falls.*

HARUKI MURAKAMI is a native of Kyoto, Japan. He has published many books, the most recent of which is *The Elephant Vanishes.* He is currently translating *The Complete Works of Raymond Carver* into Japanese for Chuokoron-Sha Publishers of Tokyo.

JOYCE CAROL OATES is the author most recently of a novel, *Black Water,* and *Where Are You Going, Where Have You Been?—Selected Early Stories.* She is the Roger S. Berlind Distinguished Professor in the Humanities at Princeton University.

BIBHU PADHI has published four collections of poems. He has also written a book on D.H. Lawrence and another on Indian philosophy and religion. He teaches in Puri, Orissa, India.

MICHAEL ROGERS has written three novels and a collection of short stories, *Do Not Worry About the Bear.* He lives in Oakland, California, and is a senior writer for *Newsweek.*

DENNIS SCHMITZ's most recent book is *About Night: Selected and New Poems.* His earlier collections include *Singing, String, Goodwill, Inc.,* and *Eden.* He is a past winner of the Shelley Memorial Award and has received fellowships from the National Endowment for the Arts and the Guggenheim Foudnation.

JEFFREY SKINNER's latest book of poems is *The Company of Heaven.* He has worked at a number of jobs, including private investigator, and is currently professor of English at the University of Louisville.

TED SOLOTAROFF teaches writing at Columbia University and writes frequently for *The Nation.* He recently edited, with Nessa Rapoport, *Writing Our Way Home: Contemporary American-Jewish Stories.*

JIM SOMERS was a renter in Raymond Carver's house in 1974. He now lives in Grants Pass, Oregon. He met Tess Gallagher in 1991 and with her help and encouragement began to write.

BARRY SPACKS has published many books of poetry and fiction. After thirty-seven years of university teaching, he has recently been sprung free to full-time writing in the piny mountains of Trinity County in Northern California.

DAVID SWANGER's poetry has won awards from the National Endowment for the Arts and the California Arts Council. He has published two books of poems, *The Shape of Waters* and *Inside the Horse,* and a book about poetry, *The Poem as Process.*

LIGGETT TAYLOR was a member of Raymond Carver's high school class, and his association with Carver stemmed from their 1986 class reunion. He is as a copy editor at the *Herald-Republic* in Yakima, Washington.

TOBIAS WOLFF was born in Birmingham, Alabama, in 1945. His books include a novel, *The Barracks Thief;* two collections of short stories, *Back in the World* and *In the Garden of the North American Martyrs;* and a memoir, *This Boy's Life.* He lives in upstate New York and teaches at Syracuse University.

JAY WOODRUFF's stories have appeared in the *Atlantic, Story,* and other publications. He is the author of *Conversations with Robert Coles* and *A Piece of Work: Five Writers Discuss Their Revisions.*

CHARLES WRIGHT is the author of *Country Music* and *The World of the Ten Thousand Things.* Raymond Carver once helped him catch three salmon. He lives in Charlottesville, Virginia.

NOEL YOUNG is the founder of Capra Press in Santa Barbara, California. In addition to having published six books by Raymond Carver and Tess Gallagher, he has edited the Capra Chapbook series and written several works of nonfiction.

THE EDITORS

WILLIAM L. STULL, professor of rhetoric at the University of Hartford, has edited four books by Raymond Carver: *Those Days: Early Writings; Conversations with Raymond Carver, No Heroics, Please;* and *Carnations: A Play in One Act.* MAUREEN P. CARROLL, an attorney and former professor at the College of the Holy Cross, has collaborated with her husband on these and other literary projects.

INDEX

Adams, Henry, 71
Agee, James, 217
Alaska, 112
Alcoholics Anonymous (AA), 122
Ambler, Eric, 57
American Academy and Institute of Arts and
    Letters, 164, 211
Amsterdam, 112
Anaheim, California, 117
Arcata, California, 28-30, 31, 91
Arkansas, 16
Aspen, Colorado, 93

Babel, Isaac, 165
Beagle, Peter, 96
Beattie, Ann, 121
Beer, Ralph, 141
Bell, Marvin, 144-45; "The Door," 144-45
Ben Lomond, California, 80, 82
Berkeley, California, 88
Best of the Small Presses, 232
Bible, 216
Binghamton, New York, 124
Blades, John, 143
Block Island, Rhode Island, 249
Bond, Morris R., 148-49; "My Crony,"
    148-49
Boston Globe, 212
Bowles, Paul, 231
Brautigan, Richard, 235
Brewster, Elizabeth, 173
British Museum, 199
Buford, Bill, 162
Bukowski, Charles, 62-65, 136, 231
Burk, Amy, 56, 77
Burroughs, Edgar Rice, 153; *The Princess of
    Mars*, 153
Burroughs, William S., 231
Buzbee, Lewis, 114-18; "New Hope for the
    Dead," 114-18

Caldwell, Gail, 212, 213
Carlile, Henry, 150-60; "Fish Stories," 150-60
Capote, Truman, 130; "The Headless
    Hawk," 130
Capra Press, 65, 67
Carpenter, David, 166-86; "What We Talk
    About When We Talk About Carver,"
    166-86
Carruth, Hayden, 251-52; "Ray," 251-52
Carver, Christine (daughter), 76

Carver, Ella Beatrice Casey (mother), 59,
    200-01
Carver, Maryann Burk (first wife), 50, 54-59,
    76-77, 80-83, 89-90, 97
Carver, Raymond: alcoholism of, 20, 49, 54,
    58, 63-64, 68-69, 76-77, 78-79, 80-81, 87-
    91, 97, 103, 117, 125, 133, 137, 143, 164,
    196, 235, 242-43, 245; and American
    dream, 104; anger and domestic violence
    of, 27, 76, 81, 82; physical appearance of,
    14, 15, 30, 53-54, 68, 82, 85, 108, 115,
    127, 133, 144, 174, 194-95, 236, 242, 249;
    autobiographical element in writings by,
    57, 81, 112, 206, 209; automobiles owned
    by, 83, 89, 92, 116, 144; boating by, 98,
    249; boyishness of, 53, 80, 81, 151, 198,
    243-44; cancer of, 85, 93, 95, 164, 192,
    197, 211, 249; cheating and check-walking
    by, 79, 109; cigarette habit of, 49, 53-54,
    58, 61, 83, 108, 174, 186, 197-98, 242; and
    coffee, 52, 85-86, 176-77, 186, 243; as
    conversationalist, 49; as critic, 82, 123; on
    criticism and literary theory, 111, 122,
    220; death of, 14, 24-25, 70, 71-72, 93,
    103, 112, 114, 198, 199, 213; dress of, 19-
    20, 53, 83, 108, 186, 194, 201, 243; early
    writings of, 28, 32; as textbook editor,
    59; in England, 199, 201; and
    expressionism, 57; feminine side of, 201;
    as fisherman, 69-70, 93, 98, 109, 112, 144,
    150-51, 162-64; and food, 80, 108, 116,
    142, 177, 184, 241-50; friendships of, 54,
    77, 142, 200, 206, 240; funeral and burial
    of, 94, 226, 228, 230; generosity of, 52,
    82, 93, 142; gentleness of, 82, 200, 248;
    Guggenheim fellowship of, 19;
    handwriting of, 196; honesty of, 113, 202,
    245; honorary degree received by, 211;
    hugging of friends, 30, 75, 198; humility
    of, 119, 125, 175; humor of, 107, 115,
    175, 242; as hunter, 148-59, 166-86,
    and Internal Revenue Service, 242;
    interjections and exclamations by, 110,
    184, 221, 244, 250; as janitor at Mercy
    Hospital; and Japan, 130-35; Lane
    lectureship of, 19; ordinary language used
    by, 51, 139, 162, 202, 242; laughter of,
    16, 17, 49, 53, 76, 110, 117, 194, 198, 200,
    247; letters by, 150, 162, 199, 210, 211,
    212-13, 234, 235, 236; as listener, 110,
    142, 197, 198, 199, 200, 244; literary
    values of, 51-52, 110-11, 115; lung surgery

of, 86, 93, 198, 211; as manager of apartment complex, 50; marijuana smoking by, 83, 116; marriage to Maryann Burk, 50, 104; marriage to Tess Gallagher, 113, 198, 212; memorial services for, 201, 204; as mentor, 78-79, 119-26; and minimalism, 106, 206; modesty of, 16, 54, 56, 77, 82, 201; and mystery, 106, 216, 244; as northwesterner, 16, 54, 77, 106, 137, 229; paranoia of, 57, 60, 249; at parties, 27, 28, 62-64, 78-79, 88-89, 90, 96, 242, 245; photographs of, 53; poetry of, 49-52, 54-55, 56-57, 115-16; politics of, 69, 95; and poverty, 58, 59, 77, 80, 164; pseudonymous writings by, 31; public readings by, 29, 103, 115-16, 117, 128-29, 167, 170, 173-75; and realism, 57, 103, 106, 120, 130, 162; restlessness of, 19, 61, 83, 96, 102, 108, 112, 242; revisions by, 51, 67, 113, 195, 197; nicknamed "Running Dog," 242; and secrets, 51-52, 86, 94, 142-43, 206, 244, 246-47; short stories of, 49, 57-58, 104, 105, 106, 120, 153-54; shyness of, 49, 61, 103, 121; as small-town boy, 54; Stegner fellowship of, 18; storytelling by, 49, 108-10, 223, 243, 244-45; Strauss Livings award of, 116, 194; and surrealism, 57; as teacher, 50, 61-62, 69, 89-90, 119-26, 127-29, 132, 144, 241, 243-44; "two lives" of, 26, 30, 82-83, 98, 108, 125, 141, 234, 241, 246; and Vietnam War, 27; speaking voice of, 20, 49, 82, 84, 103, 115, 119, 126, 133, 140, 175, 195, 244; sense of wonder of, 16, 20, 30, 49, 50, 82, 110, 116, 234, 248; working-class background of, 104-05, 115, 137-38, 174, 200, 217, 219-20; writing processes of, 77, 112, 195; and Zen, 127

WORKS: "After-Glow" (poem), 221, 251; "Alcohol" (poem), 221; "Another Mystery" (poem), 249; "Are These Actual Miles?" (story), 59, 60; At Night the Salmon Move (poems), 97; "The Autopsy Room" (poem), 50; "The Bath" (story), 138-39; "Blackbird Pie" (story), 106, 203; "Boxes" (story), 197; Carnations (play), 27; Carver Country (photographs), 75; "Cathedral" (story), 106, 142, 203, 218, 221, 224; Cathedral (stories), 115, 162; "Chef's House"

(story), 105; Complete Works of Raymond Carver (Japanese edition), 131; "Distance" (story), 167; "Distress Sale" (poem), 67; Dostoevsky (screenplay), 247; "Eagles" (poem), 244-45; "Elephant" (story), 19, 107, 223; "Errand" (story), 49, 95, 106, 117, 201, 221, 222, 236; "Fat" (story), 57, 60, 104, 218; "Fires" (essay), 165, 202, 203, 218, 247; Fires (essays, poems, stories), 65, 67, 116, 137, 139-40, 167, 247; "Friends" ["Friendship"] (essay), 197; Furious Seasons (stories), 67, 103; "The Gift" (poem), 50-51; "Gravy" (poem), 50, 200, 221, 230; "Intimacy" (story), 70, 105, 106, 208-09; "Jerry and Molly and Sam" (story), 202; "Late Fragment" (poem), 248-49; "The Mailman as Cancer Patient" (poem), 221; "Menudo" (story), 164, 197, 203-04; "The Mortician" ["Errand"] (story), 197; "My Father's Life" (essay) 218; "Near Klamath" (poem), 111; "Neighbors" (story), 57, 60, 159; A New Path to the Waterfall (poems), 55, 77, 248, 249, 251; "No Need" (poem), 221; "Nobody Said Anything" (story), 60-62, 138, 152-59; "On Writing" (essay), 139, 165, 218, Paris Review Interviews (interview), 137, 206, 235; "Poem for Hemingway and W.C. Williams" (poem), 221; "The Projectile" (poem), 134; "Put Yourself in My Shoes" (story), 96, 112, 132; "The River" (poem), 151-52; "A Small, Good Thing" (story), 29, 99-100, 139, 202, 221, 222, "So Much Water So Close to Home" (story), 67, 105, 130, 232, 234; "Son" ["Boxes"] (story), 197; "The Student's Wife" (story), 57, 223; "The Summer Steelhead" (story), 60, 61, 153; "They're Not Your Husband" (story), 202; Ultramarine (poems), 50, 197; "Viewfinder" (story), 244; Les vitamines du bonheur (French edition of Cathedral), 162; "Vitamins" (story), 218; "What Is It?" (story), 59, 60; "What the Doctor Said" (poem), 221, 251; "What We Talk About When We Talk About Love" (story), 223; What We Talk About When We Talk About Love (stories), 54, 67, 114, 195, 227; "What's in Alaska?" (story), 159, 218; "Where I'm Calling From" (story), 130; Where I'm Calling From (stories), 60, 62, 117, 202, 213; *Where Water Comes Together with Other Water* (poems), 30, 195-97; "Whoever Was Using This Bed" (story), 175; "Why Don't You Dance?" (story), 104, 109, 136, 223, 244; "Will You Please Be Quiet, Please?" (story), 57, 87-88, 203; *Will You Please Be Quiet, Please?* (stories), 18, 50, 57, 60, 109, 114, 121, 136, 241; *Winter Insomnia* (poems), 15, 56-57; "You Don't Know What Love Is" (poem), 65; "Your Dog Dies" (poem), 221

Carver, Raymond Clevie, Sr. (father), 58, 235

Carver, Vance Lindsay (son), 76

Carter, Billy, 71

Catlett, Dorothy, 194-98; "Do You Like It?" 194-98

Cheever, John, 89, 109, 116, 121, 245

Chekhov, Anton, 49, 60, 62, 94-95, 105, 106, 110, 115, 117-18, 121, 125, 165, 199, 201, 206, 217, 221, 222, 223, 249; "Anyuta," 223; "Gooseberries," 94; "In Exile," 62; "Two Tragedies," 223

Chicago Tribune Book World, 143

Chico State College [University], 124

Chuokoron-Sha Publishers, 131

City on a Hill, 82

Cohen, Olivier, 150, 161-65; "Lines of Force," 161-65

Coles, Robert, 215-24; "American Light," 215-24

College V, 62, 81, 89, 127. *See also* University of California at Santa Cruz

Corso, Gregory, 231

Coulette, Henri, 71

Crumley, James, 141

Cupertino, California, 58-59, 76, 88-90, 208

Dallas, Texas, 103-04

Dartmouth Medical School, 221

Davenport, California, 66

Day, Dorothy, 217

Day, Richard Cortez, 27, 31-32, 56, 91; "Bad News," 31-32

December, 87

Dickens, Charles, 217; *Great Expectations*, 217

Dickey, James, 77; "Deliverance," 77

Dickey, William, 117

Dobler, Patricia, 102; "Odometer," 102

Dobyns, Stephen, 108-13, 243; "Laughter's Creature," 108-13

Dostoevsky, Fyodor, 247

Duke University Center for Documentary Studies, 222

Duncan, David, 153; *The River Why*, 153

Dunn, Geoffrey, 68-70; "Tell Me More About Salmon Fishing," 68-70

Duranti, Riccardo, 74; "The Message," 74

El Paso, Texas, 102

Eliot, George, 217; *Middlemarch*, 217

Eliot, T.S., 119

Elliott Bay, 92

Elliott Bay Book Company, 75

Ellison, Ralph, 216, 217; *Invisible Man*, 216, 217

Erikson, Erik H., 215, 217

Esquire, 83, 141, 174, 196, 208, 209, 210

Ettlinger, Marion, 53

Everson, William, 96

Faulkner, William, 121

Fisketjon, Gary, 141, 234-36; "Salt Water and Fresh," 234-36

Fitzgerald, F. Scott, 121, 130, 247; "The Rich Boy," 130

Flaubert, Gustave, 165

Foley, Martha, 26

Ford, Richard, 141, 163, 166-86, 174, 220, 243, 249; "Sweethearts," 174

Fort Ross State Historic Park, 51

Gallagher, Tess (second wife), 19, 24, 26, 58, 68, 70, 75, 82, 85, 93, 94, 98, 103-07, 113, 115-16, 120, 127, 133, 134, 140, 141, 142, 151, 162, 163, 164, 171, 194, 196, 197, 198, 199, 201, 207, 212, 220, 234, 241, 244, 245, 247, 248; "The Ghosts of Dreams," 103-07; "The Harvest," 142

García Marquez, Gabriel, 212; *Love in the Time of Cholera*, 212

Gardner, John, 92, 124, 138; *On Becoming a Novelist*, 138

Glück, Louise, 243

Goddard College, 108, 109, 112, 243

Gorky, Maxim, 201, 206

Haines, John, 17, 81

Hall, Donald, 243

Hall, James, B., 62

Hardy, Thomas, 217; *Jude the Obscure*, 217

Harmon, William, 71-72; "A Nothing Generation," 71-72
Harvard University, 137, 215, 217
Harvard University Medical School, 221
Hass, Robert, 243
Hemingway, Ernest, 29, 31, 61, 120, 125, 138, 142-43, 152; "Big Two-Hearted River: Part II," 152; *The Garden of Eden*, 142; "The Old Man and the Sea," 61
Heyen, William, 14; "Carvering," 14
Heynen, Jim, 244-45
Hitchcock, Alfred, 57
Hitchcock, George, 15-16, 55-58, 62
Hopper, Edward, 219, 220, 223
Houston, James D., 15-20, 65-66, 78, 96, 130; "The Days with Ray," 15-20; *West Coast Fiction*, 130
Hugo, Richard, 81
Humboldt County, California, 27
Humboldt State College [University], 26-27, 31, 56
Hunt, Stephen, 225-33; "Stories Change You," 225-33
Hurston, Zora Neale, 217

Illinois, 109
Inadomi, Kenneth, 127-29; "Read It Again," 127-29
Intersection Gallery, 115
Iowa, 55, 56
Iowa City, Iowa, 89, 109-10, 112, 116, 139, 140, 245
Iowa Writers' Workshop, 27-29, 89, 121, 124, 139, 140, 218. *See also* University of Iowa
Irving, John, 243
Israel, David Raphael, 21-22; "Just Listening to Stories," 21-22

Japan, 127, 131-32, 134-35
Jenks, Tom, 141-43; "Shameless," 141-43
Jenner, California, 51
Johnson, Curt, 87
Jones, James Earl, 77
Jung, Carl, 151

Kafka, Franz, 104, 111; *The Metamorphosis*, 104
Karr, Jay, 26-30; "The Most Unhappy Man," 26-30
Kayak, 15, 55-58
Kenyon, Jane, 192-93; "The Letter," 192-93

Kerouac, Jack, 136, 231
Kinder, Chuck, 90
Kittredge, William, 17-18, 81, 85-95; "Bulletproof," 85-95
Kresge Auditorium, 19
Kundera, Milan, 236; *The Unbearable Lightness of Being*, 236

La Couple, 162
Lasquin, François, 105
Life, 194
Levine, Philip, 86, 217; "They Feed the Lion," 86
Lish, Gordon, 81-83; "How I Got to Be a Bigshot Editor," 82
London, Jack, 97, 98; *John Barleycorn*, 97, 98
London, 112, 199
London Times, 105
Los Altos, California, 59

Marcus, Morton, 53-67, 81, 96; "All-American Nightmares, 53-67; *Origins*, 56
Marx, Karl, 69
Maupassant, Guy de, 121
McClanahan, Ed, 90
McGuane, Thomas, 141
McHugh, Heather, 243
McInerney, Jay, 119-26, 132, 141; "Raymond Carver, Mentor," 119-26
McKinleyville, California, 91
Michaels, Leonard, 81
Miller, Arthur, 104; *Death of a Salesman*, 104
Miller, Henry, 136
Milosz, Czeslaw, 86
Missoula, Montana, 88, 89, 90
Missouri, 29
Mondale, Walter, 133
Montana, 18, 85
Monterey, California, 78
Mueller, Lisel, 243
Murakami, Haruki, 130-35; "A Literary Comrade," 130-35; "The Windup Bird and Tuesday's Women," 132

New York, 198
New York City, New York, 128, 141, 161-62, 164, 199, 201, 211
New York Times, 93, 210, 211, 212
New Yorker, 19, 113, 130, 132, 175, 210
Noonan, Peggy, 138

Oates, Joyce Carol, 24-25; "Weedy Logic," 24-25
O'Connor, Flannery, 121, 216, 217; "The Artificial Nigger," 216; "The Lame Shall Enter First," 216
O'Connor, Frank, 121
Olsen, Tillie, 217, 221
Olympic Mountains, 92
Olympic Peninsula, 85
Olympic Hotel, 87
Oregon, 235

Pacific, 207, 208
Padhi, Bibhu, 237-38; "Something Else," 237-38
Paley, Grace, 242-43
Palo Alto, California, 17, 60, 78, 90, 116, 241
Paris, 105, 162
People, 209
Percy, Walker, 217, 221, 223; The Last Gentleman, 223; Lost in the Cosmos, 223; The Moviegoer, 223
Perera, Victor, 82, 96
Phoenix, Arizona, 245
Plainfield, Vermont, 112, 243
Poe, Edgar Allan, 106; "The Purloined Letter," 106
Poetry, 152
Port Angeles, Washington, 19, 70, 85, 92-93, 94, 98, 133, 145, 160, 162-64, 165, 187, 194, 197, 209, 210, 225-28
Portland Oregonian, 209
Portland State University, 153
Pound, Ezra, 119, 139
Printer's Inc., 116
Proust, Marcel, 85; Remembrance of Things Past, 85
Publishers Weekly, 211

Quarry West, 62, 81

Reagan, Ronald, 133, 138
Reno, Nevada, 113
Rilke, Rainer Maria, 113, 223
Robison, Mary, 121
Rogers, Michael, 78-79, "A Real-Life Carver Story," 78-79
Ross, Sinclair, 181; As for Me and My House, 181
Ryan, Michael, 243

Sacramento, California, 49-50, 208

Sacramento State College [University], 56
Saint Louis Post-Dispatch, 26
Saints-Pères Hotel, 162
Saltzman, Arthur M., 159; Understanding Raymond Carver, 159
San Francisco, California, 14, 15, 24, 55-58, 66, 83, 91, 115
San Jose, California, 66, 78
Santa Barbara, California, 96
Santa Clara Valley, 18
Santa Cruz, California, 15, 18, 60, 65, 68, 80-84, 96-97
Saskatoon, Saskatchewan, 166-86
Schmitz, Dennis, 49-52, 56, 82; "Secret Places," 49-52
Schweizer, Harold, 106
Science Research Associates, 59
Scribner's Bookstore, 164
Seattle, Washington, 85, 87, 92, 107, 211
Seattle Times, 70, 207, 208
Seneca Review, 61, 153
Shakespeare & Co., 129
Shepard, Sam, 136
Short Stories from the Literary Magazines, 87
Sinclair, Giles, 28
Skinner, Jeffrey, 99-100; "The Good Story," 99-100
Sky House, 133, 163
Smith, Annick, 85, 86, 93
Socrates, 159
Solotaroff, Ted, 199-206; "Going Through the Pain," 199-206
Somers, Jim, 75-77; "Dark Days," 75-77
Spacks, Barry, 240; "Carver's Medallion," 240
Stanford University, 19-20, 21, 78, 89, 121, 124, 242
Stegner Fellowship, 89
Strait of Juan de Fuca, 106, 198
Stroud, Joe, 96
Sunnyvale, California, 81
Swanger, David, 80-84; "No Blessed Calm," 80-84
Swanton Corn Roast, 66
Switzerland, 80
Syracuse, New York, 92, 120, 124, 141, 143, 241
Syracuse University, 121, 124

Taylor, Liggett, 207-14; "Reunion in Yakima," 207-14
Tel Aviv, 50

Texas, 82
Thompson, Gary, 51
Tolstoy, Leo, 201, 127, 221, 223; *Confession*, 223
Tocqueville, Alexis de, 69
Toyon, 31
Tucson, Arizona, 19, 245
Turgenev, Ivan, 121

University of Arizona, 19
University of California at Santa Barbara, 96
University of California at Santa Cruz, 17, 60, 62, 80-82, 89-90, 127, 128. *See also* College V
University of Hartford, 211
University of Iowa, 109. *See also* Iowa Writers' Workshop
University of Saskatchewan, 170
Updike, John, 164

Vanity Fair, 26, 209
Vermont, 92, 108
Vietnam, 27, 76
Vintage Contemporaries, 141
Vivaldi, Antonio, 86
Voigt, Ellen Bryant, 243

Washington, 16, 19
Weil, Simone, 217
Welty, Eudora, 121
Western Humanities Review, 83
Westminster College, 29
Williams, William Carlos, 31, 125, 216, 217, 218, 221, 223; "Doctor Stories," 218; *Paterson*, 217, 223; *White Mule*, 218
Wolff, Geoffrey, 243, 249
Wolff, Tobias, 141, 143, 220, 241-50; "Appetite," 241-50
Woodruff, Jay, 136-40, 218; "Laundroma," 136-40
Wright, Charles, 187-89; "Twice-Touched," 187-89

Yakima, Washington, 77, 92, 207-14
Yakima Herald-Republic, 208
Yakima High School, 207
Young, Noel, 65-67, 96-98; "Happy Hour with Ray," 96-98

ZAP Comics, 77